AUTHORITY

AUTHORITY

Construction and Corrosion

BRUCE LINCOLN

The University of Chicago Press • Chicago and London

BRUCE LINCOLN is professor of the history of religions
and an associate of the Department of Anthropology at the University of Chicago. Among his earlier books are *Discourse and
the Construction of Society* (1989) and *Death, War, and Sacrifice*
(1991), the latter published by the University of Chicago Press.

The University of Chicago Press, Chicago 60637
The University of Chicago Press, Ltd., London
© 1994 by The University of Chicago
All rights reserved. Published 1994
Printed in the United States of America

03 02 01 00 99 98 97 96 95 94 1 2 3 4 5

ISBN: 0-226-48197-2 (cloth)

Library of Congress Cataloging-in-Publication Data

Lincoln, Bruce.
    Authority: construction and corrosion/Bruce Lincoln.
        p.   cm.
    Includes bibliographical references and index.
    1. Authority—History. 2. Political oratory—History.
    3. Rhetoric—Political aspects—History. I. Title.
    HM271.L53   1994
    303.3'6—dc20   94-12514
                                                            CIP

♾ The paper used in this publication meets the minimum requirements of
the American National Standard for Information Sciences—Permanence of
Paper for Printed Library Materials, ANSI Z39.48-1984.

In memory of my father

WILLIAM DANIEL LINCOLN

28 February 1920–19 November 1992

All authority is in the last analysis the authority of communications.
　— Carl F. Friedrich

It is the access to the legitimate instruments of expression, and therefore the participation in the authority of the institution, which makes *all* the difference — irreducible to discourse as such — between the straightforward imposture of masqueraders, who disguise a performative utterance as a descriptive or constative statement, and the authorized imposture of those who do the same thing with the authorization and the authority of an institution. The spokesperson is an imposter endowed with the *skeptron*.
　— Pierre Bourdieu

CONTENTS

ACKNOWLEDGMENTS

There are many people to thank for their suggestions, criticisms, guidance, and patience. Above all, I am grateful to my closest and most valued colleagues, Louise Lincoln and Cristiano Grottanelli, who read through all of this manuscript and helped me to improve it in countless ways. Others who commented on specific chapters or helped me sort through one issue or another include Wendy Doniger, Richard Leppert, Ron Aminzade, John Archer, Heidar Azodanloo, Aleta Biersack, Jimmy Bishara, Peter Bruder, Doug Catterall, Ruma Chawla, Pietro Clemente, Rita Copeland, Laurie Cozad, Arthur Droge, Bud Duvall, Gary Ebersole, Anne Enke, Paul Friedrich, Clark Gilpin, Paul Griffiths, Kaaren Grimstad, Gary Herrigel, Michael Herzfeld, Ted Huters, Allen Isaacman, Lisette Josephides, Bill Malandra, William Marvin, Ellen Messer-Davidow, John Modell, Judy Modell, John Mowitt, Gregory Nagy, Mohamed N'daou Saidou, Tord Olsson, Sherry Ortner, Carla Pasquinelli, Jim Perkinson, Diego Poli, Gianna Pomata, James Redfield, Martin Riesebrodt, Adam Rose, Martha Roth, Jim Scott, Brian Smith, Jørgen Podemann Sørensen, Pier Giorgio Solinas, George Steinmetz, Ulrike Strasser, Larry Sullivan, David Sylvan, Gary Thomas, Hernan Vidal, Marilyn Waldman, David Wallace, Morten Warmind, Luise White, Pauline Yu, Tony Zahareas, and Andrej Zaporogchenko. Institutions that permitted me to present pieces of this book while they were still very much in process include the Università degli Studi di Macerata, Università degli Studi di Siena, Københavns Universitetet, Lunds Universitetet, Novosibirsk State Pedagogical Institute, the University of Chicago, and the University of Minnesota. In each instance I benefited greatly from the discussions that followed. For the friendship, support, encouragement, generosity, and criticism of all, I am deeply appreciative.

CONSTRUCTING AUTHORITY

BUYERS, SELLERS, AND AUTHORITIES

In this book, I hope to arrive at an improved understanding of authority, which is something — an entity? a phenomenon? a status? — I have come to see as extraordinarily complex, hopelessly elusive, and almost as badly misconstrued in most scholarly discussions as it is in popular parlance. For although there exists a large literature on this topic, it generally runs in one of three ruts. First, there is the project of those political philosophers of neoconservative bent, who took the turbulence of the 1960s as a "crisis of authority" in the face of which they sought to reestablish the legitimacy of the liberal democratic state. Then there is the work of those social psychologists whose memories stretch back to events of the 1930s and 1940s, who are more concerned with dangers posed by the state than those posed to it, and who have used a variety of experimental data to point up the widespread tendency of citizens, even in liberal democracies, to follow authoritarian leaders. Finally, there is the set of sociological discussions that involve a fairly conservative manipulation of the typology introduced by Max Weber, in which Weber's subtlety and the more brooding, even ironic, qualities of his thought are mostly lost. Two of the three categories Weber posited as ideal types are thus rapidly disqualified—traditional authority being treated as obsolete, and charismatic authority dangerous—leaving legal-rational authority, the system of the modern bureaucratic state, as the only viable game in town.

In general, I have found a number of works not centrally concerned with the issue of authority a good deal more helpful than those which have it as their prime focus. In this vein, I think particularly of the writings of Pierre Bourdieu, Michel Foucault, Mikhail Bakhtin, Maurice Bloch, and James Scott, all of whom, in very different fashions, treat authority as an aspect of discourse and are more attentive to its labile dynamics than to its institutional incarnations. I read them as posing a set of interrelated questions: Who is able to speak with authority? Where and how can one produce authoritative speech? What effect does such speech have on those to whom it is addressed? What responses does such speech anticipate? What responses does it allow? And what consequences can unanticipated and disallowed responses have for the construction, exercise, and maintenance of authority?

Given these initiatives, the time seems right for a radical rethinking of authority—radical in the literal sense of returning to the roots. Such an attempt could begin at any number of points, including the obvious piece of etymological reconnaissance through which English "authority" is tracked to its source in Latin *auctoritas,* a word used with many different shades of meaning, usually in connection with the capacity to perform a speech act that exerts a force on its hearers greater than that of simple influence, but less than that of a command. If we are in search of roots, however, we can simplify things somewhat by focusing initially on the sense *auctoritas* has within legal texts, for there the term makes its first appearance and is used with greatest precision. Four types of legal *auctoritas* are specified in Roman law, and three of these reflect the capacity to make consequential pronouncements, that is, to take action through acts of speech that hearers will accept out of respect for the speaker and his (never her!) office. These are the authority of the senate (*auctoritas patrum* or *auctoritas senatus*), that of the emperor (*auctoritas principis*), and that of a trustee or guardian (*auctoritas tutoris*). There is a fourth type of authority, however, which is called into play within certain sales transactions (*auct-oritas venditoris*), and it is this form alone — the one that to our eyes is strangest and least familiar — that is mentioned in the oldest texts, the *Twelve Tables* of Roman Law, which date to the middle of the fifth century B.C.

Specifically, *auctoritas venditoris* figures in the highly formal procedure of *mancipatio* (literally "mancipation"), through which the most valuable and important forms of property — land, livestock, and slaves — were solemnly transferred from a seller to a buyer. In effect a ritual, *mancipatio* was the process through which one person's claim to these goods — living beings and the means of production — was formally and publicly dissolved (five Roman citizens had to be present and serve as witnesses), while another person's claim was publicly constructed.

Obviously, for any sale to take place it is necessary for the seller to have ownership of the goods in question, and it is here that *auctoritas* enters the scene. The seller was required to warrant that he had full title to that which he sold, and was further required to guarantee that should his title prove to be invalid, he would not only make full restitution to the buyer but would pay heavy penalties as well. Specialists in Roman law have debated for more than a half a century whether the *auctoritas* of the seller is best understood as his title to the property or the guarantee he offers, but the distinction may be artificial. The best understanding of *auctoritas* in this highly specialized context is one that connects it to the other types of *auctoritas* mentioned above. Accordingly, I would treat it as the capacity to make a consequential pronouncement, and understand *auctoritas venditoris* as the kind of speech — a guarantee of title — that brings a sale to fulfillment. Moreover, it is a speech that magically puts potentially difficult questions to rest. In this instance, the fundamental question implicit in acts of mancipation: Can one human being be the property of another?

AUTHORITY AND AUTHORITIES

These observations may help us transcend a distinction often made between executive and epistemic authority: between the authority of those who are "in authority" (e.g., political leaders, parents, military commanders) and that of those who are "an authority" (e.g., technical experts, scholars, medical specialists). Although one may distinguish between the ways in which these different types of people come to occupy their positions and the different warrants they are able to produce in support of their authority, what they have in common is precisely that which characterizes the four types of *auctoritas* recognized in Roman law: they have the capacity to produce consequential speech, quelling doubts and winning the trust of the audiences whom they engage. Thus, for example, the speech of executive authorities in its most extreme form is the military command that produces automatic and unquestioning obedience: the similarly extreme speech of epistemic authorities is the kind of pronouncement that ends all debate on a given question.

In practice, the consequentiality of authoritative speech may have relatively little to do with the form or content of what is said. Neither officers' commands nor experts' opinions need be artfully phrased or even make sense in order to yield results. (Indeed, the authority of the latter may be enhanced by a certain incomprehensibility.) Similarly, it does not arise out of some quality of the speaker, such as an office or a charisma. Rather, I believe it is best understood in relational terms as the effect of a posited, perceived, or institutionally ascribed asymmetry between speaker and audience that permits certain speakers to command not just the attention but the confidence, respect, and trust of their audience, or—an important proviso—to make audiences act *as if* this were so.

BETWEEN COERCION AND PERSUASION

Authority is often considered in connection with two other categories, persuasion and force—the processes through which one wins others over through acts of discourse or bends them to one's will through acts or threats of violence. Persuasion and force have been contrasted to one another since antiquity, persuasion generally being understood as the realm of words and the mind, and force that of deeds and the body. Authority, however, is yet a third entity, which remains distinct from persuasion and coercion alike while being related to them in some very specific and suggestive ways.

Although authority and persuasion both operate primarily through the medium of language, this superficial commonality ought not obscure their more fundamental differences. First, it is important to observe that the exercise of authority not only involves but often depends upon the use of nonverbal instruments and media: the whole theatrical array of gestures, demeanors, costumes, props, and stage devices through which one may impress or bamboozle an audience. Second, even when authority does work with and through words, it does so in a very different fashion than persuasion. Thus, one persuades by arguing a case, advancing reasoned propositions, impassioned appeals, and rhetorical flourishes that lead the hearer to a desired conclusion. In contrast, the exercise of authority need not involve argumentation and may rest on the naked assertion that the identity of the speaker warrants acceptance of the speech, as witness the classic pronouncements of paternal authority *in extremis:* "Because *I* said so," and "Because I'm your father, *that's* why!"

Anarchists and others have, on occasion, considered such blunt assertions as these to be paradigmatic of authority in general, and have taken them to reveal that by its very nature authority is both unreasoning and unreasonable. Against this charge, others have maintained that, abuses notwithstanding, the proper exercise of authority involves and rests upon what they have come to call "the capacity for reasoned elaboration." According to this line of analysis, the potential for persuasion is always implicit within authority, which is accepted not just on its own say-so but because it is understood by all concerned that if asked to explain themselves, those in authority could and would do so. Persuasion, then, is a possibility encapsulated within authority and one that may be brought forward upon demand, while authority, conversely, is a time-saving device or a shorthand version of persuasion.

Although this formulation has been widely used to defend authority against the charge of authoritarianism, I believe it is severely flawed. In actual practice the exercise of authority depends less upon the "capacity for reasoned elaboration" as on the *presumption* made by those subject to authority that such a capacity exists, or on their calculated and strategic willingness to pretend they so presume. Authorities need not be able to explain themselves so long as others are sufficiently cowed or respectful that they do not ask for explanations. Moreover, when an explanation is requested, the situation is transformed in subtle but important ways, for the relation of trust and acceptance characteristic of authority is suspended, at least temporarily, in that moment. If authority involves the willingness of an audience to treat a given act of speech as credible because of its trust in the speaker, then under the sway of authority an audience acts *as if* it had been persuaded, *when in fact it has not,* while accepting the fact that its regard for the speaker obviates the need for persuasion. In contrast, when authority is asked to explain itself and responds to that request by arguing in earnest rather than simply reasserting itself, it ceases to be authority for the moment and becomes (an attempt at) persuasion.

Other transformative possibilities also exist, and if authority's liberal defenders point proudly to its "capacity for reasoned elaboration," they are generally more reticent about another capacity, which it harbors in equal measure: the capacity for repressive violence. The fact that force is implicit within authority, however, and that authority may deploy force rather than argumentation in response to anything it regards — or chooses to regard — as a challenge is something known to all who are involved in the asymmetric relations constitutive of authority: ruler and ruled, officer and private, teacher and student, parent and child. But if force is actually used, or if threats of force are made with anything less than extreme delicacy (a delicacy that insures deniability), authority risks being perceived as a fig leaf of legitimacy that conceals the embarrassment of naked force. And when authority operates (and is seen to operate) on pain and fear rather than on trust and respect, it ceases to be authority and becomes (an attempt at) coercion.

Authority is thus related to coercion and persuasion in symmetrical ways. Both of these exist as capacities or potentialities implicit within authority, but are actualized only when those who claim authority sense that they have begun to lose the trust of those over whom they seek to exercise it. In a state of latency or occultation, persuasion and coercion alike are constitutive parts of authority, but once actualized and rendered explicit they signal — indeed, they are, at least temporarily — its negation.

AUTHORIZED AND AUTHORIZING OBJECTS, TIMES, AND PLACES

Above, I made passing reference to "the whole theatrical array of gestures, demeanors, costumes, props, and stage devices through which one may impress or bamboozle an audience." It would, no doubt, be of interest to consider the myriad trappings that serve this purpose — the precise physical postures and facial expressions that at one time and place or another have been used to convey attitudes of gravity, solemnity, decisiveness, and the like, or the seemingly endless variety of uniforms and insignia (badges, diplomas, special seats, vehicles, headgear, etc.) that are used to mark certain people as distinguished for their rank, status, office, lineage, special training, etc., and which thereby help them lay claim to an audience's attention, respect, and trust.

At a certain level, however, we can dispense with an investigation in detail that would be virtually interminable. For as an iconic emblem (if not as a practical instrument), the judge's gavel is functionally identical to the doctor's stethoscope or the athletic coach's whistle and clipboard. All of these items (and countless others) announce the authority of their bearer for a given audience and within a circumscribed context or sphere of activity. Some emblems, particularly those insignia of office associated with the most sweeping and consequential forms of authority, play a more active role than others in the construction of that authority. Thus, rituals of coronation transform pretenders (a significant title!) into kings by placing the crown on their heads, and priests cease to be priests when they are literally and ceremonially defrocked.

The conventional analysis of such data is that the king's crown and the priest's vestments are arbitrary representations of offices, and authority resides within the office. Those who wear the crown or the robes (like those who wear a policeman's badge, to cite another familiar example) signal to others that they are acting in an official capacity. When they appear without these trappings, they signal that they act with their own personal authority, not that derived from their office. The moment of coronation, then, is the moment when someone is endowed with the authority of the royal office, of which the crown is a mere sign or emblem, and defrocking is the reverse procedure with regard to the priestly office.

Such a view has much to recommend it, but there are cases that reveal its limitations. Consider the example of impostors and usurpers, who are able to wield authority effectively when they possess the insignia but not the office precisely because the insignia obtain for them the trust of those people who in the moment of trusting become their "subjects." The inverse case—those who hold the office but not the insignia—is exemplified in the story of the emperor's new clothes, which points up the shortcomings of any model that locates authority simply and straightforwardly in the person, the emblem, or the office. Although the emperor's office permitted him to demand that his subjects show their trust by acting as if his absent insignia were present, and although his subjects complied with this demand up to a point (out of respect for his authority), there were very definite limits on their willingness or ability to do so. At the moment when one member of the audience (significantly a child, which is to say, one least schooled in and least intimidated by the ways of authority) gave voice to skepticism, the emperor's authority effectively crumbled. Moreover, that delicious moment reveals to us that offices, insignia, and office holders all advance claims which are most effective and consequential when correlated with one another. When audiences accept these claims—for whatever reason and with whatever measure of sincerity—authority is the result. Finally, it is consistent with our emerging view that authority depends on nothing so much as the trust of the audience, or the audience's strategic willingness to act as if it had such trust.

Returning to the topic of insignia, insofar as a particular garment or piece of paraphernalia has come to enjoy the respect and reverence of a given audience (for whatever reasons), it focuses the attention of that audience on whomever comes to hold it, whose words will consequently be received—initially, at least—with similar respect and reverence. The same is true for certain select times and places. Consider, for example, the pulpit on Sunday mornings, the lectern at the appointed hour for a university class, or the judge's bench when court is in session. Such times and places are authorized, not only by specific institutions (church, university, government), but also by the memories, associations, assumptions, and expectations they call forth in the audiences they call together. Being authorized by the group, they are able to authorize — i.e., confer authority on — those whom the group permits to speak and that which they say within this setting.

The question of permission is an important one, for most groups treat the opportunity to speak within such places as a scarce and valued resource. Considerations of office, rank, credentials, personal qualities, and qualifications (age, gender, moral character, etc.) can be used to restrict access, but regardless of the specific criteria employed, the general principle remains the same. In order to gain admission, one must be authorized; that is, one must enjoy the confidence and command the trust of the group as a whole, or of those who have been delegated as its gatekeepers. Here it should also be noted that authorization ordinarily carries with it implicit obligations, for the group trusts those whom it expects to be respectful of its sensibilities and values as expressed in the codes of etiquette, decorum, and ritual that determine the kinds of speech and behavior considered appropriate to the setting. Violation of these codes can result in loss of the group's trust, withdrawal of authorization, and expulsion from the privileged sphere.

AUTHORIZED SPEECH AND SIGNIFICANT SILENCE

When an authorized speaker advances to an authorized and authorizing place, the audience falls quiet. This silence ought not to be taken for granted, but ought to prompt a prolonged inquiry. How does this silence come to be? How is it maintained or enforced, and how fully? What does this absence of speech signify? More pointedly, one might ask if it is the speaker (or the speaker's henchmen) who silences an audience, or if an audience silences itself in order that the speaker might speak? Further, is it really the speaker who speaks to the audience in such situations, or does an audience speak to itself through the medium of the speaker? Finally, if we combine the most challenging of these possibilities (although by no means the least probable), we are led to wonder if, at least in those situations where the audience is most respectfully attentive, it might not be silencing itself in order to hear itself speak to itself through a speaker it takes to be its own representative, delegate, or in-carnation?

Silence takes many forms, however, and one needs to take account of the nonverbal behaviors of a silent audience, for these can serve as an indication of the extent to which its members accept and acknowledge the speaker's authority or merely bow to his or her power. Resistance, for example, can take the form of simple inattention or disrespect, as every classroom teacher knows. Such resistance becomes more acute when it is signaled in visible bodily demeanor (yawns, eye-rolling, loung-ing, etc.) and threatens to spread to others in the audience. When it becomes visible to the speaker, it can amount to—or be taken for—a sign of open defiance.

If upon close examination the silence of the audience proves to be of analytic interest, so too are the moments in which this silence is broken and one begins to experience, albeit vaguely at first, the absence of the absence of the audience's speech. Here it is helpful to recall two points: first, as I have repeatedly stressed, the authority of the speaker depends on the trust of the audience (or, alternatively, on the fear that makes an audi-ence act as if it had such trust); and second, an audience has ways of talking to itself that do not require the agency of a speaker. Moreover, an audience has recourse to these ways when it begins to lose trust in those whom it has authorized to speak. Thus, when an audience starts to whisper, the authority of the speaker has been called into doubt, and a speaker who says things sufficiently jarring to cause the audience to mutter has placed his or her authority at risk. Accordingly, speakers who wish to avoid these possibilities—and this accounts for the vast majority—strive to say inconsequential and platitudinous things in a way that makes them sound fresh and stimulating, and to say challenging things in a sufficiently conventional way as to make them sound mild, navigating in this fashion between the twin dangers of shocking and boring their audiences.

CONJUNCTIONS AND DISRUPTIONS

Ultimately I want to suggest that discursive authority is not so much an entity as it is (1) an effect; (2) the capacity for produc-ing that effect; and (3) the commonly shared opinion that a given actor has the capacity for producing that effect. More precisely, I take the effect to be the result of the conjuncture of the right speaker, the right speech and delivery, the right staging and props, the right time and place, and an audience whose historically and culturally conditioned expectations establish the parameters of what is judged "right" in all these instances. When these crucial givens of the discursive situation combine in such a way as to produce attitudes of trust, respect, docility, acceptance, even reverence, in the audience, or—viewing things from the opposite perspective—when the preexistent values, orientations, and expectations of an audience predispose it to respond to a given speech, speaker, and setting with these reverent and submissive attitudes, "authority" is the result.

Although the preceding discussion may have its uses, it is meant to be no more than a set of preliminary and provisional reflections that may provide the starting point for a more empirically grounded set of inquiries. In the subsequent chapters, it is my intention to study authority not as an abstract concept, but in its concrete occurrences; not as a static entity, but in its dynamics. I am also inclined to think that the best way to study something like authority is not when it operates smoothly and efficiently, for its success in some measure depends on naturalizing itself and obscuring the very processes of which it is the product. Thus, I propose to investigate select moments of crisis. Having come to view authority as the effect produced by a specific conjunction, in chapters 2 through 4 I will consider in detail three episodes in which that conjunction is disrupted, as for example (a) when an unauthorized person starts to speak in the authorized and authorizing sphere (chapter 2); (b) when a fully authorized person is expected to say the wrong thing in such a setting (chapter 3); and (c) when people who are expected to say the wrong thing seek authorization (chapter 4). In all cases, we are able to observe the critical moments of challenge and riposte when actors who are accustomed to enjoying a relative monopoly on the privileged sphere confront the possibility that someone else will make use of it to gain authorization for acts of speech they consider antithetical to their own desires and interests. Just as the nature of the challenges varies in these three cases, so does the nature of the responses. In one instance, the challenging speaker is removed from the privileged sphere (chapter 2); in another, events are manipulated so that he loses his opportunity to speak (chapter 3); and in the third, the nature of the sphere is violently transformed, losing its authorization and its capacity to authorize (chapter 4).

The examples I have chosen are drawn from societies sufficiently removed in time from our own to provide a secure critical distance, but sufficiently connected to us by way of continuing cultural tradition that they may still afford us some feeling of recognition. In selecting these data, I began by identifying the most privileged locus for speech within three societies of ancient and medieval Europe: the Assembly (*agorē*) of the Homeric Greeks, the Roman Senate, and the Germanic *Thing*. I then looked for the most disruptive events said to have occurred within each of these settings. In the first instance, this led me to a work of poetic fiction (the episode of Thersites as recounted in book 2 of the *Iliad*); in the second, to an historic event (Caesar's assassination, as reported by Suetonius, Dio Cassius, and Plutarch); and in the third, to an intermediate form — the literary recasting of history (Egil Skallagrimsson's conflict with the Norwegian king and queen, as preserved in the saga that bears his name).

In all cases I deal with texts, not events themselves, as is always true when one studies the past (and much of the time when one studies the present). And although in the confines of the present work I cannot possibly investigate the question of how *textual* authority is constituted, I still find that my inquiry here turns back on itself, for all the texts I will be treating enjoyed considerable authority within the societies that produced them, that is, their audiences put their trust in these accounts and listened to them attentively, permitting their words to act on them. Accordingly, I am willing to grant these same texts a certain degree of authority at second hand and make use of them, not for the recovery of "actual events," but for the elucidation of what authority was and how it operated within these societies. I trust that these texts said things which their audiences found credible and which we may therefore take to reflect with some accuracy the sociopolitical processes and authority effects with which those people were familiar.

Originally, it was my intention to write a set of conclusions based upon the examples treated in chapters 2–4, and to present them in a final chapter. Research never goes precisely according to plan, however, and complex issues have a way—maddening or delightful, depending on one's disposition—of spilling beyond the bounds allotted to them, thereby defying easy closure. As I grappled with the data I had assembled, ever more questions kept arising, some of which have now been given their own chapters: "corrosive" discourses like gossip, rumor, and curses, which eat away at authority (chapter 5); the problematic situation of women (chapter 6); the role of religion in the construction of authority (chapter 7); and the question of whether authority in the modern and postmodern world differs fundamentally, or only superficially, from its premodern counterpart (chapters 8 and 9, which take up two further examples).

2

ORATORY AND RIDICULE

Thersites and the Homeric Assembly

THE HOMERIC ASSEMBLY: FORMS AND PROCEDURES

Within Homeric diction, the term *agorē* marks both a place and an institution. More specifically, it marks the place where people met to engage in certain highly patterned practices, as well as the meetings and practices which transpired in that place. The place was an open arena formed when participants sat about an open center that they could enter in order to speak. Participants came in two forms. Those of high rank were entitled to seat themselves closest to the center, where, in permanently established assembly-places, a ring of stones might be set, whose surfaces had been polished smooth by the bottoms of worthies who occupied them in assemblies past. Further from the center were the others, who sat on the ground and participated less fully in the proceedings.

Although the Homeric texts do not include anything like a copy of their *Roberts' Rules of Order,* we may infer the standard practices by noting the patterns and regularities that recur in the numerous descriptions of assemblies. Generally, then, an assembly was called by a sovereign king or high-ranking hero, who sent out his heralds to announce the meeting and to bring the (exclusively male) group of those who participation was desired to the assembly-place. Once gathered at that site, people took their customary seats, and the person who had called the meeting would speak first, although some other person of rank might also get things started by asking why this assembly was being held. To address the group, one rose from his seat and stepped into the center, receiving a sceptre from one of the heralds upon doing so. This sceptre served as the tangible token of his right to stand, enter, and speak.

In general, speeches took one of two forms, being addressed either to the group as a whole or to the preceding speaker. In the former case, a speaker resumed his seat directly he had finished, and in the latter, both persons involved in the dialogue would remain standing until their exchange was concluded. Moreover, with one exception only—which will be considered at length below—all those who stood and spoke in the center of the assembly held the rank of king (*basileus*). Others in the audience might respond to speeches with pointed silence, with shouts of approval, or might even spring into action at the conclusion of a speech, but beyond these possibilities they were expected to remain seated and silent until such time as the assembly (the group and the occasion of communal gathering) "dissolved."

A JOINTLY HOSTED ASSEMBLY

Much of the *Iliad*'s tensest and most significant action takes place within its assemblies. There is one assembly that holds particular interest, in part for the ways in which it is typical, and in part for its anomalies. This is the assembly described in book 2, which comes at a fairly delicate moment in the epic's unfolding. Prior action has included the offense of Agamemnon against Apollo's priest and the consequent plague; the assembly which Achilles called, hoping to set matters right; the celebrated quarrel of Agamemnon and Achilles, their mutual denunciations, and the latter's withdrawal from combat; Achilles' appeal to his divine mother, her intercession with Zeus, and Zeus's decision to aid him by aiding the Trojans in battle. All of these incidents are recounted in book 1. Book 2 continues the story, describing the false dream sent by Zeus, promising victory to Agamemnon, but actually leading him toward disaster; Agamemnon's decision to call another assembly; and the preliminary council (*boulē,* a term used to describe the meeting of a smaller, more select group than the more general *agorē*), in which he brought together the high-ranking kings and explained to them the plan he had developed to test his troops by disingenuously offering them the chance to return home.

With this, Agamemnon dissolved the council and moved toward the *agorē,* leading the nobles behind him. Things were considerably more complex than he believed, for he had been deceived by the false dream, which rendered him blind to the true nature of the situation. What is more, the normal lines of cleavage evident in the division of any assembly into an inner circle of kings and an outer circle of the rest was particularly exacerbated in this instance, as described in the passage in which these two groups entered the assembly ground.

Having spoken thus, [Agamemnon] went forth from the council
And they rose with him and they were persuaded by the shepherd
   of the people —
They, the sceptre-bearing kings. And the common warriors
   hastened.
Just as tribes of swarming bees go out
From a cave, ever more coming forth
And they fly in clusters to springtime flowers,
Some flying here in a swarm, and some there,
So many tribes marched in crowds from the ships
And the huts before the broad beach
To the assembly-place [the *agorē*]. And among them Rumor had
   blazed up,
Zeus's messenger, inciting them to go. They gathered.
The assembly was all stirred up, and the earth groaned
Under the warriors as they sat down. A din arose, and nine
Shouting heralds restrained them
So they might hear the kings, nurtured by Zeus.
Hastily the warriors sat down, and they were kept in their seats,
Ceasing from the clamor

                                        (2.84–100)*

---

* All translations in this and subsequent chapters are original.

Within this passage, so rich in poetic language and description, line 2.86 holds particular interest for the subtlety with
which it underscores a point of utmost importance. The line
begins by naming those whom Agamemnon led from his council to the assembly as "sceptre-bearing kings" (*skēptoukhoi basilēes*), and the syntax has been organized in such a way that these
words fall at the end of a sentence that began two lines earlier.
A period follows, breaking the line, after which a new and very
short sentence fills it out, a sentence that describes the motion
toward assembly of all those who were *not* included in Agamemnon's council. This sentence also inverts normal word order, naming these other people in the line's last word, "common warriors" (*laoi*). Kings and commoners are thus conjoined
in this line much as they were in Homeric society, the one coming first and the other last, with the caesura marking the gulf
that divides them.

Also significant is another detail that lies embedded in the
poetic diction of this passage. Whereas the participants ordinarily would be summoned to assembly by the heralds of the
king who called the meeting, such is not the case here. The
nobles who met in council received word directly from Agamemnon himself, and were led by him to the assembly-place.
In contrast, the common warriors were called to assembly by a
herald, but not one in Agamemnon's service. Rather, they were
summoned by Rumor herself, who appears in personified form
and is explicitly identified as "Zeus's messenger" (*Ossa . . . Dios
angelos*, 2.93–94).

One may, of course, dismiss this as metaphor, but something
is gained by treating it more seriously. Throughout book 2,
Agamemnon and Zeus are working very much at cross purposes, and if one accepts the text's testimony that Zeus himself
has called the commoners to assembly, acting through the
agency of his messenger, Rumor, then we recognize a new level
of complexity in the proceedings that ensued. It would then
appear that we have not a unitary phenomenon, but rather two
different, if coterminous assemblies, one called by Agamemnon
and the other by Zeus. Moreover, the two different sorts of
people who participate in any assembly—the nobles of the inner circle and the commoners of the outer—were here even
more imperfectly integrated than usual, insofar as they came at

the bidding of different sovereigns. On this occasion the commitment of the commoners to Agamemnon and to his projects was thus considerably less than total, and they remained imperfectly under his control, for all that his discipline was imposed on them when they entered the assembly-place and belatedly encountered his heralds, who forced them to sit still "so they might hear the kings, nurtured by Zeus" (2.98).

It was only at this point—when an uneasy and unstable quiet had been established—that Agamemnon arose, sceptre in hand, to deliver a crafty address in which he dwelt upon the promises of victory that had been made by Zeus, the ten-to-one superiority which the Greeks enjoyed over the Trojans, and the shame they would experience were they to withdraw. Finally, however, he concluded with a suggestion he hoped would have been rendered utterly unacceptable by all of his preceding remarks: "Let us flee with the ships to our dear ancestral land, for no longer will we take Troy of the wide streets." (2.140–41).

THE FLIGHT TO THE SHIPS

However much Agamemnon may have wanted the Greeks to reject the suggestion of flight, his concluding words had an immediate and galvanizing effect on them, particularly the commoners who had come to this assembly for Zeus's purposes and not for his. Directly they ran for the ships, shouting as they went, until their headlong flight was halted by Odysseus, who had been set to this task by the goddess Athena, and who had armed himself with Agamemnon's sceptre before setting out. The passage describing his attempts to restore order and to bring everyone back to assembly was a favorite in antiquity, and it continues to hold considerable interest, particularly for the way it falls into two parallel, but contrasting speeches directed toward the nobles and the commoners respectively (2.188–97 and 2.198–206, which are set out in table 2.1).

Both sections open with preambles (IA and IIA) establishing the social identity of the two different groups Odysseus encountered and indicating the treatment he gave them. We are told that with "a kingly and distinguished man," (*basilēa kai exokhon andra*, 2.188), he used no more than "gentle words"

TABLE 2.1: The Two Sides of Odysseus's Intervention

Section I: 2.188–97	Section II: 2.198–206
A) When he came on a kingly and distinguished man, Standing beside him, he would restrain him with gentle words:	When he saw a man of the people and found him shouting, He would drive him along with the sceptre and would urge him with speech:
B) "Good sir, it is not fitting to try to terrify you as though you were a coward.	B) "Good sir,
1) Sit yourself down 2) and make the others of the host be seated,	1) sit still 2) and listen to the speech of others who are mightier than you, as you are unwarlike, helpless, and not to be counted upon in battle or in assembly.
C) For you do not yet fully know Agamemnon's mind. He is testing you now, and soon he will press hard upon the sons of the Achaeans. Did we not all hear what he said in the council? Let him not, being angered, do some evil against the sons of the Achaeans.	
D) Great is the spirit of kings nurtured by Zeus.	D) In no way do we Achaeans all rule as kings here. The leadership of many is no good thing.
Their honor is from Zeus, and cunning Zeus holds then dear."	Let there be one leader, one king, to whom the child of deviously cunning Cronus gave the sceptre and the laws of tradition that he might counsel them."

(2.189), while with "a man of the people" (*dēmou . . . andra*, 2.198), not only was his speech unmodified by concerns of gentility, but he acted on the fellow's body as well as his ears, driving him back to the place of assembly with the sceptre as a prod.

The speeches which follow these introductory lines both begin with the same marker of polite address (*daimonie*, 2.190 and 2.200), which may, however, be used straightforwardly on the one hand and ironically on the other. After this, they proceed—after a bit of mollification in the case of the nobles—to the specific demands Odysseus made in his attempt to restore the conditions under which the assembly could be resumed. Thus, he asked that all be seated (sections IB1 and IIB1), voicing this in somewhat rougher terms to the common warriors than to the nobles: "sit still" (*atremas ēso*, 2.200), as opposed to "sit down" (*kathēso*, 2.191). His second demand was more asymmetric still, for whereas the nobles were asked to speak up and to command their subordinates to be seated (section IB2), the commoners—whose noisiness is consistently associated with dirt and disorder—were told to be silent and listen as their superiors talk (section IIB2).

Odysseus concluded both of these paired speeches (sections ID and IID) with the assertion that kingship is the basis of all order, and the legitimating claim that kings rule by Zeus's favor. When speaking to the nobles, he was able to touch lightly on these ideologically significant points, making use of familiar formulae such as his reference to "kings nurtured by Zeus" (*diotrephēes basilēes*, 2.98), for these people knew the arguments well, and they knew whose interests they served. When dealing with *hoi polloi*, however, it was necessary for him to press his case more aggressively and to uphold monarchic rule against their presumed desire for more democratic alternatives ("the leadership of many," *polykoiraniē* 2.204).

Other connections between the two speeches notwithstanding, there is one portion of Odysseus's address to the nobles (section IC) that has no parallel. Here he offered explanations and made reference to privileged communications that were accessible only to them. He reminded the kings that as Agamemnon had explained to them (and to them alone) in the preliminary council (*boulē*), he did not mean for his suggestion of flight to be accepted, but was only "testing" (*peiratai*, 2.193).

The same familiar hierarchic distinction made in so many ways between kings and commoners is structurally encoded in these paired speeches in three separate ways: (1) the speech to the nobles comes first; (2) it is longer (eight lines as opposed to seven); and (3) it contains an important section that its counterpart lacks. Yet in both, the content remains much the same, with Odysseus defending Agamemnon's intentions against his words (also, unknowingly, against the intentions of Zeus), his subtextual arguments against his explicit conclusions, and the sincere speech he delivered in the elite council against the disingenuous speech he gave to the general assembly.

The net effect of Odysseus's efforts is clear enough. By a mixture of persuasion and coercion (the latter directed only at the commoners), he managed to bring all of the Greeks back to the *agorē*, where he expected that the nobles would resume discussion and lead the group to a more suitable and decorous conclusion. At this point, however, a rather remarkable character made his appearance: Thersites, the only non-noble to speak in assembly in either of the Homeric poems.

THE BASEST, MOST HATED OF MEN

The etymology of Thersites' name identifies him as one who is marked by audacity and daring, and we meet him as he stands in defiance of the two demands that Odysseus made on the members of his class. Even as all others had fallen into compliance, Thersites alone refused to sit down and shut up. Before we are permitted to hear what he says, however, the text is at pains to describe him in such a way as to emphasize his anomalous nature, and to shape the attitude we will adopt toward him.

> Then the others sat down, and settled in their seats,
> But still Thersites of the unmeasured words alone scolded.
> He could hurl many words from his heart, disorderly ones,
> Idly and not according to order, to make strife with kings,
> [Saying] anything that he thought might be laughable

To the Argives. He was the ugliest, basest man before Troy.
Squinty he was, and lame in one foot. Both his shoulders
Were hunched and joined together over his chest;
His head was pointed, and covered with sparse hair.
He was most hated by Achilles and above all by Odysseus,
For he repeatedly reviled them.

(2.211–21)

Three closely interrelated aspects of this singular fellow are sequentially described as the passage moves from the nature of his caustic and immoderate speech (2.212–16), to his hideously deformed physical appearance (2.216–19), to the adverse reactions he prompted in others (2.220–23). That these all go together is signaled by the elsewhere unattested adjective *aiskhistos* (2.216), a superlative form that designates him as simultaneously "most ugly," "most base," "most blaming (of others)," and "most blameworthy (himself)."

With regard to this term and its broad range of meaning, Gregory Nagy has astutely written: "[Thersites] is *aiskhistos* 'most base' not only for what he says and does . . . but also for his very ugliness. And surely the base appearance of Thersites serves to mirror in form the content of his blame poetry." Yet starting from the same point — the association of an ugly language of blame with an ugly speaker of that language — one may move the analysis in a somewhat different direction by stressing that ideals of beauty and ugliness do not spring unproblematically from nature, but are themselves culturally constructed.

Blame thus originates not with "the ugly," but rather with persons who suffer the adverse judgments of others who, in one fashion or another, more thoroughly embody their society's aesthetic norms. "The ugly" thus come to experience these norms as the ultimate source of their suffering, and they can ratify or embrace society's notion of "the good" and "the beautiful" only at the cost of denouncing themselves. Yet they have another option to them, for they may also denounce the norms and those whom they profit, although in doing so they risk offending people, particularly those who are most successful and powerful under the established regime of beauty. This dynamic may be perceived in the specification that Thersites singles out Achilles and Odysseus — the two heroes consistently judged to be "the best of the Achaeans" — for criticism, and in return came to be "most hated" (*ekhthistos*, 2.220) by them.

THE TAMING OF THE SCOLD

Finally, after the text has laid this groundwork, it permits us to hear the speech with which Thersites "shouting loudly, reviled Agamemnon" (2.224):

> "Atreides, with what do you again find fault, and what is it you
>   desire?
> Your huts are full of bronze, and many women
> Are in your huts, choice ones, whom we Achaeans
> Give to you first whenever we capture a city.
> Yes, and still you want for gold, which one of the Trojans,
> Breakers of horses, might bear out of Troy as a ransom for a son
> Whom I or another Achaean might lead off, having captured him.
> Or would you mingle in love with a young woman
> Whom you keep far away for yourself? It is not seemly
> For their leader to involve the sons of the Achaeans in evils.
> You weaklings, you evil shameful things, Achaean women and
>   not men!
> Let us return home with the ships and leave him
> By himself in Troy to chew on his prizes, so he can learn
> Whether or not we bring help to him —
> Someone who now has dishonored Achilles, a much better man
> Than he. For having seized Achilles' prize, he keeps her.
> But anger does not come to Achilles' breast, and he is yielding,
> Otherwise, Atreides, you would now have committed your last
>   outrage."

(2.225–42)

Although this is fairly violent language, it is hardly unprecedented, and after his big buildup, Thersites' rhetorical performance may even come as something of a disappointment. To be sure, he makes one remark that by the normal standards of epic diction was considered coarse and offensive: his suggestion that Agamemnon liked to "mingle in love with a young woman" (2.232). This is not just an improper reference to matters sexual and therefore private, but also a pointed allusion to the episode in book 1 where Agamemnon, having been forced to give up his own woman (Chryseis), demanded that he be compensated with Achilles' favorite (Briseis), thereby provoking their quarrel. With this important exception there is little in Thersites' remarks that goes out of bounds. In truth, his speech picks up on the denunciations which Achilles himself hurled at Agamemnon and, as many critics have observed, it contains numerous phrases and passages that closely echo the latter. Francis Cairns, inter alia, has conveniently listed the points that the two speeches have in common:

> Agamemnon is greedy (1.222=2.225–33, esp. 229); he takes the loot while others, especially Achilles and Thersites (!) do the work (1.163–68=2.229–33); it would be better to go off home, leaving Agamemnon at Troy (1.169–71=2.236–38); the Greeks are slack and worthless (1.231=2.235, cf. 241). In addition there are two full lines where Thersites repeats verbatim the actual words of Achilles (*Iliad* 2.240=1.356, and 2.242= 1.232).

Essentially, Thersites says little that Achilles had not said just a short while earlier, speaking to the same person, before the same audience, in the same place, and under closely related circumstances. Moreover, it is Achilles, and not Thersites, whose rebukes were punctuated by slashing invectives, with which he excoriated Agamemnon as "wine-sodden, with the eyes of a dog and the heart of a deer" (1.225), "eater of the masses" (1.231), and "greediest for gain of all men" (1.121). Obviously, were Thersites Achilles, his discourse would have produced a different reaction, and indeed, one ancient critic observed that had he been Diomedes, nothing he said would have been treated as laughable. Far from being a figure of heroic stature, however, Thersites was a common warrior, and an ugly, crippled, unruly one at that.

Issues of content notwithstanding, the very fact of Thersites' speaking poses serious problems. In part, the question before the Greeks and before those who would interpret this text is one of temporal and dramatic sequencing. That is, did the assembly that was interrupted by the flight to the ships resume with Thersites' speech or, alternatively, did Thersites pose the last obstacle to its resumption? Resolving this issue depends, in turn, on spatial and social considerations: Did he or did he not have the right to stand up, enter the circle, and speak therein?

Again it is Odysseus who moves to resolve things, his intervention taking nonverbal form at first. He "looks darkly" at Thersites, a phrase that James Holoka studied extensively and found to denote that facial expression through which a Homeric hero announces "that an infraction of propriety has occurred, and deplores the willful traducing of rules of conduct governing relations between superordinates and inferiors." Further, "in all instances, this facial gesture charges the speech it introduces with a decidedly minatory fervency and excitement: a threshold has been reached and such inflammable materials as wounded pride, righteous indignation, frustration, shame, and shock are nearing the combustion point."

> Looking darkly at him, Odysseus rebuked him with these harsh
>   words:
> "Thersites, although a clear orator, you are indiscriminate in your
>   speech.
> Desist, and do not have a mind to make strife on your own
>   against kings.
> For I say that there is no other man who is lowlier than you
> Among those who came with Atreides to Troy.
> Therefore you ought not speak in assembly, mouthing off to
>   kings,
> Nor ought you utter reproaches to them, nor watch for a chance
>   to return home.
> We do not know at all clearly how these events will turn out:
> Whether well or badly we sons of Achaeans will return home.
> In these circumstances you are continually reproaching Atreus's
>   son, Agamemnon,
> The shepherd of the host, for all the things that the Danaan
>   heroes
> Give him, and mockingly you speak in assembly.
> But this I say to you — and it will come to pass —
> If I come upon you acting as senselessly as you do now,
> No more may the head of Odysseus sit upon his shoulders,
> And no more may I be known as Telemachus's father
> If I do not seize you and strip off your clothes,
> Your cloak and your chiton that cover your shameful parts,

And send you weeping to the swift ships,
Driving you out of the assembly with unseemly blows."
(2.245–64)

Nowhere does Odysseus really engage in debate with Thersites or dispute what he says, for the issue is not the content of Thersites' speech but his right to speak. More precisely, the issue is his right to *agoreuein,* a verb formed from the noun *agorē,* which most commonly and most literally means "to speak *in assembly.*" It is precisely this which Odysseus would deny Thersites, whom he tells "you ought not speak *in assembly* (*ouk . . . agoreuois,* 2.250), mouthing off to kings," and whom he threatens to drive *from the assembly-place* (*peplēgōn agorēthen,* 2.264) should he be found there again. That Thersites may say the same things at some other time and in some other place is implicitly left open, and prior action has shown that others (e.g., Achilles; cf. Diomedes at 9.32–33) can say them within the spatial and temporal bounds of the assembly. But the conjuncture of this particular speaker, speech, place, occasion, and audience is something that Odysseus judges improper and intolerable.

If Odysseus is to establish his point he can permit no reply, for it is precisely Thersites' right to stand and speak in the center of the assembly that is at issue. Accordingly, if Odysseus is to make good his case and to restore what he regards as proper order and decorum, he must remove the offender from the place where he does not belong and put a stop to his offending action: that is, he must render Thersites silent and seated once more in the outer circle of the assembly ground, along with the other commoners. As the action continues, we find that he has available to him the means to accomplish this.

Thus Odysseus spoke, and he struck him with the sceptre
On the back and shoulders. Thersites doubled over, shed a thick
    tear,
And a bloody welt rose up on his back
Under the golden sceptre. He sat down, terrified
And pained, and looking about aimlessly, he wiped away his tears.
Although grieving, the others laughed sweetly at him.
And thus someone would say, looking at his neighbor:
"Truly, Odysseus has done thousands of great deeds
Taking the lead in councils and preparing for battle,

But the greatest deed he has accomplished
Is keeping this outrageous word-hurler out of the assembly.
Never again will his bold spirit incite him
To strive against kings with reproachful words."

$$(2.265–77)$$

THE SWEETNESS OF LAUGHTER

The last word lies neither with Odysseus nor with Thersites but with the crowd, who pass clear judgment and whose views we are largely meant to accept as fitting and proper, for all that we may retain some sympathy for the defeated Thersites. In some measure, of course, the crowd's reaction was already prefigured by Thersites' tears, for though it is not necessarily a shameful thing to weep within the epic scale of values (witness Achilles' tears for Patroclus or Zeus's for Sarpedon), to weep as the result of physical pain is the epitome of unheroic conduct. At the moment he cries, Thersites renders himself ridiculous and contemptible in the eyes of all present, and the struggle is effectively over. Still, the fact that this man's tears, pain, and humiliation cause all of the others to laugh—and to laugh "sweetly" at that—surely must grate a bit on our non-epic sensibilities, and ought to lead us to reflect on just what the Achaeans found so funny.

Laughter, as James Redfield has rightly observed, is rare in the *Iliad,* and as a rule it seems to mark the release of social tension. Laughter that is specifically described as "sweet" is rarer still, being heard on four other occasions only. Paris laughed sweetly when he wounded Diomedes in the foot, effectively nailing him to the ground (11.378), and Zeus did so when the weeping Artemis came to him after Hera had boxed her ears with her own bow and arrows (21.508). Sweet laughter also swept over the Achaeans when Oilean Ajax, having been tripped by Athena during a footrace such that he tumbled headlong into a dung pile, came up protesting this act of divine sabotage, spitting out cow turds as he did so (23.784).

Also comparable is the story of Irus (*Odyssey* 18.1–121), a beggar described as big and greedy but lacking in strength, who encountered Odysseus outside the royal hall when the latter was himself disguised as a beggar. Resenting what he perceived as an infringement on his accustomed territory, Irus ordered the newcomer to depart, but Odysseus refused, "looking darkly" at him as he did so. Further exchanges built to a violent encounter, much to the amusement of the onlooking suitors.

> After they put up their hands, Irus struck at his right
> Shoulder, and Odysseus struck him on the neck, beneath the ear, crushing
> The bones within. And straightaway red blood came down his mouth.
> He fell in the dust, groaning, and he ground his teeth together,
> Flailing at the earth with his feet. But the illustrious suitors
> Were dying with laughter as they put up their own hands. And Odysseus,
> Seizing Irus's foot, dragged him through the doorway until he reached the courtyard
> And the gates of the portico. And he set him down, leaning him
> Against the outer wall of the courtyard. And he took his walking stick [*skēptron*] in hand,
> And uttering winged words, he addressed him:
> "Sit there now, scaring off the dogs and the pigs,
> And don't try to be the leader of strangers and beggars,
> Lest being so wretched, you bring on yourself an even worse evil."
> Then over his shoulders he flung his shabby leather pouch,
> All full of holes, its strap just a cord.
> Then, going back to the doorway, he sat himself down. And the suitors went inside,
> Laughing sweetly . . .
>
> (*Odyssey* 18.95–111)

The similarities which mark these five cases are displayed in table 2.2, which makes it clear that "sweet" laughter follows upon the physical anguish, public degradation, and crashing defeat certain characters experience in situations of open competition and conflict. It should be stressed, however, that it is not the fall of the mighty which prompts this mirthful response, nor the fall of the lowly, at least not the lowly who know their place. Rather, those whose downfall prompts "sweet" laughter are regularly presented by the text and perceived by the laughers as persons who have presumptuously

TABLE 2.2: The Components of "Sweet" Laughter

	Thersites	Diomedes	Artemis	Ajax	Irus
In a situation of open conflict or competition	Assembly	War	War	Footrace	Fistfight
A person suffers bodily violence at the hands of a superior	Beaten by Odysseus with sceptre	Wounded by Paris* with arrow	Beaten by Hera with own bow and arrows	Tripped by Athene, lost race to Odysseus	Beaten by Odysseus
Particularly involving attacks to the foot / Bringing him/her literally low	Lame in one foot (2.217) / Knocked to ground	Wounded in foot (11.377) / Arrow pins him to ground		Tripped by foot (23.782) / Falls in dung heap	Dragged off by foot (Od. 18.101) / Knocked to dust and dragged down stairs
Producing a shameful bodily discharge	Large tear, bloody welt		Tears	Spits dung	Bleeds from mouth

*It is less than clear that Paris ranks above Diomedes. Yet the superiority of Odysseus to Irus or to Ajax also was not initially evident, but was revealed in the course of the action and then ratified by the crowd's laughter. By this logic, it may be that his ability to wound Diomedes established Paris's unsuspected superiority to him, although the fact that it was Paris himself who laughed in this instance creates further problems still. Perhaps it is best to conclude that the incident demonstrated to Paris's satisfaction (if to no one else's) his superiority to Diomedes.

claimed a status that their capabilities cannot sustain, and who lose their honor when they fail to live up to the expectations an audience has for anyone cast in the role they assume. At the moment such overreachers are knocked to the ground, their bodies stained by the fluid discharges of blood or tears that confirm their inadequacy, vulnerability and disgrace, spectators understand the inherent rightness of their culture's values and the stability of their social order to have been dramatically reaffirmed, at which point they hoot with glee.

THE HALT AND THE LAME

Ancient authors also pondered over the question of what made Thersites such a figure of fun, and they often focused on a specific feature which thus far we have ignored: the fact that he was lame (*khōlos*). What is more, this debility led them to associate him with the god Hephaestus, who is the only other lame figure of the epic and who also appears somewhat ridiculous at times, as when he provoked "unquenchable" laughter among the gods. That occasion holds considerable interest, for it provides a divine counterpoint to the issues which find expression at the human level in the Thersites episode.

On Olympus, as on earth, the question repeatedly arises whether—if at all—those of lesser rank and power can effectively challenge decisions made by sovereign rulers. This is at issue, for instance, in book 1 of the *Iliad* when Zeus decides to grant success to the Trojans, and Hera (who favors the Greeks) protests vigorously. In response, Zeus orders his wife—in terms that reflect the politics of gender, just as Odysseus's similar commands in book 2 reflect those of class—to "Sit down in silence" (*akeousa kathēso,* 1.565; cf. 2.200), and he goes on to threaten physical violence against her and against any who may support her if she fails to obey. In this tense moment Hephaestus intervenes, counseling Hera to be prudent, and recalling another occasion in which, we are told elsewhere, Zeus hung her up by the hands, tied anvils to her feet, and hurled her would-be rescuer down from Olympus.

> "Endure, my mother, and submit, although you are pained,
> Lest dear though you are, with my own eyes I see you
> Smitten. And then, although grieving, in no way will I be able

To save you, for it is a difficult thing to set one's self against the
  Olympian.
Another time when I was eager to defend you
He grabbed me by the foot and hurled me from the edge of the
  divine realm
All day I was borne along and at sunset
I tumbled down in Lemnos, with little life left in me.
Then the Sintian men cared for me just after my fall."
Thus he spoke, and the goddess, white-armed Hera smiled,
And smiling, she took a cup from her son's hand.
Then he poured wine for all the other gods,
Moving from left to right, drawing sweet nectar from the mixing
  vessel.
And unquenchable laughter arose among the blessed gods
As they saw Hephaestus shuffling through the palace.

                        (1.586–600)

Several points should be made with regard to this passage.
First, Hephaestus, like Thersites, is one of the lowliest members of his relevant social group. As the craftsman of the gods he holds a menial station, and as the son whom Hera conceived without consort he is something of a bastard, lacking ties to any defining patrilineage. Second, his lowly status within the body social is mirrored in the image of his lameness, a doubly negative marker in that it calls attention first to the lowest member of his physical body (the foot) and second to its defective status. Third, this passage makes his defect follow from a foolhardy attempt to oppose his sovereign ruler, for as other texts make clear, Hephaestus was injured at precisely that moment when Zeus "grabbed [him] by the foot" (*podos tetagōn* 1.591) and cast him down from Olympus (cf. Apollodorus, *Bibliotheca* 1.3.5). Fourth, the height from which Zeus hurled him may be understood in sociopolitical as well as geophysical terms, for Hephaestus's fall marks his (literal and figurative) demotion and de-gradation. Finally, Hephaestus's station, appearance, and history conspire to render him contemptible and ridiculous in the eyes of others, for not only did the gods break into laughter at the sight of him limping about to wait on tables, but elsewhere he is heard to say "it is a *laughable* and intolerable thing that Aphrodite, Zeus's daughter, ever *dishonors*

me *because I am lame,* and loves destructive Ares because he is handsome *and sound of foot*" (*Odyssey* 8.307–10).

SILENCED SPEAKERS AND ERASED TRADITIONS

If the Homeric poems tell the story of how Hephaestus became lame, they do not do the same for Thersites. All they say of him is contained in the lines quoted above, which convey nothing about his birth, death, or other adventures. Moreover, in striking contrast to every other character who plays a role of similar importance (and many of far lesser importance), Thersites is not provided with a patronym, a genealogy, or a place of origin.

There is, however, information to be had elsewhere, for it is clear from a goodly number of scattered references and artistic representations that Thersites played a prominent role in other works of the lost epic cycle, works that drew on the same rich store of oral traditions as the Homeric poems. For example, a detailed account of his death seems to have been given in the *Aethiopis* of Arctinus of Miletus (a work almost as old as the *Iliad*), which described how Thersites was killed by Achilles after he mocked the hero's love for the slain Penthesilia. What is more, that text and others told how other Greek heroes, particularly Diomedes, were outraged at Thersites' murder and raised such violent strife on his behalf that Achilles was actually forced to offer sacrifices of atonement and to seek ritual purification for the deed.

Information on Thersites' birth and earlier exploits is also found in a scholium to *Iliad* 2.212, which cites the fifth century philosopher Pherecydes of Leros as its source: "Pherecydes said that Thersites was one of those who pursued the Calydonian boar, and having given way to the boar in battle, he was thrown off a precipice by Meleager. As a result his body was mutilated. And Pherecydes says that he was the descendant of Agrius, Dia, and Portheus." The parallel to Hephaestus is striking, for like his divine counterpart, Thersites was lamed when his sovereign superior, displeased with his conduct, hurled him from a great height to the ground below.

At this point, however, one may begin to wonder why Thersites should appear among the high-ranking heroes whom Meleager led in the fabled hunt of the Calydonian boar. What was he doing at Troy, for that matter, and who was he to enter into conflict with the foremost of the Greeks — Agamemnon, Odysseus, and Achilles? And why was another great hero, Diomedes, willing to risk confrontation with Achilles in order to avenge his death? Answers to this string of questions follow from the brief genealogical information this scholium provides, for it makes Thersites out to be a descendant of Portheus, placing him within the lineage of Aetolian kings, from which, according to the *Iliad*, Diomedes and Meleager themselves were also descended (see figure 2.1).

Pherecydes thus makes Thersites an Aetolian prince and a kinsman of Diomedes, whereas the *Iliad* makes him out to be a common warrior of unspecified origins. Experts have debated at some length whether Pherecydes or other later sources filled in what they took to be a crucial lacuna in the Homeric text or, alternatively, whether that text omitted traditional information that was preserved elsewhere. Of these, the latter view strikes me as preferable, since it is utterly anomalous for the *Iliad* to introduce an important character with no information whatever about his family or place of origin.

So singular an omission is not likely to have been an oversight; rather, it is best explained as the result of a conscious and strategic choice, the motives for which may be perceived. By erasing Thersites' genealogy, the *Iliad* was able to take a character traditionally known to be verbally abrasive, insubordinate by temperament, physically cowardly, crippled, and repulsive and to make him a social isolate, someone devoid of familial or

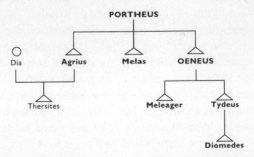

Figure 2.1 Thersites' genealogy. Figures and relations in boldface appear in *Iliad* 9.543–45 and 14.113–18. Those in lightface are given by Pherecydes, as cited in Scholium BL to *Iliad* 2.212. Capital letters indicate kings of Aetolia.

regional connections, thereby providing him with an outsider's freedom to act, while simultaneously giving others the freedom to react to him without fear of anyone leaping to his defense. Moreover, this strategic erasure of traditional information permitted the *Iliad* to transform Thersites from a nobleman into a commoner and a person utterly bereft of social standing. That this was essential both to the narrative and ideological line advanced in book 2 was already recognized by the scholiast, who, directly after quoting Thersites' genealogy, went on to worry about its implications: "But if [Thersites] were a kinsman of Diomedes, Odysseus would not have struck him, for he struck only plebeians!"

The text of the *Iliad* thereby stripped Thersites of his genealogy, much as Odysseus threatened to strip him of his clothes if ever he should be found prating in assembly again (2.258–64). One can make the stronger point that the text deprived Thersites of his genealogy (in which was embedded his claim to noble status) precisely so that Odysseus could remove him from the assembly, for once redefined as a common warrior, Thersites effectively lost his right to speak there. Further, that same loss of identity and status rendered him vulnerable to the kind of physical repression that Odysseus meted out with the sceptre "only to plebeians."

ODYSSEUS'S WEAPON AND THE LEGITIMACY OF KINGS

In many ways, all the action we have been considering is dominated, start to finish, by the image of the golden sceptre. Immediately upon awakening from his false dream, Agamemnon dressed in royal raiments, taking up last of all "the sceptre of his fathers, ever undecaying" (2.46). The nobles whom he led from his preliminary council to the general assembly are similarly described as "sceptre-bearing kings" (2.86). At the moment Agamemnon rose to open the assembly, the text shows him holding his sceptre (2.100–101), and pauses to recount that sceptre's sacred history: how it was made by Hephaestus for Zeus; how Zeus had Hermes deliver it to Pelops, the founding king of Argos who was, according to some sources, his son; and how it descended from Pelops through the line of Argive kings down to Agamemnon (2.101–108).

That passage is a subtle one, for not only does it assert the divine origin and nature of the sceptre, but also it charts several different sorts of involvement with it. Most important is the distinction between kings, who derive their powers and legitimacy from its possession, and those whose contact with the sceptre is instrumental only, and who derive no privileges from it. Of the latter, two sorts of persons are specified and given divine prototypes: artisans (represented by Hephaestus), who may fabricate a sceptre but not own one; and heralds (represented by Hermes), who convey it from one king to another, but never possess it themselves.

After this mythologic excursus, the text returns to Agamemnon, who now leans on the sceptre (2.109), supporting himself physically as well as ideologically on a staff that is also the legitimating emblem of kingship. Later, use value and sign value converge once more when Odysseus, having obtained the sceptre from Agamemnon (2.186), employs it both as a material goad with which to drive the commoners back to assembly (2.199), and as an item of discourse with which to repersuade them of the legitimacy, even the necessity of kingship:

> In no way do we Achaeans all rule as kings here.
> The leadership of many is no good thing. Let there be one leader,
> One king, to whom the child of deviously cunning Cronus [i.e.,
>   Zeus] gave
> The sceptre and the laws of tradition in order that he might
>   counsel them.
>
> (2.203–206)

The sceptre is thus represented as Zeus's gift to those who rule, and with it comes the bundle of powers and prerogatives that constitute kingship. Among these, the last line of this passage calls particular attention to the kings' right to render judgment in matters of law and their right to speak in the privileged spheres of council and assembly, tasks which they undertook with the sceptre in hand. For possession of a sceptre mystified the monopoly that kings held on speech within the most solemn, effective, and consequential arenas of the Homeric world. To grasp a sceptre and stand in the center of the assembly was tantamount to representing one's self, one's office, one's speech, and also one's right to speak in that place and on that occasion as authorized by the divine powers from whom the sceptre was claimed to descend. It was this which Thersites lacked, this which he challenged, and ultimately this with which he was beaten.

Odysseus thus deployed the sceptre against Thersites in a double sense, for it was not just a cudgel with which the king swatted the unruly commoner, but the emblem of authority itself. And although the exercise of this authority depends ultimately on a set of mystificatory claims and arguments embedded in iconic and narrative representations, when an audience is genuinely persuaded by such mystifications (or simply when it dares not challenge them), they can and they will assume considerable social, political, and material force.

3

RUMORS AND PROPHECIES

Lucius Aurelius Cotta and the Roman Senate,
15 March 44 B.C.

POWER AND AUTHORITY IN THE MAKING OF KINGS

Everyone who has read their Shakespeare, or a high school text-book in world history for that matter, knows that the Romans hated kings. The Roman sources — Livy, Dionysius of Halicar-nassus, Cicero, et al., and the now-lost annals from which they drew their information — tell us much the same thing, although they do so in a more nuanced way than is usually recognized. They describe the founding of the city by a heroic first king (Romulus), and an initial period of rule by three other good kings, followed by a slide into tyranny that ended only when kingship was overthrown and the Republic founded (510 B.C., according to tradition). We also have to recall that many of the testimonies on which we rely come from the first century B.C., when the Republic itself was sliding into terminal crisis, and the topic of kingship acquired new interest for some of the most powerful Romans, who looked back to the ancient period of the kings as they sought solutions to that crisis, while also seeking ways to improve their own particular positions.

It is this historic moment which interests me here, this struc-ture of the conjuncture, when actors of one age looked to their stories of an earlier age in search of the models and instruments

37

through which they might rethink the structures of their society, plot their own actions, and interpret the actions of others. Specifically, I want to take as my point of departure the way in which Julius Caesar and his contemporaries understood the procedure their ancestors supposedly used in the selection and installation of their kings after Romulus's death. Close examination of these procedures is rewarding and reveals that they involved — or were believed to have involved — a finely calibrated cooperation between the two principal constituent groups of the Roman polity, the Senate and the people (*Senatus populusque Romanus,* S. P. Q. R.). Such cooperation reflected and helped to define the asymmetric nature of relations between these two groups. The relevant texts state clearly and explicitly that although the people possessed the power (*potestas*) to select a candidate for the throne, exercising their voice through the popular assembly or simply through acclamation in the streets, the choice of the people always remained provisional until it was ratified by the authority (*auctoritas*) of the Senate. Only when these two separate and sequential steps had been accomplished could a new king properly and legitimately assume the throne, robes, responsibilities, and prerogatives of royal office.

According to the annalistic accounts (and the later sources dependent on them), the people and the Senate cooperated in this fashion when selecting Romulus's first three successors: Numa Pompilius, Tullus Hostilius, and Ancus Marcius, all of whom were regarded as exemplary rulers. Subsequent kings, however, violated these procedures in increasingly flagrant ways, with the result that their legitimacy gradually diminished, their reigns became ever more troubled, and the institution of kingship fell ever further into disrepute (table 3.1). Tarquin the Elder erred by actively campaigning among the people, thus intruding his agency into theirs and compromising their independence. Then he offended in similar fashion by packing the Senate with his supporters before seeking its approval. Upon Tarquin's death, Servius Tullius, his protégé, immediately assumed the royal robes and the throne, and only afterward did he seek ratification by the people of what was already a fait accompli. To make matters worse, he did this after bribing the

TABLE 3.1 Accession to the throne of all Roman kings after Romulus

	King's Election Effected		Power Taken By	
	By power of the people	By authority of the Senate	Assuming robes and throne	Killing predecessor
NUMA POMPILIUS	1	2	3	—
TULLUS HOSTILIUS	1	2	3	—
ANCUS MARCIUS	1	2	3	—
Tarquin the Elder	(1)	(2)	3	—
Servius Tullius	(2)	—	1	—
Tarquin the Proud	—	—	2	1

Note: Kings listed in boldface capital letters were regarded as good rulers; those in boldface were kings of dubious legitimacy; and those in lightface letters were regarded as tyrants. Numbers indicate the sequence in which various steps were accomplished. Parentheses indicate that a given step was accomplished in a fashion that was tainted with some measure of impropriety.

lower orders with rich gifts of land, and he ignored the Senate altogether. Finally, Tarquin the Proud murdered Servius, donned the purple, occupied the throne, and never bothered to secure acclamation by the people, the Senate, or anyone else. As a result, his rule came to be understood as the model of tyranny, and the excesses committed by him and his sons so outraged the people and Senate that under the leadership of Lucius Junius Brutus — the first Brutus — they drove the Tarquins from the city and put an end to kingly rule.

The making of kings was thus understood as a process that involved two complementary forms of creative action. Both of these were necessary, and neither sufficient: omission or compromise of either step led to trouble (trouble that was not inherent in the nature of kingship per se). Further, these two forms of creative action resided in and characterized two different social groups along the lines of the general principle articulated by Cicero: "Power [*potestas*] should be in the people and authority [*auctoritas*] in the Senate." Within the context of royal election, *potestas* (from the verb *posse*, "to be able") designated most precisely the capacity to generate novel but as yet unrealized possibilities (cf. *possibilitas*, also from *posse*). These possibilities could then be brought to fulfillment by a vote of ratification, through which the Senate invested them with its full *auctoritas* (from the verb *augere*, "to increase, augment, complete"). The contrast is as clear as is the complementarity of the two capacities and that of the two social bodies with which they were correlated. Thus, the power of the people was understood as the voice of initiative that could transform a citizen into a candidate, while the authority of the Senate was seen as the voice of consequentiality that could transform a candidate into a king.

ATTEMPTS AT PROMPTING THE VOICE OF THE PEOPLE

After his victory at the battle of Munda (17 March 45 B.C.) put an end to the Civil War, Julius Caesar held a virtual monopoly on political power, and in the following months he solidified his control as a docile Senate showered unprecedented honors upon him. No end to this seemed imminent, and by the early months of 44 B.C., many observers believed that Caesar was trying to produce a situation in which the Roman people would hail him as king, based on their reading of three separate episodes.

The first of these was an incident of uncertain date, in which laurel diadems wreathed in white fillets mysteriously appeared on the two golden statues of Caesar that, by order of the Senate, stood on the speaker's platform at the head of the Roman Forum. Ordinarily one of these statues bore a wreath of oak (the *corona civica*), honoring Caesar as Rome's savior and the other, a wreath of grass (the *corona obsidionalis*), honoring him as the city's liberator. The new headgear, however, suggested still greater honors, for the white diadem was a standard emblem of royal status in antiquity. Persian kings had worn them first; subsequently, they were adopted by Alexander the Great and his successors, and ever since the second century B.C., statues of the ancient Roman kings had been similarly adorned.

Some said the diadems were set in place by Caesar's henchmen, and others claimed it was the work of enemies, who sought to discredit him in the public eye. But if responsibility for the deed remains muddied, the reaction it prompted is clear enough, as the Roman people regarded the diadems "very suspiciously," and took them to be "a symbol of slavery." Responding to the crowd's discomfiture, two tribunes of the *plebes* promptly removed them from the statues and arrested a man who was said to have been responsible.

Then there were the events of 26 January 44 B.C., when Caesar returned from Mount Alba, where he had just finished presiding over the Feriae Latinae, a ritual with some interesting associations. Among the most ancient of all Latin rites, it was originally celebrated by the kings of Alba Longa, the foremost city in the Italian peninsula before the emergence of Rome. According to legend, Alba Longa had been founded by Julus, Aeneas's son, from whom Caesar's family (the *gens* Julia) took its name and traced its lineage. For this occasion Caesar coyly signaled these connections by exchanging his normal senatorial footgear for red boots, which he wore "after the fashion of the Alban kings, for he proclaimed that he was related to them through Julus."

Returning to Rome, Caesar was given an official *ovatio* and secured the right to enter the city on horseback, something normally forbidden one holding the office of dictator. Ordinarily, an *ovatio* was a reduced-scale version of a triumph, and like a triumph it was a parade that served to honor a victorious general as he reentered the city. But Caesar, unlike all other attested recipients of this honor, was returning from a ritual celebration, not from battle, and the only victory he might conceivably be said to have won on this occasion was his success in representing himself as a(n Alban?) king within the context of the Feriae Latinae. Further events could only heighten suspicion that the purpose of this extraordinary ceremony was for Caesar to be hailed by the Roman people in similar terms. Yet if this was so, the plan miscarried, as Plutarch recounts:

> When Caesar was descending from Alba to the city, they dared
> to hail him as king. But the people were thrown into confusion

by this, and being vexed, he said "I am not called 'King,' but 'Caesar.'" And when this produced a general hush, he passed on—not very cheerful or well-disposed.

It appears that Caesar's remark—"I am not called 'King,' but 'Caesar'"—was intended as a joke, through which he meant to extricate himself from a potentially embarrassing situation. For in addition to being a suspect title, *Rex* ("King") was also a common cognomen in the lineage of his father's mother—the Marcii *Reges* ("The Kingly Marcii") took this name as part of their claim to descend from the ancient king, Ancus Marcius (figure 3.2). The quip's humor, lame though it was, thus came from Caesar's feigned belief that some poor soul had mistakenly—but altogether innocently—used a matrilineal form, *Rex,* in place of his proper patrilineal cognomen, *Caesar.*

Once more it appeared to many that Caesar had tried to organize a situation in which the Roman people would publicly hail him as king. But if this was so, being a shrewd tactician he had an escape route ready when the crowd again refused to play its part as scripted and balked at the very mention of kings. Again the same tribunes of the *plebes* intervened, arresting the man who first took up the cry of "King." Bad jokes notwith-

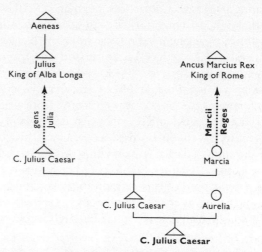

Figure 3.2 Caesar's genealogy, indicating the interplay of the cognomens "Caesar" and "Rex" that were found in his father's patrilineal and matrilineal lines respectively.

standing, Caesar was not amused, and at his insistence these tribunes were summarily removed from office, threatened with death, and banished from Rome.

Finally, there was the famous scene played out some weeks later, during another important ritual of considerable antiquity: the Lupercalia, which was celebrated each year on 15 February. On this date in 44 B.C., Caesar for the first time in his career wore robes of purple and sat on a golden throne, having just been granted the right to do so by the Senate. Some, however, had doubts about the propriety of his comportment on this occasion, for throne and robes were said to have been established by Romulus himself as emblems of royalty, and there were critics who judged such honors to be "greater than human rank." Indeed, some argued that Caesar's enemies were deliberately playing on his vanity, bestowing excessive honors on him as a means of leading him to his doom. For at the moment he cloaked himself in the purple and took his place upon the throne without benefit of popular election or senatorial confirmation, Caesar could be understood to be repeating the acts of the archtyrant Tarquin.

Celebration of the Lupercalia was meant to invoke a very different set of associations, focused on the first and greatest of the ancient Roman kings rather than the last and worst. Normally, it involved two bands of young men called *Luperci*, who ran around the city clad only in goatskin loincloths, ritually reenacting events that took place in the precivilized time immediately prior to the founding of Rome. One of these bands, the Luperci Fabii, was closely associated with the followers of Romulus, while the other, the Luperci Quintilii, stood in similar relation to the members of Remus's band. As they ran about the Palatine Hill, the site of the city's most ancient origins, they reenacted a mythic race that figured prominently in the rivalry of the two brothers, which culminated in Remus's death and the installation of Romulus as the city's first king. In the year 44 B.C., however, the scenario of this mythico-ritual drama was given a different twist, since the Senate had voted to introduce a *third* troop of Luperci in that year's celebration, a troop that would bear Caesar's name: the Luperci Julii. Obviously more than a symbolic gesture of vaguely and innocuously honorific intent, this innovative addition to the ritual claimed for the dictator a status comparable to that of the city's founding heroes and its first king. Further, a victory of "his" Luperci could easily be used by those so inclined to treat Caesar as a new Romulus.

At the head of the Luperci Julii was Caesar's co-consul and closest aide, Marc Antony. It was in this specific capacity "On the Lupercal," as Shakespeare's Antony put it:

> I thrice presented him a kingly crown,
> Which he did thrice refuse.

The "crown" in question, of course, is none other than the diadem, which Antony at the conclusion of the race attempted to place upon Caesar's head, while claiming for the record that he did so "by order of the people" (*populi iussu*). The people's reaction, however, hardly supported so bold an assertion. Cicero, who was an eyewitness (albeit an unsympathetic one), states that when Antony first held up the diadem, there was a "groan from all the forum," and he describes the events which followed as a sort of test in which crowd reactions were closely monitored as Antony "placed the diadem [on Caesar] to the lamentations of the people, and [Caesar] rejected it to their applause." Plutarch states that "a few of Antony's friends applauded when Antony was forcing the crown on him, but all the common people applauded with a roar when Caesar declined." Appian also speaks of "applause from a few, but groans from the majority."

STRATEGIC MANEUVERS: MILITARY AND POLITICAL

Few could doubt that Caesar had repeatedly sought to win acclamation by the voice of the people in January and February, or that he had failed in these attempts, having encountered on three different occasions a resistance that consisted of nothing more (and nothing less) than the people's refusal to cheer when invited to do so. Experienced military men do not ordinarily abandon their projects directly when they encounter resistance. Rather, when frontal assaults founder, they find ways to test their enemy's flanks. In truth, military and political strategy seem to converge during February and March of 44 B.C., for Caesar seems to have been determined to be named king before his scheduled departure on 18 March for a massive expedition against the Parthians, who were at that time Rome's most dangerous foe.

March was, of course, the month of the war god, Mars, and army campaigns regularly commenced with the advent of spring weather in its latter half. Normally, the ruling magistrates presented their military plans for the Senate's ratification at meetings scheduled for the Ides of March. It was for this purpose that Caesar, acting in his capacity as consul, dictator, and commander-in-chief, called the Senate to meet on that date at the Curia of Pompey. No doubt he expected easy approval of his plans, for not only did he have firm control of the Senate, but few senators were likely to underestimate Parthian power, given the disaster of nine years prior, when Crassus blundered into the most humiliating Roman defeat in centuries, losing seven legions, his life, and his honor in the process. Obviously Caesar was taking no chances, for he had assembled a massive army of sixteen infantry legions and ten thousand cavalry which stood ready to depart. Yet he wanted more than men and materiel, for the fullest account we have (Appian *Civil War* 2.110) suggests that Caesar also wished to be named king, in order to command greater respect and obedience as he traveled through the Hellenistic east, an area steeped in monarchic rather than republican institutions.

His last chance to accomplish this before departing was the Senate's meeting on the Ides of March. For the Senate to consider such a motion, a candidate ought to have been acclaimed properly by the voice of the people. This Caesar sought — and failed — to engineer in January and February. In early March, it appears he initiated a second and rather different attempt to have a proposal for his kingship placed before the Senate. At least that is the impression one gets from a rumor that spread rapidly through the city at the time, which suggested that a certain Lucius Aurelius Cotta would report to the Senate a newly discovered Sibylline prophecy which stated that the Romans would never conquer Parthia *until they were led by a king.*

ENLISTING THE VOICE OF THE GODS

The phenomenon of a rumored prophecy is striking for the way it encompasses two very different forms of discourse in which we pass from the voice of the people to the voice of the gods. For if rumor is the speech that comes from below — the anonymous, collective, and scurrilous voice of the streets — prophecy is that speech which comes from above. The Sibylline books represented themselves as texts of revelation that recorded things spoken by gods through the medium of inspired priestesses at Cumae, Dodona, Erythraea, and elsewhere. We should note, however, that Romans regarded the phenomenon of prophecy with a certain degree of ambivalence and anxiety. Although they accepted as a matter of course that a deity could speak through the mouth of a Sibyl, they also recognized the possibility that unscrupulous persons could modify, distort, or even fabricate prophecies for their own benefit (an offense for which Catiline and Publius Lentulus Sura were prosecuted).

As a result, the Roman state was careful to exercise control over all discourses that claimed prophetic status and to evaluate them critically. Initial screening was carried out by a specialized college of fifteen priests, known accordingly as the Quindecemviri ("Fifteen-men"), to which only persons of great experience, stature, and proven probity were named. Once a Quindecemvir determined that a given text was authentically Sibylline, it was his responsibility to inform the Senate, which in turn considered and voted upon his report. Thus, the discursive chain was understood to run from a deity through a Sibyl (and a scribe) to a Quindecemvir, and then to the Senate, where the discourse itself and its divine origin might be finally and authoritatively validated.

In passing, we might note that Roman data force some modification of those models of prophecy which stress the frequent opposition of prophets to kings and/or priests, as in Biblical, Islamic, and select anthropological examples. Such a perspective is valuable, to be sure, and helps us to see the opportunities that an ideology of direct revelation can afford to those at the bottom or on the margins of a sociopolitical order because of the threat it can pose to those who hold other, more institutionalized forms of power. Further, it lets us see why the latter sorts of people might like (and often try) to assert some form of control over prophets and prophecy. In Rome that sort of attempt was quite successful, and gave rise to a specialized bureaucratic organ — the priestly college of the Quindecemviri — as well as a set of formal procedures specifically designed to ensure state control of prophecy.

A novel sort of problem arose in March of 44 B.C., however, when one fraction of the Roman state and ruling stratum came to believe that another fraction — one that was centered on the state's most powerful member — had found a way to subvert the bureaucratic organ of the Quindecemviri and to use it not just for the suppression of unwelcome prophecies, but for the production of prophecies that would serve its purposes by expanding and solidifying Caesar's control over state power. In the report that Cotta was scheduled to make, it is as difficult for a critical observer to construe prophecy as an oppositional voice as it is to hear in it either the voice of the people *or* the voice of the gods.

Consideration of this example should caution us, inter alia, against any simplistic attempt to read a specific political position, agenda, or set of interests from the fact of a prophetic utterance. What does emerge clearly is that prophecy and the claim of prophecy can provide the terrain for political maneuvers of varying sorts, and that a hermeneutic of suspicion, both political and scholarly, has its uses. For while it is the fundamental claim of prophecy that the gods can speak through the mouths of select humans, we should also recognize that this process is eminently reversible and that select human actors are also capable of speaking their own interests and desires through a complex system of mediations such that they ultimately represent themselves as "the voice of the gods."

THE SIXTEENTH QUINDECEMVIR AND THE ASIAN KING

The rumor that Cotta would make such a report possessed a certain measure of credibility, for he was, indeed, a Quindecemvir, and it seems probable that he was appointed to that office by Caesar himself, who expanded the number of Quindecemviri from fifteen to sixteen after his victory at Munda. Cotta was one of three brothers, all of whom served as consul in the 70s and 60s, and all of whom had shown special favor to Caesar. A highly respected figure now nearing the end of his political career, Lucius Cotta had helped Caesar launch his political career, had gained control of the Roman treasury for him at a critical moment in the Civil War, and had provided him with important support on a number of other occasions, as had his brothers. In this there is nothing terribly surprising, for after all, the Aurelii Cottae were Caesar's uncles (figure 3.3). To say they were his uncles, however, distorts matters somewhat, for within the logic of the Roman kinship system, the relations of a nephew or niece to an "uncle" or an "aunt" varied strongly according to the gender of the parent through whom the relation was traced. The father's brother (*patruus*) was thus something of an auxiliary father, and like the father was expected to be stern, demanding, and severe. In contrast, the mother's brother (*avunculus*) was a sort of male mother: nurturing, protective, affectionate, and easily approachable—a person in whom a nephew could freely confide and from whom he could ask important favors.

If the rumor was reasonably credible, so too was the prophecy, since similar Sibylline utterances were well known and had long circulated, particularly among nationalist movements in the eastern provinces. Consistently they foretold that a king would arise out of Asia and would put an end to Roman rule. Mithridates of Pontus made use of such predictions in his propaganda, and unimaginatively enough cast himself in the leading role. Persians looked for the return of their mythic king Vishtaspa (or "Hystaspes" as his name was transliterated in Greek). Judaeo-Christian messianic speculations were part of this same pattern, which is why Roman governors became nervous when anyone assumed—or was said to have assumed—the distinctly royal title of "the Anointed One" (Hebrew *mā-*

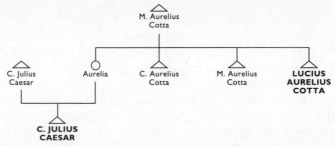

Figure 3.3 Caesar's matrilineage, showing his relation to the Aurelii Cottae brothers.

šiaḥ = Greek *khristos*). The Parthians, against whom Caesar would shortly be marching, were led by their own "king out of Asia," and in the past they had enjoyed considerable success against Roman arms, of which the Romans were all too conscious.

Obviously, there was a certain measure of variation among the specific prophecies that drew on the "king out of Asia" theme. Some were more vague, others more pointed in the indications they were willing to give about just who this king might be. Variation also existed in the rationales they implicitly or explicitly offered for his anticipated triumph. In general, two broad lines of argument diverged, each of which involved a set of binary oppositions so structured as to force the desired conclusion. Thus, one system took the *Asian* identity of the conqueror to come as its point of departure and then proceeded as follows:

Asia	:	Europe
East	:	West
Sunrise	:	Sunset
(Imperial) Growth	:	(Imperial) Decline

Cotta's prophecy, however, took the alternate tack, and starting from the conqueror's *royal* identity, deployed the following set of oppositions:

Parthia	:	Rome
Monarchy	:	Republic
+King	:	−King
+Power	:	−Power

From this symbolic structure, a practical conclusion obviously followed (indeed, this was its very point), for a political system is open to modification in ways that a geographic locus is not. If ratified, Cotta's report would be treated as an authoritative prophecy, and its content would exert considerable pressure on the Senate to name Caesar king. At that point, the prophecy would effectively function as if it were a nomination that had been brought forward, not by the voice of the people (as in the traditional practices Caesar tired to replicate in January and February), but by the voice of the gods, *vox dei*, doing service where *vox populi* was lacking.

PROPHECIES AND RUMORS

I do not want to underestimate the indeterminacy of the situation in the days just before the Ides, during which time Roman senators confronted not the word of the gods, but a widespread rumor. And even if that rumor did prove true, they would not yet have confronted the word of the gods, but only a Quindecemvir's report, which they could still reject. Technically it was the vote of the Senate (and that alone) that was capable of investing such a report with authority, thereby transforming a somewhat suspect discourse (one that *purported* to be a divine voice) into one that was ratified, certified, and authorized as such. If senators feared that it was not a deity but Caesar who spoke — ventriloquistically — through the mouth of the Sibyl or of the Quindecemvir, they were free to vote their doubts. Yet given Caesar's power, the prospect of rejecting Cotta's report can hardly have been an attractive one. Indeed, we are told there were senators who contemplated other sorts of action, particularly Marcus Junius Brutus, who during these tense days suddenly encountered graffiti and catcalls throughout the city that urged him to emulate his ancestor and namesake: the Brutus who centuries before had rid Rome of kings.

The conjunction of rumor and prophecy in a *rumored prophecy* is something of an intermediate form, in which a self-consciously serious and highly consequential discourse is encapsulated within another that carries no such weight, with the result that listeners are left free to place greater or lesser credence in what they have heard. Should they choose to dismiss the rumor, however, they face the possibility that the prophecy may emerge from its encapsulation, at which point it will exert powerful demands on them and on others as well. And should they be determined to escape those demands for one reason or another, ignoring the rumor affords no security. Better to act as if the rumor were true, and to take preemptive steps so that the prophecy never comes to be spoken in such a manner and within such a context as will lead to its status as prophecy being recognized and ratified. It is precisely this strategy which Brutus and his co-conspirators adopted, as the parallel accounts of Dio Cassius and Suetonius make clear.

Dio Cassius 44.15.3–4

A rumor — whether true or
false — such as people love to
fabricate, was spreading that
the priests called the
Quindecemviri were giving
out that the Sibyl had said
the Parthians would never be
conquered except by a king,
and they were going to
propose that this title be
given to Caesar. Believing
this to be true, and given
that a vote would be
required of the magistrates,
including Brutus and
Cassius, on so important a
resolution, and neither
daring to oppose it nor
wishing to remain silent,
they hastened the plot along
. . .

Suetonius, *The Deified Julius*
79.3–80.1

A variety of rumors circulated
[. . . including] that at the
next meeting of the Senate
Lucius Cotta would
announce the judgment of
the Quindecemviri that since
it was contained in the
books of fate that the
Parthians could not be
conquered except by a king,
Caesar ought to be named
king. This was the reason
that the conspirators
brought the business on
which they were resolved to
fruition, so that it would not
be necessary to give their
assent to this proposal . . .

Cotta, of course, never got the chance to report his prophecy
to the Senate, if that indeed was his intention. Before the session could be called to order, Brutus and the other conspirators
brought forth their daggers. With twenty-three blows, they reduced Caesar to a corpse and Cotta to silence.

THINGS SAID AND UNSAID

There are many ways one can think about the Ideas of March.
Authors from Plutarch to Shakespeare and beyond have dwelt
upon issues of character in the conflict that pitted Brutus, "the
noblest Roman of them all," and the other conspirators against
Julius Caesar. Others, including most of the actors themselves,
understood the same events in less immediately personal terms
as a conflict between those who wished to preserve the Repub-

lic and those who wished to (re)construct a monarchy. More recently there are those who would stress the social, rather than the personal or political aspects of the struggle, and who point out the ways in which the conspirators' defense of the Republic was also an attempt to preserve against the threat of radical change a highly conservative social order in which they and their families enjoyed considerable privilege.

All of these views have their merits, but it is also useful to consider the conflict of Brutus and Caesar, the Senate and the (presumed) would-be king in somewhat different terms. Accordingly, I would focus for a moment on issues of power and authority, understanding that the principal actors in this drama all possessed some measure of both, with Caesar having far the greatest power, while the Senate remained foremost in authority, albeit by a much lesser margin. From this perspective, the initiative that would have been taken had Cotta's prophecy been announced on the floor of the Senate may be understood as a moment in which that person most possessed of power (i.e., Caesar) sought to deploy such authority as he had at his disposal to win, first, a greater level of authorization for his exercise of power, and second, a greatly enhanced and much more autonomous authority for himself. Moreover, these were to be wrested from that group and institution which traditionally had held the most authority, but which saw its authority to be rapidly shrinking, never so much as in that moment. In similar fashion, the assassination may then be understood as a riposte, in which the group and institution most possessed of authority deployed such power as they had remaining to put an end to that attempt, and to the attempter as well.

Given our primary interest in the dynamics of authority, it is also worth paying attention to the role played by a supporting character in this drama, whom history has largely consigned to oblivion, but who effectively catalyzed the action on the Ides of March. This is Lucius Aurelius Cotta, who closely resembles Homer's Thersites in many ways. Both men provoked crises, and in both instances the crisis derived from their actual or expected utterance of certain things within an authorized and authorizing sphere of speech: challenging, even dangerous things that were being said by other people and in other places, but which powerful actors very much wished to keep from being said on official occasions and in privileged spheres. Here, however, the two stories begin to diverge, for whereas Thersites actually spoke his piece in the center of the assembly, after which he was silenced, Cotta never entered, never spoke, and never suffered direct repression.

Unlike Thersites, who had no right to stand and speak in the midst of the Homeric assembly, Cotta was eminently entitled to hold forth in the Senate. Thersites entered the assembly unexpectedly, catching the others unaware. Cotta, in contrast, was very much expected to speak, and prior discussion of that prospect caused his adversaries considerable tension and anxiety. As an unauthorized person, Thersites could enter by surprise, but his forcible ejection could also be easily arranged and would produce no serious objections. In order to deal with the threat posed by Cotta, however, one had to anticipate the likelihood of his entry and find a way to bar it, for once this man began to speak on the Senate floor, his speech could not easily be stopped, nor could its consequences be avoided. Ironically, then, it was because Thersites *lacked* the right to speak in assembly that he was, in fact, able to do so, and it was precisely because Cotta *had* the right to speak in the Senate that others organized to keep him from exercising that right. Odysseus's violence fell on the speaker; that of Brutus and the conspirators fell somewhere else. But a secondary result of Caesar's assassination — one that was neither unintentional nor trivial — was cancellation of the Senate's scheduled session for the Ides of March. That is to say, the conspirators' violence fell on Caesar, not on Cotta, but it still managed to deprive the latter of his opportunity and his occasion for speaking within the privileged sphere.

Other actors also deserve our attention, although we will remain forever ignorant of their names. These are common persons, the faces in the crowd and the people who spoke in whispers, none of whom had much power or authority, but who still had a significant role to play. The Roman people spoke decisively in January and February of 44 B.C., and in many ways their very nonauthoritative discourses were more consequential than anything said by senators, priests, dictators, or Sibyls. Through their muttering and their groans, their halfhearted applause, and even their silence, they manifested their resistance in ways that had collective force and had the advantage of shielding them against individual risk. In this fashion, they were able to deny Caesar the kingship on three different occasions. Then, in March, when it appeared that the question of kingship might be moving toward resolution of a very different sort in the halls of the Senate, the people asserted themselves once more, speaking this time in rumors, gossip, catcalls, and graffiti in so effective a fashion that they persuaded an irresolute and wavering group of conspirators to take up their daggers.

LAW, CURSES, AND DERISION
Egil Skallagrimsson and the Gula Thing

VIOLENCE AND THE VOICE OF THE LAW

In the preceding chapters, I have been concerned with episodes in which someone sought to enter and speak within an authorized and authorizing sphere in a fashion others found challenging, so much so that they responded to this attempt with violence. In both cases, those who felt threatened were successful in suppressing a speech unwanted and unwonted alike, although there are some significant differences in the way they accomplished this. Whereas Odysseus's violence fell directly on Thersites and had multiple effects — cutting his speech short, removing him from the privileged sphere, and making him laughable in the eyes of the audience — the violence of Brutus and the other conspirators fell not on Cotta but on Caesar, the prime beneficiary of the speech that Cotta was to have given. In certain ways they went considerably further than Odysseus, for whereas the latter rendered Thersites' speech ineffectual, the Roman tyrannicides obviated Cotta's speech entirely by preemptively depriving it of its raison d'être, while also eliminating the occasion in which it was to have been given.

In the present chapter, I want to consider a third episode that has a number of similarities to those I have already treated, but which differs from them in at least one important respect, for here the violence in question is directed not at the speaker, would-be speaker, or any other actor, but rather at the privileged sphere of speech itself. That sphere is the Old Norse *Thing*, a place and institution that stood at the center of medieval Scandinavian society as the place to which legal disputes were regularly brought for resolution. As in all civil courts, resolution was accomplished though a dialectic and dialogic process in which the voices of two adversaries encountered one another, and then yielded to a third, authoritative voice: that of the law, which transforms disputation into *legal* disputation. This voice serves to regulate the way in which procedures are conducted, and ultimately it is called upon to adjudicate between the contending parties, insofar as it is (or, more accurately, insofar as it claims and is perceived to be) a voice that speaks through select persons — here, a set of thirty-six judges — without belonging to them or being their creation. It is a voice that presents itself as both disinterested and transcendent, faithful to established principles and devoted to the common good. In general, it speaks coolly and dispassionately, but with imperative force, and ideally, the last word is supposed to rest with the law. Occasionally, however, things work out otherwise.

THE DISPUTED INHERITANCE OF BJORN BRYNJOLFSSON

The particular case I want to consider stands at the structural and thematic center (chapter 56) of *Egil's Saga*, one of the oldest and literarily most accomplished of all the Icelandic family sagas, where an account is given of a case that was heard at the Gula *Thing* of southwest Norway in A.D. 934. This was a case of inheritance law, in which Egil Skallagrimsson, the hero of the saga, brought suit against his brother-in-law, Berg-Onund, for a share of the lands and wealth left by their wives' father, Bjorn Brynjolfsson, who had died two years earlier.

There are few areas of Old Norse law that are spelled out in such detail as those regarding inheritance, and the text which preserves the *Laws of the Gula Thing* elaborates a system of inheritance that rendered the fundamental principles of the social order evident and operative in concrete practice, mandating that property should pass first on the basis of kinship proximity and then on the basis of gender. Six different degrees of kinship relation are listed in rank order, with preference being given to men first and then to women in each instance. Only the first two of these need concern us here, as spelled out in the *Laws of the Gula Thing* section 103, which stipulates that males at one generational remove in the direct line of the deceased (sons and fathers) have first claim on an estate, followed by females at one generational remove and males at two removes (daughters and sons' sons), who share second claim (figure 4.1).

As Bjorn had no sons and his father had died some twenty years before he did, it would seem that his property ought to have passed to his two surviving daughters, Asgerd (the elder) and Gunnhild (the younger). Or rather — since the law not only tilted toward male heirs in its order of preference, but also made it impossible for a married woman to hold property in her own name — it would be more accurate to say that Bjorn's property ought to have passed not *to* these women, but *through* them to their husbands, Egil and Berg-Onund respectively.

As the actors in this drama sought to apply this law to their case, however, they discovered complexities and ambiguities

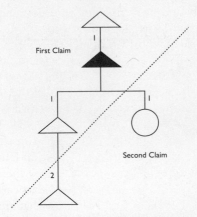

Figure 4.1 The initial rules of the medieval Scandinavian inheritance system, as set out in the *Laws of the Gula Thing*, sec. 103. Numbers indicate generational removes from the deceased.

that presented strategic opportunities to some and difficulties to others, for insofar as kinship relations are never governed by unmediated and self-evident biological "facts," but rather by the social and legal interpretation that is put upon them, the nature and significance of these "facts" remain ever disputable. Nowhere is this clearer than in struggles over inheritance, where (1) persons' relations to property depend on their relations to other persons; (2) the definition of those relations depends on judgments that actors make about a wide-ranging set of actions, persons, and relations, both past and present; and (3) those judgments are informed by categories and criteria that are given their most formal and consequential articulation in law.

In the case at hand, these rather abstract points find concrete expression in the highly charged question of whether Asgerd was to be considered Bjorn's legitimate daughter. For it so happened that Asgerd and Gunnhild were born to different mothers, and whereas Bjorn's marriage to Gunnhild's mother (Alof Erlingsdaughter) was quite unexceptional, he earlier took Asgerd's mother, Thora Lace-Sleeve, to be his bride in a manner that was sufficiently irregular as to permit Berg-Onund (Gunnhild's husband) to raise the question many years later of whether this had been a legal marriage at all (figure 4.2). Such a question was hardly idle, and the stakes were high, for Bjorn was quite rich, and were this not a proper marriage, it would follow that Asgerd was illegitimate and as a result, Egil would lose all rights to any portion of her father's estate.

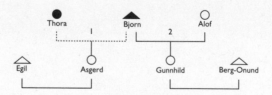

Figure 4.2 The marriages and children of Bjorn Brynjolfsson. The boldface dotted line represents an ambiguous union that actors favorably disposed to Egil considered to be a legal marriage and those favorably disposed to Berg-Onund did not, portraying it as a relation of concubinage.

THE RAW, THE COOKED, AND THE ROYAL

While *Egil's Saga* focuses most intensively on Egil Skallagrims-son, it sets his story within a much longer history that begins with his paternal grandfather, Kveld-Ulf, and continues through the lives of that man's sons and grandsons, and an elegant structure holds together the narratives that are told about the five men in question. There is a sharp distinction in the lineage between those whom we can characterize as the "savage" and the "courtly" members of the family. The former (Kveld-Ulf, Skalla-Grim, and Egil) are described as ugly, obstreperous, and suspicious of the Norwegian kings, with whom their relations are often antagonistic. In contrast, the "courtly" members of the family (Thorolf Kveldulfsson and Thorolf Skallagrimsson), who take after their matrilineal side, are handsome, well-mannered, and likable, and they eagerly enter royal service (figure 4.3). Whereas the "savage" trio consistently succeed in their acts of resistance, albeit with occasional risks to their lives and safety, the two "courtly" men, who appeared to have taken the safe and prudent course, ultimately run afoul of the kings whom they serve and go to an untimely death.

Early chapters of the saga describe the difficulties that Kveld-Ulf and Skalla-Grim had with Harald Fairhair (circa 850–933), the founder of the Norwegian monarchy, and those that Egil had with his successor, the aptly named Eirik Bloodaxe

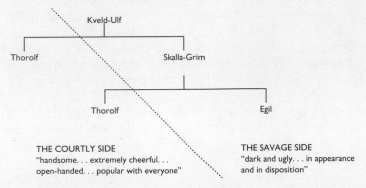

THE COURTLY SIDE
"handsome. . . extremely cheerful. . .
open-handed. . . popular with everyone"

THE SAVAGE SIDE
"dark and ugly. . . in appearance
and in disposition"

Figure 4.3 Structural bifurcation in the lineage of Kveld-Ulf. The descriptions of these individuals are quoted from *Egil's Saga*, chapters 1 and 31.

(reigned 930–35). Such troubles were common during the period when the Norwegian state was being aggressively constructed, and like many others unwilling to accept royal rule, Kveld-Ulf, Skalla-Grim, and Egil decided to leave Norway for Iceland, which at that time was unsettled and offered them the opportunity to develop a society more to their liking. Others, however, chose to remain in Norway, where they were able to cultivate the king's favor and to exploit the opportunities it afforded them. Among these was Egil's brother-in-law, Berg-Onund, as the saga spells out in the same passage that tells how Egil heard of Bjorn's death and learned how his estate had been treated.

> One summer, a ship came from Norway to Iceland, bearing the news from the east that Bjorn was dead. The report was also brought that Berg-Onund, his son-in-law, had taken over all the wealth that Bjorn had owned. He had carried all the movable property to his home, had settled the lands, and had reserved for himself all the land-rents. He had also taken possession of all the lands that Bjorn had owned. And when Egil heard that, he carefully asked whether Berg-Onund would have done all this on his own authority, or had he the support of men greater than himself. He was told that Berg-Onund had come into a great friendship with King Eirik, and what is more, to Queen Gunnhild he was very dear. (*Egil's Saga* 56.20–22)

Egil's chance of recovering the property seized by Berg-Onund — who was now the queen's favorite — could hardly be called strong. Nevertheless, he was determined to press his claim, and toward this end he returned to Norway, where straightaway he took counsel with Arinbjorn, a man who occupied a pivotal position within a complex web of relations. He was at once Egil's closest friend, Asgerd's first cousin (mother's brother's son), Bjorn's nephew (wife's brother's son), the king's foster brother and valued retainer, as well as the dominant nobleman in the Fjord shire, one of the three communities that together composed the area under the laws of the Gula *Thing*.

Egil's request for assistance notwithstanding, Arinbjorn, who throughout the saga shows a fine strategic sense, came straight to the point, and advised him that the case looked "unpromising" (*óvænligt*), not on legal, but strictly on political grounds, as a result of the royal support that Berg-Onund enjoyed. To this argument, Egil responded not at all, but instead asserted flatly one of the dominant ideals of medieval kingship, in which the king was represented as guarantor of all that is right, bound above all else to render justice. As Egil put it: "*The king will let us obtain law and justice in this case* [*Konungr mun oss láta ná lǫgum ok réttendum á máli þessu*)], and with your support, it does not seem a big thing in my eyes to seek law with Berg-Onund" (*Egil's Saga* 56.28). This same phrase recurs when Arinbjorn, having announced Egil's suit to King Eirik and heard the latter voice his displeasure (with the queen scowling ominously in the background), says directly to the monarch, in terms both portentous and formulaic, "You will let us obtain law in this case" (*Egil's Saga* 56.39).

IN THE SACRED SPHERE OF THE LAW

Egil and Arinbjorn thus put their trust in the third voice: that of the law. In their view — and 'it is hardly theirs alone — not only does the law speak with an authority that stands above and beyond that of the contending parties in any dispute, but its authority is also understood to stand above and beyond that of the king, whom it commands to set aside his arbitrary will when this conflicts with the overriding demands of justice.

The arena in which the law was expected to prevail was the *Thing,* which remained a legal, political, and social institution of fundamental importance in tenth-century Norway, although the king's court was just beginning to take over some of its functions. The relatively recent emergence of a unified nation under the rule of a single monarch notwithstanding, Norwegian society in this period continued to be organized in segmentary fashion, the smallest settlements (*bygðir* or *héruð*) being grouped together to form "shires" or "folk" (*fylki*), which in turn were grouped together to form a "law" (*lǫg*). This last term strikingly denoted not only an authoritative discourse that regulated social practice, but also the territory in which that discourse prevailed and the social group whose (comm)unity was based upon their submission to it, as in the Old English *Danelaw.*

If the "law" simultaneously denoted a group of people, their territory, and their normative (and norm-enforcing) practices, the *Thing* was central to this "law" in all its aspects. Every spring the people of its three constituent shires assembled at the Gula *Thing* to hear the fully body of their law publicly proclaimed and to settle any disputes that may have arisen, according to its dictates. Cases were heard within a "court-circle" or "judgment-ring" (*dóm-hringr*), the physical structure of which is described as follows:

> There was a level field where the court was established, and hazel staffs were set in the field in a circle, and a cord was placed around them. These were called the bonds of consecration (*vé-bǫnd*). Within this circle sat the judges: twelve from the Fjord shire, twelve from the Sogn shire, and twelve from the Hardaland shire. These thirty-six men would judge men's lawsuits there. (*Egil's Saga* 56.42)

The spatial structures of this court-circle reflect the nature of the processes which were expected to transpire within it. Its ground had been made level, smooth, or polished (*sléttr*), which is to say that people had worked to remove any inequities, slants, or points of roughness that may have been naturally present. And having made this ground simultaneously pristine and egalitarian, they gathered upon it a social microcosm: twelve men representing each of the three shires or "folks" (*fylki*) that together constituted the community of and under the laws of the Gula *Thing*. Finally, the ground on which they met was separated from the surrounding space by staffs made of hazel, a wood that had strongly ritual and apotropaic associations in medieval Norway and among other Germanic peoples.

These staffs and the cords which connected them one to the other were called "bonds of consecration" (Old Norse *vé-bǫnd*), and other Norwegian texts tell us that it was an "ancient law [or custom]" (*fornr réttr*) to erect them at the *Thing*-place (*Frosta-thing Law* 1.2). Places of judgment were also marked off in similar fashion among other Germanic peoples. Thus, for example, in Gothic the term *staua* (literally "staff") also denotes "court" and "judge," while in English, entry to the *bar* still signifies admission to the legal profession and the court spaces in which it operates, although originally it referred more specifically to "the barrier or wooden rail marking off the immediate precinct of the judge's seat, at which prisoners are stationed for arraignment, trial, or sentence" (*Oxford English Dictionary,* 1971).

The second element of the Old Norse compound *vé-bǫnd* (literally "bonds") refers to the willows and cords that separated the legal from other spheres of existence, and as such it is readily comparable to the Gothic "staff" or the English "bar." The compound's first member, however, adds a semantic precision that is lacking in these other terms, for as an independent noun, Old Norse *vé* means "temple." Further, it is cognate to a large set of words throughout the Germanic languages that are used to denote things, people, or spaces that have been set apart in time, space, or status and marked as pure and holy, deserving of special reverence, and demanding special attitudes and decorum (e.g., Old Saxon *wîh-dag* "holy day," Old English *wîg-bed* "altar" [literally "holy bed"], or German *Weih-nacht* "Christmas" [literally "holy night," cf. *weihen* "to consecrate"]).

The cords thus separate a sacred space from its profane surroundings, just as they separate a sphere of speech from one of violence; all who entered the *Thing*-place had to leave their weapons behind and those inside were treated as inviolable. Yet the court-circle was also very much a political arena, as is apparent from the sentence that directly follows the passage above, for we are told: "Arinbjorn decided who the judges from the Fjord shire were, and Thord of Aurland those from Sogn. They were all of one party" (*Egil's Saga* 56.43). One third of those to whom justice was entrusted were thus selected by—and presumably clients of—the plaintiff's chief advisor, in a case where questions pertaining to the legitimacy of his own cousin (Asgerd, his father's sister's daughter) and the honor of his aunt (Thora, his father's sister) were being hotly contested. What is more, the judges named by Thord of Aurland were "of one party" with those named by Arinbjorn, which is not so surprising, for Thord was himself Asgerd's paternal uncle (figure 4.4).

THE CONTESTED MARRIAGE OF THORA LACE-SLEEVE

A sacred space, a social microcosm, and a political arena: inside the court-circle there gathered the judges and the disputants. Outside stood others, whom the text is careful to categorize as

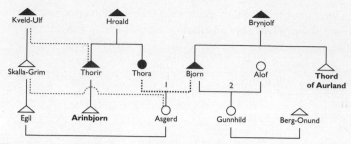

Figure 4.4 Participants in the lawsuit. Those whose names appear in boldface each appointed one-third of the judges. The lightface dotted lines represent relations of fosterage.

clients of Arinbjorn, those of the king, and those unattached to either. And although Arinbjorn prudently brought with him "a large crowd" (*fjǫlmenni mikit*), the king's forces outnumbered his by at least three to one. Hardly an "ideal speech situation," it was rather a social and political arena in which speech, action, and strategy were all profoundly influenced by considerations of power, as Egil, Berg-Onund, and Arinbjorn spoke in turn.

At issue was the union of Asgerd's parents, Bjorn Brynjolfs- son and Thora Lace-Sleeve, whose story is recounted much ear- lier in the saga (chapters 32–35). Having asked Thora's brother, Thorir Hroaldsson, for her hand and been refused, Bjorn car- ried Thora off, fleeing first to his father's home, and then to the Shetland Islands, where directly upon arrival, Bjorn "made a wedding for Thora" (*Egil's Saga* 33.2: *gerði hann brúðlaup til þóru*). Thereafter, the couple departed for Iceland, where they took refuge with Egil's father, Skalla-Grim, and where a daugh- ter, Asgerd, was born to them. Then, following several years of negotiations in which Skalla-Grim played mediator, Thora and Bjorn returned to Norway and sought reconciliation with Thorir, while leaving Asgerd under the fosterage of Skalla- Grim. The actual reconciliation — which would be the crucial point on which the law case turned some thirty years later — is described in only the briefest of terms:

> Then word was sent to Thorir Hroaldsson. He and Brynjolf
> arranged a meeting and Bjorn came there to their meeting. Then
> Thorir and he ratified the settlement between them. Thereafter,
> Thorir paid out that money which Thora had in his keeping,

and Thorir and Bjorn established friendship and affinal kin-relations. (*Egil's Saga* 35.10)

The issue of Asgerd's legitimacy was vexed indeed. The first point to observe is that a "wedding" was performed before there were any sexual relations between Bjorn and Thora, and that the text (33.2) employs one of the two closely related, but subtly differentiated terms that are used to denote a proper legal ceremony of marriage: *brúð-laup*, the "bride's leap," which refers to her change of residence. Other conditions were also legally requisite for a proper marriage, however: (1) *mundr*, "bridewealth," which was paid by the would-be husband to his bride in the presence of witnesses (whence the second term for a wedding: *brúð-kaup*, literally the "bride's purchase"); and (2) *festar*, "betrothal," in which the male relative who was responsible for a given woman (normally her father or her brother, should the father be deceased) formally granted his permission for the marriage to take place. It is this latter step, one which was essential to a patriarchal system in which men exercised control over the sexual and reproductive powers of their female relatives and employed their daughters and sisters as instruments through which they could establish alliances with the men of other families, which was lacking in this case. Since Thorir had refused to give his permission prior to Thora's wedding or Asgerd's birth, Berg-Onund was able to claim that there had been no marriage at all and to argue that Thora had been "taken in concubinage, without the consent of her kin" (*Egil's Saga* 56.48). Were that so, it would follow that Asgerd would have been born outside of wedlock and, accordingly, would forfeit her claims to any portion of her father's estate.

The trump card, however, lay with Arinbjorn, who now led in twelve eyewitnesses, all prepared to swear oaths "that it was decided in the settlement of Thorir, my father, and Bjorn Brynjolfsson, that Asgerd, the daughter of Bjorn and Thora, was entitled to an inheritance from Bjorn, her father" (*Egil's Saga* 56.54). The importance of this testimony becomes clear in light of a pattern within the Old Norwegian codes of law that Laurence Larson has discussed at length:

> Throughout all this legislation one finds the same fundamental principle, namely, that the dealings of man with man should, as

far as possible, be made a matter of public knowledge. It was, therefore, held necessary to have a record made of the important features of every transaction that might later become a subject of litigation. Inasmuch as it was not possible to make written records in every case, even after the Christian clerk had brought an improved art of writing into the land, the record had to be made on the minds of men. Where a modern litigant would bring a written deed or contract into the court, the Norseman of the eleventh century would bring a group of men who had at some earlier time been called together to witness the arrangement that had since led to litigation.

Within the *Laws of the Gula Thing* (section 124), it is specified that in order to resolve cases of disputed inheritance, both sides might offer testimony from people who had witnessed the contracting of a marriage the validity of which was subject to question, and judges were directed to rule in favor of whichever side was able to produce the most witnesses. Now, Arinbjorn was Thorir's son and he still resided on the estate that had been his father's. As a result, he had privileged access to those people—servants, retainers, members of the local community, etc.—who would have been called to witness the critical events of three decades past. In contrast, it is virtually unthinkable that Berg-Onund could have produced someone who could knowledgeably contradict the testimony given by Arinbjorn's witnesses, let alone thirteen such people.

Once these witnesses tell their story inside the court circle, the case is as good as settled, for their words will have official status and, upon their ratification by the judges, they will attain the force of law. At this point, however, there is a vertiginous swing in the course of the narrative. Just as resolution of the lawsuit comes into view, the struggle which two men were waging over possession of an inheritance segues into an infinitely more important and more dangerous struggle waged between the monarchy and the premonarchic structures of Norwegian society over possession of the law itself at the moment we are told of the judges' hesitation in the presence of royal power: "[The witnesses] asked to swear oaths before the king and the judges. The judges wished to take the oaths, *if the king did not forbid it*" (*Egil's Saga* 56.56).

KING, QUEEN, KNAVE

This is to say that the witnesses sought permission to enter and speak within the authorized and authorizing sphere. Permission being granted, their words will command the attention and trust of all assembled, and their speech will have profound consequences. At this critical moment, King Eirik equivocated. His queen did not, but spoke with the fourth voice, the voice of state power.

> The king said that he would take no position, either to permit or prohibit this. Then Queen Gunnhild took up the case and said: "This is extraordinary, King, how you let this big fellow Egil entangle all the cases before you. Perhaps you might not even speak against him if he claimed your very kingdom. Although you will not grant a decision that would be of help to Berg-Onund, I will not endure if that Egil thus tread my friend under his feet and wrongfully take Berg-Onund's wealth from him. Where are you, Alf Shipman? Come here with your company, where the judges are, and do not permit this wrongful judgment." Then Alf Shipman and his company leapt into the court. They cut apart the bonds of consecration, broke down the staffs, and set the judges running. Then there was a great tumult in the *Thing*, but all the men were unarmed there. (*Egil's Saga* 56.56–59)

At the queen's pronouncement ("Come here . . . *where the judges are,* and do not permit this wrongful judgment.") armed men appear, under the leadership of Alf Shipman, her brother and henchman. Possessing a monopoly on the use of force (all others being unarmed, in accordance with the rules of the *Thing*), Alf Shipman and his company waste no time in demolishing the sacred precinct of the court and silencing the voice of the law. And in the process of foreclosing any verdict against the queen's favorite, they also disrupt the existing social, political, legal, and ideological order in ways that were hardly accidental, but intimately connected to a broader historic development.

If the discovery that the legal sphere was neither sacred nor inviolable caused shock in the tenth century, it is perhaps only slightly less shocking for us to recognize that the sphere of the law has not always been encompassed by that of the state. Yet a central theme of medieval history is the struggle that was waged by ruling dynasties throughout Europe to transfer the law from the sphere of the holy to that of the state, which in most instances meant replacing canon with civil law. In Norway, this same struggle took slightly different form, since the national monarchy was consolidated before the conversion to Christianity, during the reign of Harald Fairhair, who abdicated in the year 930, just four years prior to this trial. Harald accomplished his project of state construction through a series of military campaigns in which he systematically eliminated or subordinated all of his rivals, transforming a situation of multiple competing chieftains into the unified monarchy that he turned over to his favorite son, Eirik Bloodaxe, who, as his epithet suggests, continued in his father's ways.

Although these early kings possessed sufficient armed force to conquer a kingdom, the instruments of administration which they had at their disposal — for tax collection, to name an obvious example — were still quite rudimentary. The system of law they inherited, as evidenced at the Gula *Thing,* was one in which judicial power resided with representatives of the shires, levels of social integration that were both geographically smaller than and historically prior to the Norwegian state. Moreover, the traditional circumscription of the law as a sacred sphere claimed for these courts an independent and inviolable status, their "bonds of consecration" being also lines of defense against incursions and intrusions, conceivably even those of the king. Confronted with such an ideology, some monarchs chose to coopt it, others to attack it, and the latter found that ropes strung on hazel staffs offered little enough resistance to the power of the state.

Obviously, resistance did not reside in the staffs and ropes themselves, but in the ideology which found expression in those objects, or — more precisely still — in the extent to which persons within the relevant sociopolitical field were persuaded by that ideology. Thus, those among the king's subjects who sincerely understood the "bonds of consecration" to separate off a sacred space for the practice of the law might be expected to resent any assault on them, and fear of their possible reactions could inhibit a king from mounting such an assault. Insofar as the king himself and those around him held these views, an assault became even more unlikely, but should they become more skeptical, such an assault might be launched as a practical exercise in iconoclasm or demystification.

TOWARD THE FIFTH VOICE

The trend of history since 934 has favored Queen Gunnhild's initiative, as the voice of the state has tended to displace all others that claim some measure of control over the authorized and authorizing spheres that are consecrated to legal discourse and practice. Yet within *Egil's Saga*, the victory of the state is less than complete, and the voice of state power is not the last to be heard.

Driven from the sphere of privileged speech by the violence of the royal assault, Egil took refuge in an unauthorized place outside the *Thing*, from which he deployed an unauthorized — and, what is more, a de-authorizing — sort of speech against those people who used their power to deprive him of what he regarded as rightfully his: not just his inherited property, but his right to speak in the court-circle. After calling Arinbjorn and others to witness what had transpired, he cried out: "I curse you, Berg-Onund, and all other men — native and foreigner, highborn and low — who have done this: I charge you with breaking the laws of the land and with breaking the truce [of the *Thing*], and I call down the wrath of the gods" (*Egil's Saga* 56.66). By virtue of its inclusive clauses ("all other men . . . highborn and low . . ."), the curse is obviously meant to fall upon the king, a point that is reinforced in a poem which is written in an older dialect than the prose portions of the saga, and which most critics believe to have been composed in the tenth century by the historic Egil Skallagrimsson:

> So shall the gods repay
> the theft of my wealth:
> May the binders drive the fiend-king away.
> Wroth be Odin and the rulers!
> Frey and Njord, make him flee from the lands —
> that one who mows down the folk!
> Lord of the land, make him hated —
> he who brings grief to the people,

he who does injury to the sanctuaries!
(*Egil's Saga* 56.91)

The saga chapter we have been considering ends with this poem in which a group of pagan gods are invoked and called to take vengeance. More precisely, it ends with the line in which King Eirik is denounced as one "who does injury to the sanctuaries" (*þanns vé grandar*), a direct reference to the violence of his troops against the "bonds of consecration" (*vébǫnd*) of the Gula *Thing*. From here, the narrative rushes ahead, recounting how, in apparent fulfillment of Egil's curse, the Vík and Trondheim shires rose in rebellion against Eirik and sought to drive him from the land, naming others as king in his stead. Before leaving to quell this uprising, Eirik took time to proclaim Egil an outlaw, an act which made it licit for anyone to kill him should he be found on Norwegian soil. Meanwhile, Berg-Onund returned to protect his still-disputed estate from any possible attack.

When he heard of the sentence the king passed upon him, Egil spoke another poem, in which he pointedly denounced the king not as an "outlaw," but rather as a "lawbreaker" (*lǫgbrigþer, Egil's Saga* 57.11); not just a man who has transgressed a particular law, but someone who has broken faith with the law *in general* and done violence to it. Then, after making his way to Berg-Onund's lands, Egil employed a set of ruses and stratagems through which he managed to kill his enemy and plunder his wealth, while also despatching a son and a foster-son of the king who had been left to Berg-Onund's safekeeping. The final act of this expedition is, however, the most significant of all, for just before departing Norway for Iceland, Egil once more cursed the king and his realm.

> He took a hazel staff in his hand and went to a certain rocky projection that overlooked the land. Then he took a horse's head and set it up on the staff. Next, he recited a prayer, and said thus: "Here I set up a staff of mockery [*níð-stǫng*], and I turn this mockery toward King Eirik and Queen Gunnhild" — and he turned the horse's head in toward the land — "I turn this mockery toward the land's guardian spirits, who dwell in this land, so that they may all go astray and no one will reach or find his

home, until they drive King Eirik and Gunnhild from the land."
Next he thrust the staff down into a cleft in the rock and let it
stand there. He turned the head in toward the land and cut
runes in the staff, and they state the prayer in full. (*Egil's Saga*
57.55–57)

Both the carving of the staff and the utterances that accompanied this gesture were drawn from a repertoire of formal behaviors that were known collectively as *nið*, "mockery" or "derision." These are of considerable interest and have been
studied extensively in recent years. In general, they involve the
charge — made openly or by insinuation — that the person
against whom they were directed was unmanly in one sense or
another. The charge of cowardice thus often looms large in the
conventional language of mockery, as does that of having broken one's word. The specific insults which appear most frequently, however, involve the accusation of sexual inversion, as
when one charged that a man has borne another man's child,
that he has been sexually penetrated, or compared him to a
mare, bitch, or other female animal (*Laws of the Gula Thing* section 196; cf. *Frostathing Law* 10.35). Mockery in these and
other forms was taken extremely seriously, and was treated as a
legal offense equal in severity to rape and murder (*Laws of the
Gula Thing* section 138; cf. *Grágás* 2.392). Although striking,
the logic which leads to this conclusion is not difficult to understand, for like rape and murder mockery was regarded as a violent assault that could destroy a man's life and well-being by
destroying his reputation.

Curses, insults, mockery, and derision, like gossip, slander,
heckling, and jokes, are not genres normally employed by the
law or the state, both of which regularly attempt to discourage
them. Yet in medieval Norway, as elsewhere, the success of
those who engage in a project of inhibiting or suppressing the
speech of blame and lampoon falls considerably short of total,
for irreverent popular discourses can always be produced and
circulate in the spaces that fall outside the censor's control. And
in these discourses, as Bakhtin recognized, one hears the fifth
voice: the voice of the people that exercises a devastatingly corrosive effect on the pretensions and the claims to authority of
those who hold office, prestige, and/or power.

EPILOGUE

In the summer of 934, Eirik Bloodaxe suppressed the rebellions in Vík and Trondheim. The next spring, he was not so lucky. Chapter 59 of *Egil's Saga* opens as follows:

> King Eirik ruled over Norway for one winter after his father's death before Hakon [the Good], another son of King Harald, came to Norway from England. That same summer Egil Skallagrimsson went to Iceland. Hakon went north to Trondheim. There he was made king. For one winter, he and Eirik were both kings in Norway, and in the spring both drew up their hosts. Hakon had many more men, and Eirik saw that he had no choice other than to flee the land. He then went abroad with Gunnhild, his wife, and their child. (*Egil's Saga* 59.1–3)

Other sources, most notably the *Heimskringla,* recount these same macropolitical events, making no mention of Egil, his curses, or his staff of mockery, to which *Egil's Saga* implicitly attributes causal efficacy in Eirik's deposition. One might well wonder, then, about the historicity of these "events." Yet to do so overmuch is to miss the most important issues, which emerge precisely when we acknowledge that we are dealing not with an unmediated *event,* but with an *account* of an event, and inquire why this account was of interest to the audience for whom it was intended, and why its author told it as he did.

We are thus led to ask, not what "really happened" in Norway during the year of 934–35, but what stake Icelanders of the early thirteenth century had in the reports of these events. Here, it is crucial to recall that the Icelandic Commonwealth, alone of all nations in western Europe at that time, *had no king.* Moreover, this was a point of fierce pride, as is evident in the Icelanders' myths of national origin, which consistently stressed the view that their Commonwealth had been settled and its institutions created by "founding fathers" (*landnámsmenn*) who left their houses in Norway in the period between 870 and 930 rather than submit to the oppressive kingly rule that was then being established by Harald Fairhair. In truth, Iceland consciously and explicitly understood itself as a "society against the king," in which the court-circle of the national *Thing*-place, and not the royal household, served as the central unifying institution, for as a famous text observes, Iceland was a place where "there is no king, but only law" (Scholium to Adam of Bremen, *History of the Archbishops of Hamburg and Bremen* 4.36). In the thirteenth century, however, the Commonwealth was riven by internal rivalries and came under increasingly heavy pressure from the Norwegian crown, to which it ultimately acceded, accepting Norwegian rule in 1264.

At the time *Egil's Saga* was written (most likely some time between 1220 and 1230), these pressures were evident, but the outcome still in doubt. The act of remembering Egil Skallagrimsson's story may thus be understood as a strategic part of the Commonwealth's resistance to the Norwegian throne, for the past events that figure in this saga were re-collected and re-presented (also, no doubt, modified where useful) for purposes of the present. This is particularly clear in the way they show Norwegian state power in the persons of Eirik and Gunnhild to be something arbitrary and violent, willing to pit itself against religion and law alike, but something that could be successfully opposed by determined and resourceful Icelanders like Egil Skallagrimsson. No less than Egil's "staff of mockery," his saga was — and remains — a corrosive discourse that undermines the authority of the state whenever it is recounted, and an instrument through which those who would resist the state's incursions can be mobilized and emboldened.

5

AGAINST AUTHORITY
Corrosive Discourses

CHALLENGES TO AUTHORITY AND VIOLENT RIPOSTES

Even if it were within my power to produce an authoritative account of authority, I would be loath to do so, for I do not claim nor do I wish to be the right kind of speaker for such a project. Rather, I would far prefer to dish up a set of gossipy stories, scurrilous comments, and irreverent jokes that have some — perhaps only tangential — bearing on so august a topic. And within the limits of an overly stodgy academic diction, that is what I have tried to do in the last three chapters.

The stories I told there were meant to be juicy and revealing, embarrassing in certain ways (also for certain types of people and interests), liberating in (and for) others. In general I have not attempted to treat authority in the abstract, nor in its essence, but have chosen to focus on a few episodes of crisis to explore the dynamics of authority: to catch authority in moments of revealing disarray, where one can see how it responds to challenge, and how challengers respond to authority's responses. To this end, I began my inquiry by identifying the single most disruptive events attested within three settings, each of which was the prime "authorized and authorizing place" of a given society: the Homeric assembly (*agorē*), the Roman Senate, and the Scandinavian *Thing*.

Surprisingly, none of these crises involved a frontal assault in which some actors sought to strip others of the authority the latter enjoyed. Rather, they were catalyzed either by the entry of an unauthorized person into the privileged sphere (Thersites, Egil's witnesses), or alternatively, when it appeared that an authorized person (Cotta) would make use of his access to say things judged intolerable. In all cases, the period of crisis ended in violence: violence deployed by people who were determined to prevent an act of speech that threatened not only their interests, but also their relative monopoly on access to the privileged sphere.

Conventional wisdom deplores such violence for the way it puts an end to all opportunities for discussion. While it is hard to be critical of so mild and well-intentioned a view, its inadequacies are clear. First, it makes a special case of violence, which ought to be seen in connection to other, related phenomena. Although the direct exercise of physical force may be rare (and therefore shocking), the threat of force is present in every speech situation, being implicit in the unequal power of those who are parties to it. This threat always inflects and distorts the nature of the speech, creating opportunities for some and restrictions for others. Accordingly, it may be more important to explore (and deplore) the subtle processes of inhibition and intimidation that run through every conversation than to concentrate attention on the relatively few occasions in which the implicit threats of force are spectacularly realized.

Second, even the most flagrant use of force cannot extinguish speech in any absolute sense. At most, violent acts can do no more than deprive certain actors of certain forms of speech and certain opportunities for speaking. In so doing, however, they will surely provoke other sorts of speech (lamentations, accusations, denials, etc.) by other actors in other places and on other occasions. Moreover, if one broadens the notion of "speech" to include signifying practices in general, it follows that even lethal force is incapable of reducing those on whom it falls to absolute silence, for the graves or corpses of the slain, and the absences of the *desaparecidos* themselves become signs that "speak" what has been done and denounce those responsible.

Finally, violence itself can be understood as a form of speech through which actors announce the power they have and their willingness to use it. As such, it reaches and affects not only those whose bodies feel it directly, but also those who see or hear about it at second and third hand: This, precisely, is the terrorizing effect of terror. Yet it is also important to recognize that those who speak through the medium of force implicitly acknowledge their inability to command the obedience or even the respectful attention of their interlocutors by any less strenuous means. That is to say, in the moment they resort to force, they abandon their claim to authority, and one can thus describe violence as a speech that delegitimates itself in the very act of speaking.

ATTACK AND COUNTERATTACK: AUTHORITY AND ITS CORROSION

In each of the cases I have considered, violence forced the protagonists to retreat from the places they had assumed within the privileged sphere. Beyond this, their actions differed significantly, as did the stances they adopted toward those who drove them out. Thus, Thersites and Cotta accepted defeat: The former returned to his seat and wept, while the latter retired from public life after the Ides of March, explaining to friends that he did so "out of a certain fatal despair" (*fatali quadam desperatione*). In contrast, Egil's immediate, almost instinctive response was to meet violence with violence, and when he found this possibility blocked, he then sought other modes of action.

> Alf Shipman and his company leapt into the court. They cut apart the bonds of consecration, broke down the staffs, and set the judges running. Then there was a great tumult in the *Thing*, but all the men were unarmed there. Then Egil said: "Can Berg-Onund hear my words?"
>
> "I hear," he said.
>
> "Then I offer you a duel, and we two will fight, here at the *Thing*. He who gains victory will have the livestock, the land,

and the money. And if you dare not, you will be everyone's object of mockery."

Then King Eirik answered: "If you are eager to fight, Egil, we will grant that to you."

Egil answered: "I will not fight against you, nor against overwhelming numbers of troops. But I will not flee from an equal number of men, if this be granted to me. And in that case, I'll make no distinction among men."

Then Arinbjorn said: "Let us leave. We can't do anything here that helps us at present." Then he turned away, and all his troops went with him.

Then Egil turned back and said: "I call you to witness this, Arinbjorn, and you too, Thord, and all those men who can hear my words now: nobles and lawmen and commoners. I curse all the lands that Bjorn had, curse them for dwelling and for cultivation. I curse you, Berg-Onund, and all other men — native and foreigner, high-born and low — who have done this. I charge you with breaking the laws of the land and with breaking the truce of the *Thing,* and I call down the wrath of the gods." (*Egil's Saga* 56.59–66)

At first, Egil continues to define the situation as a struggle between himself and Berg-Onund, to whom he offers a stark alternative: "I offer you a duel, and we two will fight . . . And if you dare not, you will be everyone's object of mockery" (*hvers manns nið-ingr*). This choice involves several linked alternatives. Berg-Onund can face either Egil or the community at large, but in either case the weapons and the stakes differ sharply. In a duel, the two opponents will use weapons of metal and both will risk their lives equally. Should Berg-Onund decline, however, he will face countless, nameless adversaries, all of whom wield words as their weapons: words of scorn and ridicule (Old Norse *nið*) that inflict wounds of shame, and in this form of combat he alone will take the risks, particularly that of lost reputation.

In effect, Egil asks Berg-Onund to choose between facing physical violence (which, as we have seen, is also a form of speech) and speech, which can also be a form of violence. Berg-Onund is rescued from these bleak alternatives by the king, who insists on his own role in the dispute, and offers to enter the fray. At this point, bluster notwithstanding, Egil cannot realistically hope to accomplish anything through force of arms. Still, Arinbjorn's counsel of prudence — "We can't do anything for the moment that will serve us" — is less than fully correct, since there *is* something Egil can do, even in the face of superior force. Quite simply, he curses Berg-Onund and King Eirik alike, as he will do once more when planting his "staff of mockery" (*níð- stǫng*).

Ultimately, Egil wins a much larger victory than he could have hoped to achieve in the *Thing*-place or in any court of law. Moreover, he does so by using a blunt, coarse, and caustic speech of calumny and denunciation that is utterly different from the speech of authority, but no less consequential. Within the context of chapter 4, I referred to this as "the fifth voice" to distinguish it from the other voices there at issue: those of the two rival disputants, that of the law, and that of (monarchic) state power. Beyond this specific context, however, we might do better to call this form of speech "corrosive discourse." Under this term might then be included all those sorts of speech which are not only nonauthoritative, but downright antithetical to the construction of authority, given their capacity to eat away at the claims and pretensions of discourses and speakers who try to arrogate authority for themselves: gossip, rumor, jokes, invective; curses, catcalls, nicknames, taunts; caricatures, graffiti, lampoon, satire; sarcasm, mockery, rude noises, obscene gestures, and everything else that deflates puffery and degrades the exalted. Other differences notwithstanding, all of these discourses lead audiences to hold someone or something in diminished regard, and as an audience turns irreverent, authority crumbles.

Ironically, corrosive discourses themselves suffer from a bad name, largely because of their ad hominem quality, although this also gives them much of their piquant appeal. Not only do they concern themselves with specific, named and well-known individuals, they freely delight in their foibles and failings. Virtually nothing is off limits to them, and in tone they can range from jocular innuendo to merciless censure. Charges of sexual impropriety, cowardice, and self-indulgence of various sorts (drunkenness, gluttony, laziness, etc.) are common, since in these both moral and physical shortcomings are equally evi-

dent. Although true, it is quite inadequate to say that they focus
on the private, not the public persona. Rather, they focus on
the private *at the expense of* the public persona, stressing the inevitable contradictions between the two, as when they—with
obvious delight—speak of the body that lurks beneath and
brings discredit to the robes or uniform. In short, corrosive
discourse restores to the level of the human those frail and falli-
ble individuals who would prefer to represent themselves as the
embodiment of some incontestable office or some transcendent ideal.

NOT TO PRAISE, BUT TO BURY

According to the saga that bears his name, Egil was ultimately
able to unseat a king through the agency of corrosive discourses. He triumphs where Cotta and Thersites are defeated
precisely because he will *not* be silenced, but keeps on speaking.
In extremis, he has recourse to a new and different form of
speech, a speech with emancipatory potential that is appropriate to and effective within the new situation and position
into which he has been thrust. Hardly authoritative, it is a
speech that eats away at the authority—and ultimately the
power—of those who deprived him of his rights to the other
form of speech which originally he sought.

Although Cotta may have been reduced to silence, there
were other Romans who traded in corrosive discourse during
February and March of 44 B.C. with devastating results.
Among these, as we have seen, are the anonymous rumormon-
gers who sowed suspicion about Caesar's motives, prompting
the conspirators to kill him, and the invisible graffiti artists who
so taunted Brutus that he joined the conspiracy rather than risk
the loss of his (and his family's) good name. Several other telling examples may be drawn from the hectic and confused period following Caesar's assassination, when numerous actors
sought both to gain authority for themselves and to discredit
their rivals, the dead and living alike.

If we follow the conspirators on the Ides of March, we find
them alternating between unsuccessful attempts to speak with
authority and counterproductive acts of corrosive discourse.
Thus, we are told that immediately after the assassination Bru-

tus tried to deliver a formal address on the floor of the Senate
to justify their act as a defense of traditional Roman values:
libertas and the Republic. Unfortunately — but not surprisingly — he found himself in that moment without an audience,
since all save the conspirators had fled. Accordingly, he and his
comrades marched through the city to the Capitoline hill, waving bloody daggers, parading a liberty cap (the mark of men
freed from slavery) on the point of a spear, reviling Caesar as a
king and a tyrant, and calling on bystanders to come and join
them. Then, on the following day:

> The Senators and many of the common people went up to the
> men on the Capitoline. When the multitude had gathered, Bru-
> tus conversed with them in ways that were inviting to the
> people and fitting to the occasion. When they advised them to
> come down, Brutus and the others confidently descended to the
> forum. The other conspirators went together, but many distin-
> guished men escorted Brutus most respectfully from the heights
> of the Capitoline and installed him on the rostrum. At the sight
> of him, the masses trembled [*hoi polloi dietresan*]. Although it
> was a mixed crowd and they were prepared to create a distur-
> bance, they listened to what was forthcoming in perfect order
> and silence. When he came forward, all were quiet and they
> gave themselves up to his words. But it became clear that the
> assassination had not brought pleasure to everyone when Cinna
> began to speak and to make accusations against Caesar. At that,
> the crowd broke into a rage and spoke so badly against Cinna
> that the conspirators withdrew again to the Capitoline. (Plu-
> tarch *Brutus* 18.4–6)

Two performances are here contrasted. First, there is that of
Brutus, stage-managed by members of the senatorial elite, who
install him on the rostrum at the head of the forum — the most
privileged position for any public address — in a manner that
announces his authority so forcefully that even the most hostile
members of the crowd are obliged to give him a courteous
hearing. Matters change abruptly, however, when a man who
was not so painstakingly identified as the right kind of
speaker — Cornelius Cinna, a praetor who owed his office to
Caesar — begins to give the wrong sort of speech, abusing Caesar's memory and denouncing his benefactor. At this shift to

corrosive discourse, the crowd recovers its voice. Indeed, its shouts drive Cinna from the rostrum and the conspirators from the forum.

If Brutus and his colleagues fluctuated between attempts at authoritative and corrosive discourse, supporters of Caesar accomplished a more subtle and sophisticated interweaving of the two, most notably in the funeral oration given by Marc Antony on 20 March. Antony spoke from the rostrum, but unlike Brutus, he spoke as the Republic's highest ranking official, for in 44 B.C. he was Caesar's co-consul, as well as his most trusted assistant. Nor was it an impromptu meeting in which he spoke, but a solemn, state funeral authorized by the Senate as part of a compromise voted on the seventeenth which reaffirmed all the honors given and due to Caesar, while also granting amnesty to his assassins. The right speaker, Antony thus spoke at the right time and in the right place, and the nature of his speech was also judged "right" by the large majority of his audience. Still, much of his success resulted from the corrosive elements he skillfully inserted within an act of authoritative discourse.

Accounts differ, and none is more than a paraphrase of what Antony actually said, but of those texts which give anything approaching a full description, Appian's is usually considered the most trustworthy.

When Calpurnius Piso [Caesar's father-in-law, who had been entrusted with his will and his corpse] had borne the body to the forum, a vast multitude drew together to guard it with their weapons. With shouts and great ceremony, they placed it on the rostrum. Again there was lengthy wailing and lamentation. The men at arms clashed their weapons, and they began to repent of the amnesty that had been granted to the assassins. Antony, seeing how things were going, did not change his purpose, but having chosen himself to deliver the eulogy as a consul speaking for a consul, a friend speaking for a friend, and a relative speaking for a relative (since he was related to Caesar on his mother's side), he once more exercised his craft and spoke thus:

"Citizens, it is not fitting that the eulogy of so great a man should be declaimed by me alone, just one person; rather, it should come from his whole country. Insofar as you all voted honors to him, the Senate and the people being equally admiring of his excellence, I will read these decrees, using your voice and not that of Antony." Then he began to read, with his face both angry and sorrowful, pausing and emphasizing each decree with his voice, especially those which treated Caesar as divine, or which named him sacred and inviolable, father of the fatherland, benefactor, or patron like no other. At each of these, Antony turned his eyes and his hands toward Caesar's body, giving an illustration of his speech through his action. (*Civil Wars* 2.143–44)

At its boldest, Antony's goal was to reshape social sentiments and allegiances, particularly those involving himself, the Senate, and the people. Thus, he is at pains to connect his voice to that of the people so tightly as to make it seem they are virtually one. To this end, he begins by effacing his own voice as he says, "It is not fitting that the eulogy . . . should be declaimed by me alone . . . rather, it should come from his whole country," and "I will read these decrees, *using your voice and not that of Antony.*" Over the course of his address, however, Antony gradually repositions himself so that where initially he claims that the people spoke through him, by the end they see him as speaking for the people.

By reading the aforementioned decrees (the extraordinary honors the Senate bestowed on Caesar and reaffirmed in its postassassination meeting of 17 March), Antony also works to drive a wedge between the voice of the Senate and that of the people. When Antony states that "the Senate and the people [*hē te boulē kai . . . ho dēmos*] were equally admiring of [Caesar's] excellence," however, he does so with more than a trace of irony, as is underscored by the gestures and tone of voice he uses while quoting the Senate's resolutions. Through these paralinguistic cues, he insinuates that whereas he and the people of Rome are sincere and loyal in their admiration for Caesar, Caesar's assassins — all senators — were hypocritical and deceitful when they initially voted these honors and, more recently, when they voted to reaffirm them. With this maneuver, he laid the groundwork for transforming the traditional Rome of "Senate and people"(*Senatus populusque Romanus*, S.P.Q.R.) into Rome of the Civil War, in which a Caesarophile faction, initially consisting of Antony and the people, confronted the faction of Caesaricides centered on the Senate.

Appian goes on to describe how, in subsequent portions of his oration, Antony quoted the oaths sworn by the Senate to defend Caesar; sang hymns to him as if to a celestial deity (*ōs theon ouranion hymnei*); recounted Caesar's victories and other glorious deeds; pitched his voice into a high register, as if speaking in a state of inspiration (*epitheisas*), then dropped it again as he mourned, wept, and vowed his willingness to give his own life in exchange for Caesar's. Then, in the culminating moments:

> Completely carried away with passion, he uncovered Caesar's body, and lifting his toga up on a pole, brandished it, torn as it was from the blows of the daggers, and stained with the ruler's blood. At that, the people engaged in the most mournful lamentations with him, singing like the chorus in a tragedy, and out of his sorrow, they were filled once more with anger. (*Civil Wars* 2.146)

Although other versions differ in certain details, they consistently report that the Senate's decrees honoring Caesar were quoted verbatim, as was the oath ensuring Caesar's safety. They also agree there was a display of Caesar's bloody toga, although some say his body was also exhibited, and some speak of a wax effigy, in which all twenty-three wounds were fully evident. Virtually without exception they emphasize how Antony aroused in his audience the sentiments of pity for Caesar and rage or indignation at his murderers.

Here, Antony exposed himself to criticism as he violated the norms of rhetorical practice, under which eulogists were expected to concentrate on evoking admiration for the deceased and for his family. Dio Cassius judged Antony's unveiling of the corpse to be "most unthinkable" (*anoētotata*), and took the speech itself to be "very beautiful and brilliant, yet not fitting for the occasion." Cicero went further, thundering at Antony in a pamphlet of denunciation that purported to be a speech delivered on the floor of the Senate (i.e., a corrosive discourse masquerading as authoritative).

> You presided at the tyrant's funeral (if funeral it was!) in a most infamous fashion. That beautiful eulogy was yours, the appeal

to pity was yours, the incitement was yours. You, I say, you lit those torches — those with which Caesar was only half cremated, and those with which the house of Lucius Bellienus was burned down. You instigated the attacks on our houses by those lost souls — slaves, for the most part — which we repelled by the force of our hands.

FIRE, SWORD, AND INVECTIVE

Here, Cicero gives Antony more than his due. Granted he undercut the conspirators' authority, helped reorganize Rome into Caesaricide and Caesarophile factions, and effectively established his own authority within the latter faction; still, one ought not grant all agency in this volatile moment to him alone. Although some accounts — not least of them Shakespeare's — are written in such a way as to make Antony the puppetmaster and the crowd his marionette, there is no mistaking the fact that the Roman crowd had wishes, agency, and a highly corrosive language of its own, as becomes clear in the tumultuous events to which Cicero made reference.

Antony intended that upon conclusion of his eulogy, Caesar's body would be carried in a spectacular procession to the Field of Mars, where it would be cremated and the ashes buried, in accordance with ancient practices that forbade disposal of a body within the walls of the city. Apparently the people judged these arrangements inadequate and a quarrel broke out. Ultimately, the crowd decided to cremate Caesar in the forum itself as a signal honor, and conceivably part of an attempt to effect his apotheosis. In this act — part ritual and part riot — they dragged tables and benches from nearby shops and set them ablaze. Then, with brands drawn from this improvised pyre, the mob marched on the assassins' houses, burning one down and turning back from others only after pitched battles. On the way back, they encountered Helvius Cinna, a tribune and ardent Caesarophile. They mistook him, however, for Cornelius Cinna, the Caesaricide praetor who had antagonized the crowd when he spoke against the slain Caesar on 16 March. Falling on his hapless namesake, they ripped the man literally limb from limb, and paraded his head through the streets of the city.

This savage act so terrified the conspirators that many of them decided to make an early departure from the city. But the story does not end here. On the day after the funeral a certain Amatius, who also called himself Marius and claimed to be Caesar's cousin, erected an altar at the site of the pyre and offered sacrifices to Caesar, in effect raising him to the status of a deity. Later a memorial column was added, with the inscription "To the Father of the Fatherland." These initiatives potentially had profound consequences, both religious and political. Not only did they create a new piece of sacred space within the topography of Rome, they also established a staging ground where the most militant of Caesar's devotees could be mobilized. Through March and into mid-April an unruly group of men, army veterans and others from the lower orders of Roman society, gathered at Amatius's altar and became the scourge of those conspirators who still had not fled.

In all of this, as Guy Achard has shown in detail, the Roman people called on a rich ensemble of practices from the militant funerals and violent demonstrations they had been staging for almost a century whenever one of their popular champions died at the hands of the senatorial elite (as in the case of Tiberius and Gaius Gracchus, Gaius Marius, Catiline, and Publius Clodius Pulcher). For his part, Antony employed a few select items from the symbolic repertoire of these rituals; above all, the public display of a wounded body. But in their impromptu pyre, incendiary assaults, ad hoc establishment of a new cult place, and continuing violence, the people made fuller use of many more items from the same repertoire, and in so doing they went far beyond anything Antony either wanted or anticipated. Indeed, it was Antony himself who put a violent stop to these practices, for on 13 April he had Amatius arrested, executed without trial, then dragged through the streets on an iron hook and flung in the river Tiber.

CRIME AND PUNISHMENT

It is hard not to feel some measure of sympathy for poor Amatius on his hook. One can recognize in his brutal treatment a ritual means of execution, in which the bodies of particularly notorious criminals were denied the purifying effects of fire.

Indeed, in such cases it was Rome that needed purification, and the city sought to rid itself of the pollution such people inflicted upon it by dispatching their corpses through the alternate media of water (the Tiber) or air (when they were thrown down from the Tarpeian Rock). Unmistakably, these practices were also intended to degrade and disgrace their victims.

Inflicting disgrace and effecting degradation are complex social processes, however, not transitive actions that can be accomplished by physical means alone. Rather, their accomplishment depends on the judgment of some audience, and it is always the audience that has the last word. Operations intended to disgrace can fail or backfire, as when an audience judges the victims of such treatment to be martyrs and their authors to be bullies.

Apparently, Antony viewed Amatius as a rival for leadership of the Caesarophile faction, and decided to deal with him lest his popularity grew too large and his actions too daring. The reaction to Amatius's repression, as one might have predicted, was different among Caesaricides and Caesarophiles, but not in ways beneficial to Antony's interests. Thus, we are told that the Caesaricides in the Senate were astonished at the violence and the lawlessness of his behavior, but chose not to object, since this rough action had helped to ensure their safety. In contrast, not only Amatius's followers, but most Caesarophiles among the common people were outraged at what he had done. They rioted, seized the forum, burned buildings, and demanded recognition for their altar and for their popular cult of Caesar. Throughout, they cursed Antony (*Antōnion eblasphē-moun*), who responded by putting their movement down in blood. For this he won the very temporary gratitude of the senatorial elite, and more lasting resentment from the Roman plebs, in whose eyes it was not Amatius, but Antony who was disgraced and degraded. In April, Antony thus managed to undo much of what he had begun in his oration, and in the following months he was forced to look more to the army—and less to the people—for support of his cause.

This example makes clear two points of broad importance. First, there are multiple audiences for any speech or action, and different groups (or fractions within a group) are capable of responding in quite different ways. Second, responses may change over time as a group reconsiders its initial reactions, particularly as new events prompt such reconsideration. To these, we can add a third point, for it remains ever possible that at some later date a new audience will emerge and for reasons of its own will choose to take interest in an old case. This brings us back to Thersites.

THE TEARS OF A CLOWN

From the *Iliad*'s description, it is abundantly clear that Thersites was a master of corrosive discourse, and for years had been slandering the mighty, trafficking in scandals, and freely delighting in ridicule. An "outrageous word-hurler" (2.275), he shrieked reproaches at kings (2.214, 2.222, 2.224, 2.277) and subjected them to mockery (2.215, 2.256), using speech that others — his adversaries and his audience — considered a model of and a provocation to profound disorder (2.214–15). Readers of the *Iliad* encounter Thersites, however, in a place normally reserved for other sorts of speakers (also other sorts of speech), and the tension of the narrative derives from his paradoxical attempt to gain authorization for a discourse that is, by its very nature, antithetical to the construction of authority.

Consider, for instance, the characteristic relation of these two forms of discourse to the category of space. In general, authoritative discourses tend to be disseminated from places that are symbolically, and often physically, both lofty and central. As a result, attention is focused on those who speak within such a setting at the same time that the members of the group defined by this central point also are made to look up to them. This is evident not only in the examples we have considered (Assembly, Senate, and *Thing*), but also in such contemporary settings as the pulpit, the podium, or the judge's bench. In contrast, corrosive discourses seemingly come from nowhere and no one in particular, circulating, as it were, through back alleys, servants' quarters, toilets, locker rooms, and other low places. As such they can represent themselves and be regarded as nothing other than "the voice of the people." Seemingly spoken by everyone, they are also spoken by no one. As products of an invisible, anonymous collectivity, they are attached to no identifiable speakers: No one takes responsibility for them, and no one runs risks on their account.

Things are different, however, when some rash soul gives full voice to things that are more safely (and no less efficaciously) spoken in whispers and titters, or when she or he brings the speech of the gutters and lavatories into a privileged — and eminently public — place. We thus come to understand that by placing himself at the center of the assembly, instead of continuing to operate at its margins, Thersites committed a tactical blunder, relinquishing the anonymity that protects those who trade in corrosive discourse, and exposing himself to easy repression. Once visible, he becomes vulnerable, as Odysseus recognizes.

The physical and verbal beating that Odysseus administers also takes place in full public view at the center of the assembly. Vulnerable in his visibility, Thersites is also painfully visible in his vulnerability. Driven from the center, smashed to the ground, bloodied and reduced to tears, the scold becomes an object of scorn; the maker of jokes becomes the butt of others' laughter, and in its laughter, the audience pronounces judgment:

> Thersites sat down, terrified
> And pained, and looking about aimlessly, he wiped away his tears.
> Although grieving, the others laughed sweetly at him.
> And thus someone would say, looking at his neighbor:
> "Truly, Odysseus has done thousands of great deeds . . .
> But the greatest deed he has accomplished
> Is keeping this outrageous word-hurler out of the assembly."
>
> (*Iliad* 2.268–75)

Within the text of the *Iliad,* this stands as the final word on Thersites, and for many generations it held more or less unquestioned sway. Other audiences, however, who stand outside the text and maintain some critical stance toward its authorial designs, are capable of reaching other judgments. Each time these lines are read, other possibilities emerge, and if Thersites' tears rendered him ridiculous to the Achaeans, they have come to evoke rather more sympathy from many modern readers. Millennia later, the tears shed in pain, fear, and humiliation by this master of corrosive discourse continue to eat away at any respect one might conceivably have for Odysseus, Agamemnon, the golden sceptre, or the symbolic and sociopolitical system that endowed them with authority. Discourses of all sorts can be very rapid or slow and gradual in gaining — or altering — their efficacy. This text, like many others, continues to speak, and as it is read or heard in novel ways by novel audiences, it has come to inflict shame on those who were once its heroes.

6

AND WHAT ABOUT THE WOMEN?

QUEENS AND LOVERS

In all the materials we have considered, there is only one woman who managed to speak within an authorized and authorizing place. This was Gunnhild: "A small woman to look at, but large in her voice," according to one description. Still, in considering what she said at (and did to) the *Thing*-place when Egil's lawsuit was being heard, I argued that Gunnhild's large voice might best be understood as a voice of power, not one of law or authority: the fourth voice, that is, and not the third, to use the terminology of chapter 4. And if authority can be understood as the effect produced by a conjuncture of the right speaker, the right speech and delivery, the right staging and props, and the right time and place as I suggested in chapter 1, it is clear that audiences of several sorts (those at the trial, as well as readers of *Egil's Saga*) have harbored doubts as to whether Gunnhild was the right kind of speaker. They have not doubted that she delivered very much the wrong speech.

Considerations of context and precise dramatic sequence are important here. Thus, we should recall that when Arinbjorn attempted to swear in his witnesses, they asked permission to testify, and the judges were agreeable, provided the king would also consent. Although undoubtedly the right speaker—as established by his office and the deference shown him by all other actors—King Eirik then spoke in so equivocal and irresolute a fashion as to settle nothing. Enter Gunnhild.

As queen, Gunnhild apparently could claim the right to speak in the *Thing*-place, much as the king could. Yet the two gender-specific royal offices are not identical. Chief of their differences is the fact that a king (normally) acquires his office by descent, a queen by marriage. The terms of such a marriage establish that the queen will devote her sexual capacities exclusively to the king and her reproductive capacities exclusively to the royal lineage so that she can produce heirs whose legitimacy is absolutely secure. It is in return for this invaluable and indispensable service that she is accorded royal status.

Given this, it is a bit jarring to recognize that Gunnhild's speech in the *Thing*-place called into question her relation to the man through whom she obtained her rank, and with it the right to speak there. Yet her words were addressed directly to Eirik, and constituted a stinging rebuke. What is more, certain details were potentially compromising.

> Then Queen Gunnhild took up the case and said: "This is extraordinary, King, how you let this big fellow Egil entangle all the cases before you. Perhaps you might not even speak against him if he claimed your very kingdom. Although you will not grant a decision that would be of help to Berg-Onund, I will not endure it that Egil thus tread *my friend* under his feet and wrongfully take Berg-Onund's wealth from him . . ." (*Egil's Saga* 56.57–58)

Here, just before ordering her troops to demolish the court-circle, Gunnhild shockingly contrasted King Eirik to three other characters. First, she compared his weakness and timidity with Egil's strength, going so far as to portray Egil as a threat to the throne. Second, she compared her own willingness to take action with Eirik's waffling and hesitation. Finally, most subtly and insidiously, she measured the king against Berg-Onund. More precisely, she measured her feelings for each man, and showed by her words and behavior that she would rather herself inflict shame on the king and cause him loss of pride than let his indecision cause Berg-Onund loss of property.

And when, in this context, Gunnhild refers to Berg-Onund as "my friend" (*vini mína*), one perhaps begins to wonder just what their friendship entails.

Actually, the text has laid some groundwork for suspicion, particularly when it said to Berg-Onund "to Gunnhild he was quite dear," using a term (Old Norse *kærr*) that is tantalizing in its ambiguity. While it signals affection, it leaves utterly unclear whether that affection is innocent, erotic, or somewhere in between. Suspicions, in truth, may be more important than realities, for whenever an audience believes there have been sexual improprieties between a queen and her favorite, this can open (or widen) a breach between her and the king, with potentially severe consequences for her royal status, as well as that of her children.

Ultimately, what a queen says may be of less importance than what is said about her, since the latter will inevitably condition reception of the former. And about Gunnhild, a great deal is said. Throughout Old Norse literature, she figures as something of a stock character, and is consistently portrayed as beautiful, cruel, crafty, and unprincipled. The *Heimskringla* says it was she who poisoned Halfdan the Black, Eirik's popular half-brother and rival for the throne, and the *Ágrip* makes her responsible for other atrocities, saying, "Eirik was so receptive to her counsel of cruelty and of tyranny over the people that it was heavy to bear." *Theodricus* attributes further deaths and persecutions to the counsels she gave their son, Harald Graycloak (reigned 961–70). *Njal's Saga* and *Laxdæla Saga* also describe Gunnhild's activity during Harald's reign, but dwell on her sexual appetites and recount how, as aging Queen Mother, she still took good-looking visitors to bed, after which she secured them other sorts of favors at her son's court. Most telling, perhaps, is the story of how Eirik came to marry Gunnhild. While traveling in the extreme north (a wild area strongly associated with sorcery), his men encountered a beautiful woman, who shared a hut and a bed with two Finnish wizards, in hopes of winning their magic lore. When the king's soldiers arrived, the wizards were out hunting, and after the briefest of conversations, Gunnhild suggested to the soldiers that together they ought to kill the Finns. Then, after turning her bed into the wizards' deathtrap, she departed with the soldiers to meet and to marry Eirik.

Tempting as it is to admire Gunnhild as a woman who used men for her purposes and her pleasure, this is hardly the attitude adopted by these texts. Rather, they depict her as a witch, a murderess, a harridan and an insatiable seductress: in short, the hyperbolic incarnation of the negative characteristics conventionally associated with women in a patriarchal society. Discrediting one powerful woman, however, is only part of their intent, and beyond Gunnhild they are after bigger game. For in their treatment of Gunnhild, these Icelandic texts sought also to discredit the Norwegian kingship, which they portrayed as so deeply flawed an institution that it could permit a woman — and a woman so debased as Gunnhild — to speak with devastating power. Against the powerful speech which she, like all monarchs, was able to wield; *Egil's Saga* counterposed a corrosive speech of gossip, scandal, and innuendo, in which the wanton and violent queen was made to represent monarchy *in general,* and provided the point of vulnerability through which its claims to authority could be nullified.

THE WISE WOMAN AND THE DUMMY

After Gunnhild, the woman whom we saw coming closest to the authorized and authorizing sphere was the Sibyl. Yet she, too, on occasion, could become little more than a counter in other people's games, an object or instrument of their discourse rather than the subject of her own. In some ways, the Sibyl's situation resembled that of a queen, since she too acquired her capacity for authoritative speech only through the mediation of others: a deity in the first instance and priest in the second. But whereas a queen's relation to the king may permit her to speak in privileged places and to make serious claims on the attention of audiences, the Sibylline ideology insisted that a Sibyl does not really speak: At least, she does not speak in her own voice. Rather, in a form of divine ventriloquism, a deity spoke through her, just as "she" spoke only through the agency of a Quindecemvir.

As might be imagined, this ideology was extremely useful to

anyone who could control what the Quindecemvirs said. Legally, it was the Senate that exercised this sort of control and, as Jerzy Linderski has rightly observed, throughout the Republican period it was the Roman ruling elite that acted as master ventriloquist, speaking through the god, through the Sibyl, through the Quindecemvir, and ultimately through the Senate. In the last years of the Republic, however, others—above all, Julius Caesar—learned how to manipulate this system of mediations in order to make "the gods" and "the Sibyl" speak their interests, even when these ran directly counter to those of the Senate and the traditional elite. As we have seen, the threats posed by one such act of ventriloquism—the one scheduled for the ides of March—prompted Brutus, Cassius, and the other conspirators to overcome their hesitation and kill the puppetmaster. Shortly thereafter, it prompted Cicero to mount an attack on the Sibylline system itself, in some crucial paragraphs he added to his treatise *On Divination* in the days following the assassination.

> What authority (*Quid . . . auctoritatis*) has that madness you call "divine"? Can the insane see things that the wise do not, and can those who have lost their human senses be attendants to the gods? Ought we pay attention to the lines of the Sibyl, which she is said to have uttered while raving mad? Recently there was a false rumor, which was believed by certain men, that an interpreter of these verses would announce in the Senate that if we wanted to be saved, the man who ruled *de facto* as our king, ought also be given this title. But if this is in the books, to what man and what times does it refer? Whoever composed these verses finished them shrewdly, so that whatever actually happens seems to have been predicted, all specification of persons and time having been omitted. Further, he employed a cloak of obscurity so that the same verses might seem suitable to other circumstances. . . . Therefore, let us have Sibylline things set apart and kept secret, according to our ancestral traditions, so that these books are not read against the will of the Senate, and help dispel, rather than sustain superstitions. And let us press the priests so that they bring forth from those books anything but a king, which is something that henceforth neither the gods nor the Roman people will endure. (*On Divination* 2.110–12)

Although Cicero discreetly avoided mentioning Cotta by name, and feigned disbelief in the rumors, it is clear that he took the events of the Ides seriously, and understood them to reveal that the system designed to exercise control over prophecy no longer operated as it had in the past, but had been effectively subverted. Perceiving grave dangers in this novel situation, he therefore sought to discredit all Sibylline texts by depicting them—somewhat contradictorily—as both the ravings of madwomen and the deliberately obscure compositions of willful deceivers, which obscurity provided room for maneuver to whomever controlled the entry of these utterances into public discussion.

Cicero thus urged that these dangerous texts be "set apart and kept secret," so that they might never be read "against the will of the Senate," although it would have been less disingenuous to say "against senatorial *interests*." In the turbulent period that followed, however, the Senate could no more reestablish its control over prophetic discourse than it could reestablish itself as the leading institution of the Roman state. Rather, such control was secured as a very late step in the emperor Augustus's consolidation of power. For it was only after he had been named Pontifex Maximus in 13 B.C. (eighteen years after he defeated Antony at Actium and won full military and political hegemony) that Augustus was willing to undertake such a task. Once he had this supreme priestly office, however, he made it his very first order of business to collect all prophetic texts from throughout the empire, and to burn those he considered suspect. Only a portion of the Sibylline Books was spared from the blaze, and these writings he transferred from the temple of Capitoline Jupiter (chief god of the Republic) to that of the Palatine Apollo, his own patron deity, where he had them locked away and kept under close control.

Again, it is tempting to think that what Cicero urged and Augustus accomplished was the suppression of powerful women and the eradication of a site from which women's speech could win authorization. Undoubtedly there is some validity to this view, but it is not the full story, for it does not take into consideration the extent to which sibyls were already controlled by men through the institutions of the Quindecemviri and the Senate. The struggle was not just one of men against women, although this was part of it. Some men contended with others for an invaluable symbolic resource that was associated with, but not independently controlled by women: Sibylline prophecy, an instrument through which they could represent their own speech as the voice of the gods.

DREAMS AND NIGHTMARES

What, then, was a woman to do if she wished to speak, not only with authority, but on her own behalf and in her own voice? As we have seen, most women were barred from the places where speech was authorized, and even those few who could gain entry might still fall victim to ventriloquistic manipulations of one sort or another. Ventriloquism, however, is a supple technique, adaptable to a variety of purposes. Indeed, there are even forms in which an apparent dummy casts its voice through what is only seemingly the puppeteer, in a tour de force that permits the knowing "dummy" to speak its own lines through its own mouth with a voice that no one recognizes as its own.

Although important, Sibylline prophecy was not the only way of predicting the future in ancient Rome. Prognostications were also advanced by those who could read the entrails of sacrificial victims or interpret portentous events, flashes of lightning, astrological patterns, and the casting of lots. On all of these, we are moderately well informed, largely due to Cicero's *On Divination,* a text that takes the form of a dialogue or debate. Book 1, set in the mouth of Cicero's brother, Quintus, who represents the Stoic school of philosophy, offers a defense of such practices, while in book 2 Cicero lets himself offer a critique of them, speaking on behalf of the New Academy. One of the few things on which the brothers agree, however, is that all forms of divination can be classified within two broad categories: the "natural" (*naturalis divinatio* or *a natura*) and the "artificial" (*divinatio . . . artificiosa* or *ex arte*), each of which is further divisible into two subcategories, as shown in figure 6.1.

Every taxonomy involves a logical analysis, and in this case the organizing principles were the distinction between intellect and soul and that between specialists and others. Thus, the artificial types of divination were understood as intellectual opera-

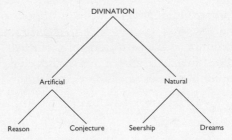

Figure 6.1 Cicero's taxonomy of divinatory practice. Version 1.

tions, forms of knowledge that could be taught and learned. In this category fall extispicy (divination from entrails), augury, astrology, and the interpretation of lots and omens. Specialists like haruspices and augurs who had sufficient intellectual gifts, training, experience, and institutional authorization to employ these techniques with a high degree of confidence (on their part and that of their audiences) could make predictions based on "reason," while others — nonprofessionals, with lesser skills and science — might still offer their "conjectures." In contrast, the natural types of divination depended on the soul's inherent powers of perception and understanding, which were taken to be enormous, however much one's capacity to exercise them was normally limited by the soul's dependence on the body. Specialists in seership (*vaticinatio*), like the Sibyl, activated these powers in states of high mental excitation or madness (*furoris divinationem*) in which they liberated the soul from its bodily prison. And just as anyone with a little learning could practice conjecture alongside the specialists of reason, so too a more democratic form of natural divination accompanied the seership available only to spiritual virtuosi. This came in dreams, when, according to Quintus, "the soul in sleep is called away from society and from the body's contagion, and it remembers the past, understands the present, and foresees the future." By way of further explanation, he quotes from a lost work on the interpretation of dreams by the great Stoic philosopher Posidonius, who suggested that in this state of liberation, the soul is able to gather information on its own, from other souls, or directly from the gods.

Beyond logical analysis, one can also perceive in this taxonomy, as in many others, the outlines of a social order; more specifically, a system based on gender. Thus, although women are barely mentioned in discussions of "artificial" divination, they figure prominently when the text turns to "natural" forms, reflecting an implicit understanding that the intellect is to the soul as the male is to the female. To cite an obvious example, the ideal division of divinatory labor appears in the household of Priam, whose son was an augur and whose daughter was a sibyl.

The system establishes four basic types of divinatory practice. One is the domain of specialists who employ the intellect ("reason"), another that of specialists who employ the soul ("seership"), and of these the first is male and the second female. A similar, but somewhat weaker distinction marks the nonspecialist forms. Thus, in theory, most anyone could practice either one, but it appears that men were particularly drawn to conjecture and women to dreams (figure 6.2).

So much for theory. Let us now consider a specific case: the curious events reported for the night preceding the Ides of March. According to Plutarch:

> Caesar was sleeping, as usual, beside his wife, when all at once the doors and windows of their bedchamber flew open. Having been thrown into confusion by the noise and the light of the moon shining down, he noticed that Calpurnia, sleeping deeply, was emitting faint words and inarticulate moans in her slumber, and it seems she held his murdered body in her arms and mourned him. Others say this was not the woman's vision. As Livy reports, by vote of the Senate a pediment had been attached to Caesar's house, to give it decoration and solemnity, and according to them, when Calpurnia saw this crumble and fall in her dream, she cried out and wept. At daybreak she

	Specialist	Nonspecialist
Intellect (Male)	Reason	Conjecture
Soul (Female)	Seership	Dreams

Figure 6.2 Cicero's taxonomy of divinatory practice. Version 2.

begged Caesar not to go forth, but to put off the meeting of the
Senate . . .

Whether this actually took place or whether these stories
were invented after the fact need not concern us here. In certain
ways, the latter case may be the more interesting, as it shows
us the sort of behavior Romans in the first century B.C. thought
a woman in Calpurnia's situation would be likely to adopt: the
most effective way that a woman, frightened for her husband's
safety, might try to persuade him to take care. Similarly, it is of
little concern whether Calpurnia actually dreamed these dreams
or made them up and only claimed to have dreamt them, for
in either event we (if not the Romans) will take them to be her
product, the set of images in which she encoded and communi-
cated her fears.

The meaning of the dreams themselves is not difficult to
fathom, as consultation of ancient dream manuals makes clear.
The downfall of Caesar's house is tantamount to his death, and
through this, or through the more graphic image of his bloody
corpse, Calpurnia sought to warn him. Worried, undoubtedly
she was — and with good reason, as events proved — but she
claimed that her fears were based not on any observations or
ruminations of a personal (and therefore untrustworthy) nature, but from a prophetic vision that had been obtained in
dreams by her disembodied soul.

This was the highest authority that any woman short of a
sibyl could ordinarily muster. Even so, it might well be dis-
missed, for it was the weakest of all divinatory forms. Not only
was it both female and nonspecialist, but it was unclear, as
Quintus's quotation from Posidonius shows, whether the voice
one heard in dreams was that of the gods, of other souls, or
simply one's own voice, albeit in a particularly lucid state. And
when the discussion turns critical in book 2 of *On Divination*,
Cicero employs a decidedly gendered vocabulary to heap scorn
on dreams and on those who respect them:

> How many people are there who follow their dreams? Who un-
> derstand them? Who remember them? And how many are
> there, truly, who disdain a belief in dreams and regard it as the
> superstition of a weak and old-womanish soul (*imbecili animi
> atque anilis*)!

Anticipating the possibility of such dismissal, Calpurnia decided not to stake her case entirely on the authority of her dreams. Rather, she urged Caesar, "if he took the least notice of her dreams, to consult other means of divination and sacrifices concerning the future" — that is, the "rational" practices of male specialists. Her gambit succeeded, initially at least. Plutarch tells us that on the fatal morning, Caesar was prone to believe his wife, and for an interesting reason. Although she made a female appeal, using a female form of authoritative speech, ordinarily she was not given to such female ways: "Never before had he observed a womanish propensity (*gynaikismon*) for superstition in Calpurnia, and now she was all distraught." Accordingly, Caesar performed sacrifices so that his haruspices could read the victims' entrails. The signs being bad ("fearful," according to Appian), he decided to remain at home and cancel the meeting of the Senate. Such, however, was not to be.

> At this point, Decimus Brutus (a man Caesar so trusted that he made him one of his heirs, but who was part of the conspiracy with Cassius and the other Brutus), feared that if Caesar escaped this day their action would be discovered. Accordingly, he scoffed at the diviners and chided Caesar that he would win for himself the accusations and slanders of senators, who would think themselves treated contemptuously. For they came at his bidding, and all were ready to vote that he be named king of the provinces outside Italy and be permitted to wear a diadem while traveling to other lands and seas. But if someone should tell them to go away, *and to come back when Calpurnia meets with better dreams,* what sorts of talk would malicious people make?

In this sinister project of persuasion, Decimus Brutus succeeded, in part, by ridiculing Calpurnia's dreams and playing on Caesar's ambitions, but more importantly, he managed to link these themes together, while also joining them to a third. Initially, then, the question he posed was whether or not Caesar ought to accept the authority of Calpurnia's discourse: Should he put his trust in the dreams she reported? The choice was important, Decimus argued, for consequent on it Caesar could expect to figure in one of two radically different sorts of discourse. If he chose to disbelieve his wife — so the tempter promised — he would hear the Senate hail him as king. But if he chose to believe her, the senators' acclamations would turn to insults, and there would be no end of taunts, gibes, gossip, and innuendo from those who gathered from this incident new grist for their ugly mills. The alternatives were as clear as their differences were stark. As Decimus Brutus framed the issue, for Caesar to accept the authority of Calpurnia's dream was not only to forfeit the fulfillment of his ambitions, but also to expose himself to the dangers of corrosive discourses that potentially could make him a laughingstock and rob him of all the authority he had.

CORROSIVE DISCOURSES AGAIN

With rare exceptions, in the societies and historic periods with which we have been concerned — as in all too many others — women were unable to speak with authority. Gatekeepers and potential audiences judged them, because of their gender, to be "wrong" speakers, and denied them access to authorized and authorizing places. In a few cases, women who enjoyed a privileged position of one sort or another (usually as a result of their relation to some even-more-privileged man) were able to gain entry (Gunnhild), to have a male representative speak their words for them inside the privileged sphere (the Sibyl), or to speak outside the sphere in a way that claimed a special status for what they had to say (Calpurnia). Even so, the results are not encouraging. In all the instances we have studied, authority proved hard for even these specially favored women to come by: not so, slander, manipulation, and ridicule.

This is not to say that the kinds of speech to which women were restricted were also inconsequential. Important possibilities remained, and for those to whom opportunities for authoritative speech are closed, those for resistant, subversive, and corrosive speech remain not only open, but eminently attractive. Informal, unofficial exchanges of information and opinion ("gossip"), for example, can have enormous effects. As individual acts of discourse, they may be insignificant and invisible (at least, from the point of view of society as a whole) but collectively, they are neither inaudible nor ineffective. As the "wrong" kind of talk from the "wrong" kind of speakers, circulating in the "wrong" kind of place, they elicit no reverence from their

hearers, yet such is hardly their intent. Indeed, frequently glee-
ful in their irreverence, they not only ask no respect for themselves, but urge that respect be withdrawn from those of whom
they speak, and in extreme forms, they move toward a world
in which the very possibility of reverence and authority seems
to disappear.

Powerful men fear the effects of these corrosive discourses,
and rightly so. Eirik Bloodaxe lost his following and his throne
when his subjects started to curse him and to spread gossip
about him and his wife. Caesar marched to his death, against
his better judgment, rather than face the risk of malicious talk.
And Agamemnon lost control of his army when the troops
were stirred up by Rumor: the kind of corrosive speech that in
antiquity was occasionally personified as a goddess, and that,
according to Hesiod, the gods placed in women as part of their
revenge upon men.

7

RELIGION AND THE CONSTRUCTION OF AUTHORITY

GODS AND GOLD

It doesn't take a Shakespeare to recognize the dramatic potential of discussions chez Caesar on the morning of the Ides. There, the pleas of a wife were weighed against the jibes of an aide, as the life of the man who did the weighing also hung in the balance. In this tense scene — whether it actually transpired or was the product of some rich imagination — we can recognize a classic encounter between authoritative and corrosive discourses, albeit with an intriguing reversal of the usual gendered roles.

On that day, it was a woman who claimed authority and sought to organize a situation in which others would be brought to respect what she said and to act as she wanted, while a man deployed scorn and sarcasm to undercut her claims and thwart her goals. That he succeeded and she failed ought to come as no surprise, but remains worthy of comment and critical attention. Also intuitively obvious, but highly significant, is the fact that Calpurnia's project of authorizing her speech was grounded in and dependent upon a set of religious assertions, specifically those regarding the origin and nature of dreams.

Upon fuller reflection, it is striking how prominently religious claims figure in all of the cases we have considered. In varying fashion, each one involved an attempt to endow certain places, persons, instruments, and acts of speech with sacred warrants of one sort or another. What is more, processes of authorization that invoke the divine or transcendent at some crucial point of their operation seem typical of societies in which the foundational assumptions (one might also speak of the critical posture or regime of truth) made normative by the European Enlightenment have not acquired hegemonic status. It would be foolish — not to say presumptuous and ethnocentric — for those of us who stand on one side of this divide to underestimate the complexity, seriousness, efficacy, and importance of the differing ideological styles more commonly employed by our counterparts located on the other.

We have considered, for example, the myth that accompanied Agamemnon's sceptre and described in detail how it was produced by Hephaestus, the divine artisan, for Zeus, the king of the gods; how Zeus bestowed it on Pelops, the primordial king of Argos; and how it subsequently passed to all Pelops' successors on the Argive throne. Through this narrative, a claim of divine origin was advanced, such that whoever spoke with this sceptre in hand implicitly asserted a connection to the gods, mediated through a line of kings. The precise ways in which the sceptre was described, and its very material substance, also served to reinscribe its sacral nature. Thus, we are told at one point that a sceptre is a bough of a tree that has been cut, trimmed, and ornamented with gold. Obviously, this process transformed an item of nature into an item of culture, but at another level, the golden trappings placed it *beyond* human culture, for gold, being most impervious of all metals to rust, was understood as a form of matter not subject to the degenerative forces of time. As a result, golden objects in Homer always have a vaguely sacred aura about them, and this general tendency was particularly stressed in the case of six objects marked by adjectives that signal their imperviousness to death and decomposition. Of these items, five belonged to deities. The sole exception — and that only partial, given its original ownership — is Agamemnon's sceptre (table 7.1).

Beside Agamemnon and his royal compeers, the Greek epics mention three others who owned sceptres: Chryses (a priest),

TABLE 7.1: Golden Objects as Either "Undecaying" or "Immortal"

Gold Item	Adjective	Owner	Maker	Text
Sceptre	Undecaying	Originally Zeus, now Agamemnon	Hephaestus	*Iliad* 2.46 and 2.186
Chariot felly	Undecaying	Hera		*Iliad* 5.724
Palace	Undecaying	Poseidon		*Iliad* 13.22
Throne	Undecaying	Hera	Hephaestus	*Iliad* 14.238
Sandals	Immortal	Hermes		*Iliad* 24.341
Sandals	Immortal	Athene		*Odyssey* 1.97

Teiresias (a seer), and Hesiod (a poet). Although we rarely group poets and kings together (not to mention the others), within the logic of Greek cultural categories one could temporarily efface the differences among these various specialists and view them all as sceptre-bearers, people whose defining characteristic was their capacity to speak with authority. Further, the sceptre was both a preeminent sign of this authority and the chief instrument through which it was constructed, precisely because it was regarded as a gift of the gods.

One last piece of evidence may give an idea of the religious reverence the sceptre commanded, not only within the Homeric texts, but also in those who read them. Writing in the second century A.D. (almost a millennium after the epics were composed), Pausanias reports as follows:

> Among the gods, the Chaeroneans honor most of all the sceptre which Homer says Hephaestus made for Zeus. They worship this sceptre, and it is something divine [*ti theioteron*], as is proved, above all, by the distinction that comes to men from it.

Pausanias goes on to provide a provenience for this sceptre, telling how Agamemnon's daughter, Electra, brought the sceptre to Chaeronea after her father's death. He also notes that the Chaeroneans had priests devoted to its care and who sacrificed to it on a daily basis. Moreover, he is convinced of the importance and authenticity of this object, and lest we think him unduly credulous, he is at pains to reassert his normally skeptical stance and to underline the exceptional nature of this case: "Poets have sung about many things made by Hephaestus, and people's gossip has followed them in this, but none are worthy of belief, save only Agamemnon's sceptre." Most interesting of all, however, is the way he — following the lead of the Chaeroneans — viewed the sceptre's capacity to confer distinction as proof of its sacred nature. A less mystificatory interpretation, however, would modify the Pausanian formulation, for the sceptre's authorizing capacity hardly constitutes post facto proof of its divine status; rather, *belief in* its divinity is the precondition for its authorizing capacity.

RAPE, INSPIRATION, AND EFFLUVIAL FUMES

That the authority of Lucius Aurelius Cotta involved religious claims is perhaps so clear as to need no discussion. Still, one should observe that the chain of mediations connecting Cotta and his speech to the realm of the gods was rather more tortured than he or his fellow Quindecemvirs would have cared to admit. By the first century B.C., most sibyls had fallen inactive and their utterances were known only from a set of scrolls in the Quindecemvirs' keeping. These texts had been gathered and brought to Rome only a few decades before, as replacements for others that were lost in a catastrophic fire of 83 B.C. The latter, according to legend, were obtained in the sixth century by Tarquin the Proud from a strange old woman (presumably the Cumaean Sibyl, but possibly an imposter), who offered to sell him nine scrolls at a seemingly astronomical price. When he refused — so the story goes — she burnt three of the scrolls and offered him the remainder at the same price. And when he refused again, she repeated the gesture. Confronted with such unorthodox sales tactics, the king belatedly decided it might be prudent to accept her offer and to acquire the last three scrolls, which he entrusted to two priests for safekeeping. Over the years, other prophetic texts were added to a collection that was maintained as a monopoly of the Roman state and entrusted to a college of priests that slowly grew with them.

After the fire of 83, commissions sent by the Roman Senate scoured the Mediterranean in search of replacements for the lost scrolls, and the college of Quindecemvirs devoted itself to the task of authenticating the new acquisitions. Thus, had Cotta been permitted to speak on the Ides, in order to make his case he would have needed to assert first that the prophecy he had found accurately replicated one from the older collection and, more importantly, that it accurately preserved the speech of a Sibyl. Beyond these more secular issues of textual transmission and fidelity, his case would have rested on a religious claim: that Sibylline speech was divinely inspired.

Here, it is important to note that Romans understood the phenomenon of inspiration in terms that were concrete and physical, not metaphoric. Consider, for example, Virgil's account of the Cumaean Sibyl, which details a set of corporeal signs indicating onset of the state Romans called *afflatus*. Although this term is most often translated as "inspiration," examining its precise etymological sense yields a more nuanced understanding of this phenomenon. The past passive participle of a verb that means "to blow or breathe on" (*ad-flō*), it most literally denotes the situation of someone who has become "inspired" or "in-flated" by a god, when the latter breathed his divine spirit into her body.

> Suddenly her expression and color change,
> Her hair refuses to stay fixed and her breast is heaving.
> Her heart swells with a wild madness, and she seems larger.
> Nor does she sound mortal, for she is inflated [*adflata*] with the
>   divine power
> Of her own god . . .
> Not yet patiently bearing Apollo, the fierce seeress
> Raves like a bacchant in the cavern, as if she could
> Discharge the great god from her breast. So much more does he
>   tire.
> Her rabid mouth. Taming her wild heart, he molds her.

Quite bluntly, this text describes a rape: a rape of rather special and rarefied form, to be sure, but a rape nonetheless. Thus, without getting graphic, Virgil still manages to make it clear that Apollo takes forcible, erotic possession of the Sibyl's body through such details as her disheveled hair, wild eyes, and heaving breast. Although the Sibyl resists, she can neither avoid nor refuse her assailant. Of particular interest is the precise site on which the god seized: her breast, which is not only the locus of her heart and emotions, but also of her lungs and breath. It is, however, something of a misnomer to speak of the breath as "hers," for in the moment of in-spiration (literally, "breathing in," from *spireō* "to breathe"), the god penetrated the Sibyl's body and lodged in her lungs. Moreover, this process was manifest in the physical signs noted by Virgil at 6.49–50: her body appeared larger than usual because, quite literally, it had been blown up with Apollo's breath, and her voice did not sound mortal, because its material substance was nothing other than the same divine breath, as it issued from her.

Compared to others who described this phenomenon, Virgil was actually rather demure. Lucan's account of the *afflatus* experienced by the Pythia at Delphi, to cite a prime example, was simultaneously more rationalist and more pornographic. At one point he speaks of how Apollo "breaks in, drives out her prior thoughts, and orders her to surrender to him all that is human in her breast," after which the god "lashes her womb with stinging goads and sets flames within her vitals." Elsewhere, in a variation on the *Liebestod* theme, Lucan suggests that the repeated entry of a god into this woman's breast leads her to an early death, since a human body is entirely too fragile to long endure such rough handling.

Lucan, like Virgil (and like other Romans), understood the experience of inspiration to be acutely physical: legible in the priestess's body and audible in a voice that came from her mouth but was not her own. This is also clear in another passage, where he sought to reconcile traditional beliefs with contemporary ideas of natural science. To this end, he advanced the decidedly curious suggestion that a deity had somehow managed to fall from the heavens and become embedded deep in the earth. Taking the form of certain effluvial vapors, this divine being (possibly "a portion of Jupiter") drifted slowly back toward the empyrean through a network of subterranean channels and caverns, within which Sibylline temples had been established, as at Delphi and Cumae. When a priestess of these temples inhaled the fumes, this temporarily (but quite literally) nebulous god entered her body and filled her lungs, with predictable results.

Who from the above lies hidden here? What deity pushed from
the aether
Deigns to dwell confined in these dark caverns?

What god of heaven fell to earth, holding all secrets of the eternal
   course of things,
Sharing in knowledge of the world to come, and ready to reveal
   himself . . .
Perhaps a portion of Jupiter is inserted in the earth to rule it
And sustains the planet, which is balanced in empty air.
This part comes out through the great Cirrhaean caves
And draws itself toward conjunction with the aetherial
   Thunderer.
When this deity is received in a virgin's breast,
It strikes her soul and calls out, setting free the seer's mouth,
Just as Mount Aetna roils with urgent flames,
Just as Typhoeus, hidden in the eternal cliffs of Inarime,
Roars and fills the rocks with steam.

GODS, OATHS, BLUFFS, AND CURSES

If religious claims were inscribed on an authorized and authorizing instrument in Homer, and on the body of an authorized
and authorizing speaker in Sibylline practice, our Scandinavian
materials show a third possibility. Here, as we have seen, the
claims were written most obviously and concretely on an authorized and authorizing place: the circle of the *Thing*, which
was defined and delimited by "bonds of consecration" (*vé-
bǫnd*) that set it apart from the surrounding profane space.

There is no rule, however, that limits each society to one and
only one of these systems (or styles) for investing human
speech with sacred status. Thus, the Homeric *agorē* no less than
the Old Norse *Thing* could be regarded as a "sacred circle"
(*hieros kyklos, Iliad* 18.504), although statements to this effect
are infrequent. In both the Greek and Scandinavian settings,
moreover, select actors — kings above all — could claim divine
favor, and the gods themselves could be called upon to guarantee the things that humans said. For example, when Agamemnon sought to make peace with Achilles by returning Briseis,
the woman he had earlier taken from him, he spoke in assembly
as follows.

"Let Zeus know first, he who is highest and best of gods,
Then Earth and Sun and the Furies, who under the earth
Punish people, including anyone who would swear a false oath:

I never laid a hand on the maiden Briseis,
Not desiring her in bed, nor in any other way,
But she remained untouched in my huts.
And if any of this is a false oath, may the gods give me pains,
A great many of them: as many as they give to someone who,
    having sworn, transgresses against them."

As a variant on the general theme "May God strike me dead if I'm telling a lie," Agamemnon's oath is one of the more audacious, not to say riskier, speech acts in the epic. Swearing by a set of all-seeing and unforgiving deities who encompassed heaven, earth, and underworld, the lord of the Achaeans courted a veritable host of dangers, some more openly than others. Among these, we might mention the Furies' chastisement, Zeus's wrath, Achilles' rejection, and also the possibility that his audience would greet his pious assertions with smirks or snickers. These dangers, however, fall into two broad groups — divine retribution and human disbelief — that he played against one another in such a way as to accomplish his difficult project of persuasion.

Appreciating Agamemnon's discursive tactics begins with the recognition that the supernatural dangers he courted so boldly are not the ones he actually feared. He courted them (or went through the motions of doing so) chiefly as a means to defuse those other dangers, about which he remained silent. Essentially, he asked: May any nontruth in my oath produce divine vengeance, a statement which may be represented as follows:

$$\{-\text{Truth} \rightarrow +\text{Vengeance}\}$$

His goal, of course, was not to call lightning down on his head (a delightful possibility that experience and chutzpah led him to believe might safely be ignored), but rather, to constitute the absence of a bolt from the blue as tangible proof of his veracity. The logic here neatly inverts that of his initial proposition:

$$\{-\text{Vengeance} = +\text{Truth}\}$$

Through a strategic recoding and an accompanying bluff, Agamemnon thus effectively recruited the gods as supporting witnesses for his testimony. In so doing, moreover, he seems to have rendered credible an otherwise implausible description of the extreme delicacy and sexual tact with which he handled (or rather, did not handle) Achilles' woman. At the very least, we may conclude that he created a situation in which members of his audience, Achilles included, felt constrained to act as if they believed him.

Whereas Agamemnon elected to use an oath in order to cope with a ticklish situation, similar oaths were required of all who took part in the legal proceedings of ancient Scandinavia. After the conversion to Christianity, these took the form of "book-oaths" (*bók-eiðr*) sworn with one's hand on the Bible, a practice we retain. Prior to that period, "ring-oaths" (*baug-eiðr*) were the norm. Practices for these are described as follows:

> There is more that should lie on the altar in every major temple: the ring every chief should have on his wrist at all meetings of the Law-*Thing,* and which he should hold and redden in the blood of an ox that he has sacrificed there himself. Every man who needs assistance in legal proceedings to perform a judgment should take an oath by that ring and invoke two or more deities.

As Hermann Güntert first recognized, the Old Norse altar ring, like wedding rings more familiar to us, gave physical representation to a complex set of legal, social, and religious bonds that permit human beings to establish relations and to transact business with one another, confident that the veracity of the speech-acts they perform under oath will be assured by the divine powers invoked. Further, we should note that temple, altar, and ring together formed a sacred ensemble, each piece of which was consecrated by and consecrating of the other two. Of this ensemble, the ring was the mobile part. Removed from the temple to the *Thing* (and there recharged by an infusion of sacrificial blood), it could be used to consecrate — that is, to authorize in a sacred fashion — the speech of anyone who swore by it.

Had Arinbjorn's witnesses been permitted to testify, under the normal procedures of the Gula *Thing* they would have been required to swear on the altar ring as follows: "I take an oath by this ring — an oath under the law. Help me, Frey and Njord and the all-mighty lord [Odin], so that I may bear witness as I know to be most right, most true, and most lawful." By refusing to let these oaths be sworn, however (and also by their destruction of the *Thing*-circle), Eirik and Gunnhild created a situation in which not only the resources of law, but also those of religion passed rapidly outside their control. In the volatile days that followed, it was Egil who availed himself of these resources, denouncing the king himself as a "law-breaker" and setting against him the very same deities who should have figured in the abortive oath:

> So shall the gods repay
> the theft of my wealth:
> May the binders drive the fiend-king away.
> Wroth be *Odin* and the rulers!
> *Frey* and *Njord*, make him flee from the lands.

At this peculiar point, where oaths become curses, we may begin to see why religion figures so prominently in the discourses and processes we have been exploring, and may also perceive some unexpected possibilities that reside within religiously-oriented systems of authority production. Here, I would begin by observing that religious claims are the means by which certain objects, places, speakers, and speech-acts are invested with an authority, the source of which lies *outside the human*. That is, these claims create the appearance that their authorization comes from a realm beyond history, society, and politics, beyond the terrain in which interested and situated actors struggle over scarce resources. Among these resources figures prominently one that is both a prize and a weapon in such struggles: the capacity to speak a consequential speech and to gain a respectful hearing. With religious claims, the attempt is made to naturalize (indeed, to supernaturalize) this capacity, thereby placing it — and some people's hold on it — beyond the possibility of contestation.

Such a move, however, cannot succeed in any final or definitive fashion, as we may recognize in Egil's curse. In a general way, one can observe that those who seek to insulate themselves against criticism inevitably open themselves up to a new kind of critique. More specifically, those who wrap themselves in the cloak of religion make themselves vulnerable to the charge that they are insufficiently, inadequately, or improperly religious, for the proposition

$$\{+\text{Religion} \rightarrow +\text{Authority}\}$$

is potentially subject to a most strategic inversion:

$$\{-\text{Religion} \rightarrow -\text{Authority}\}.$$

Egil's curse, no less than Agamemnon's oath, was an act of religious speech that took place in a system where religious claims played a major part in the construction of authority. Here, however, the gods — whether these be understood as a discursive counter or a supernatural force — were turned against the people whom they more usually served. Making use of possibilities present within the system, Egil thus denounced a powerful ruler for certain actions that he construed as so grievous a negation of religion that they ought negate the authority of the offender. And as the Norwegian people were persuaded by this argument, Eirik's days on the throne came to be numbered.

SCHOLARS AND COLD WARRIORS

Some Discussions of Authority in the 1950s

A WOMAN SPEAKS WITH AUTHORITY REGARDING ITS DISAPPEARANCE

Among the issues I have never resolved to my own satisfaction is the question of whether the modern—or postmodern—world differs fundamentally from that which preceded it, or whether the similarities are more significant than the divergences. On any given terrain I find myself able to muster arguments in support of continuity and rupture alike. Implicit here is a host of conundrums: Is the human species one or many, and if many, how—also where, by whom, according to what principles, and to what end—is it parsed? Are some or all others so alien as to be virtually unknowable, and if so, at what point of difference does this radical alterity begin? Further, if there be others who *are* knowable to some degree (while still remaining other), can one study their universe of thought and experience in, of, and for itself, or is an implicit comparison with one's own situation inescapable? And if such comparison is inevitable, what is its purpose? Are there options less distorting and more morally justifiable than the classic strategies of valorizing one's self at the expense of a denigrated other or imagining a romanticized other to celebrate at the expense of one's self?

The problem arises at present as a result of the fact that within what purports to be a discussion of authority in general, I have thus far treated examples, the most recent of which is separated from us by a shade more than a millennium. Moreover, the last two chapters have dealt with two aspects of authority where the situation of the past seems noticeably different from that of the present: the consistency with which authority was previously grounded in claims of a religious nature, and the near total exclusion of women from situations in which they might speak with authority.

It is thus rather striking to find a woman in the middle of this century speaking in what seems an authoritative voice, and advancing the proposition "that authority has vanished from the modern world" as the result of changes in the way it interacts with religion, and also with tradition. And yet, it is just this which no less a figure than Hannah Arendt argued in an essay bearing the provocative title "What was Authority?".

As always, Arendt's analysis was subtle, complex, enormously learned, and a bit idiosyncratic in places. She began by asserting that not only the word "authority," but the concept itself is of Roman origin. Within that context, she maintained, authority emerged, existed, and operated, always with the most intimate connection to religion and tradition, for those in authority were charged with extending into the present the sacred principles evident in (and responsible for) their society's foundation: principles established by Aeneas, Romulus, and the other most ancient ancestors, and faithfully transmitted through subsequent generations. The stability of the Roman order thus rested on a triadic nexus of authority, tradition, and religion, as did the medieval order that inherited these structures and understandings from Rome. But within a line of historic development that began in the Reformation, picked up speed in the Enlightenment, and culminated in the writings of Kierkegaard, Nietzsche, and Marx, tradition and religion were subjected to a critical interrogation that left them debilitated, with the result that by the twentieth century, authority, bereft of their support, was no longer viable.

Authority as we once knew it, which grew out of the Roman experience of foundation and was understood in the light of Greek political philosophy, has nowhere been re-established, neither through revolutions nor through the even less promising means of restoration, and least of all through the conservative moods and trends which occasionally sweep public opinion. To live in a political realm with neither authority nor the concomitant awareness that the source of authority transcends power and those who are in power, means to be confronted anew, without the protection of tradition and self-evident standards of behavior, by the elementary problems of human living-together. Historically, we may say that the loss of authority is merely the final, though decisive, phase of a development which for centuries undermined primarily religion and tradition. Of tradition, religion, and authority, the Roman-inherited trinity, authority has proved to be the most stable element. With the loss of authority, however, the general doubt of the modern age also invaded the political realm, where things not only assume a more radical expression, but become endowed with a reality peculiar to the political realm alone. What perhaps hitherto had been only of spiritual significance for the few, now has become a concern to one and all. Only now, as it were after the fact, the loss of tradition and religion have become political events of the first order.

Against this line of analysis one can raise any number of objections, from the most picayune (e.g., the sleight of hand Arendt employed regarding the etymology of Latin *religio*) to the most sweeping and categorical. I take three points to be most important. First, as I have tried to make clear, I do not view authority as an *entity,* still less one that came into existence in one historic era and disappeared in another. Rather, I take it to be an *effect* (and the perceived capacity to produce an effect) that is operative within strongly asymmetric relations of speaker and audience. Further, this effect can be exercised whenever certain rather general features are brought into conjuncture: the right speaker, the right speech and delivery, the right staging and props, the right time and place, and an audience, the historically and culturally conditioned expectations of which establish the parameters of what is judged "right" in all these instances. I thus take authority to be much more supple, dynamic, and situationally adaptable than does Arendt. Second, I would maintain that like religion and tradition, authority was contested and contestable long before the Reformation or Enlightenment. What is more, it has always been so, although contestation most often is directed against specific uses (and users) of authority, rarely against authority as such. To date, no critique of which I am aware has been sufficient to render any of the "Roman trinity" nonexistent.

Finally, I would acknowledge that the ideological warrants used in support of authority changed — as they have at other times in history — when religious institutions and discourses lost their hegemonic position. Within the realm of epistemic authority, for instance, appeals to "reason" (itself a constructed notion, operative within a specific and historically emergent regime of truth) have replaced claims of "revelation" or "inspiration," just as advanced degrees and professional training have supplanted the notion of a "calling." Likewise, within the sphere of executive authority, invoking the will of the people now does service where rulers once appealed to divine right. Yet real as they are, these may be differences more of style than of substance: I would suggest that authority not only survives such changes, but operates in similar fashion whether it is legitimated through a religious ideology or through mystificatory claims of other sorts.

RIGHT SPEECH AND SPEAKER

There are also other reasons why one ought to hesitate to accept Arendt's analysis, but in order to recognize these, it is important to know a bit about her life and the context in which she offered this understanding of authority. Regarding her intellectual gifts and powers of articulation, there can be no doubt. She was marvelously erudite in a number of fields, philosophy and political theory above all. Extraordinarily perceptive at the level of details, she was also challenging at the level of generalization. The views she offered were difficult to locate within the available systems of disciplinary or ideological classification, and she took some pride in the fact that she was regularly considered a "liberal" by "conservatives" and vice versa.

Above all, she possessed the ability to put subtle and complex ideas into a language that was forceful and provocative, and one senses both moral urgency and intellectual courage in her writings. She was not only willing but eager to engage the most pressing and controversial issues of her day.

At the time of her death in 1975, Arendt held near legendary status, but when she wrote and delivered "What was Authority?" she was just hitting her stride. Born in 1906 to a prosperous and cultured German-Jewish family, she studied first at Marburg under Martin Heidegger (who became her lover), then at Heidelberg under Karl Jaspers (whom she regarded as her chief mentor). Fleeing Germany in 1933, some months after Hitler came to power, she made her way to Paris. There she established friendship with other émigrés including Walter Benjamin, whose last papers she carried to New York in early 1941, when she escaped occupied France after a brief period in an internment camp.

Although she was not particularly religious, Arendt devoted herself to writing about Jewish issues and working for Jewish causes from the time of Hitler's accession until the end of the Second World War. Toward the war's end, however, she began to conceive a book in which she would identify the elements that came together in Nazism and trace their development. Moreover, she would set the unprecedented horror of the concentration camps at the very center of her analysis, describing a system that was driven — and defined — by its desire to exercise everywhere the total domination it established experimentally in the camps, where humans were stripped of all freedom and "everything is possible."

Provisionally entitled *The Elements of Shame*, this book was to consist of three sections, each of which was announced in its original subtitle: *Anti-Semitism — Imperialism — Racism*. From 1945 to 1949 Arendt labored on this massive tome, which would be her first book in English and on which her reputation would be founded. Although she retained her initial vision of the project until 1948, thereafter she modified it in ways consistent with other changes in her world and in the world at large. By then, the tentative and initially hopeful postwar period of 1945–46 had given way to the Cold War, and as the international situation turned ever more grim in the last years of the decade, with Mao's victory in China, the Berlin Airlift and the explosion of the first Soviet nuclear device, the investigations, prosecutions, and national hysteria that came to be known as McCarthyism rapidly took shape. Meanwhile, through contacts she made in her position as a senior editor at Schocken Books, Arendt — who had never held an academic position — began reaching beyond her immediate circle and established relations with the group of liberal but aggressively anti-Communist thinkers who are usually referred to as the New York Intellectuals.

Influenced by events, by changing perceptions of the Soviet Union, by new evidence concerning Stalin's crimes, and also by the views of those with whom she now found herself in conversation, Arendt decided to transform part 3 of her book, which in earlier drafts had been titled at one time or another "Racism," "Nazism," and "Race-Imperialism." In 1948, however, she expanded her discussion to include the Soviet, as well as the Nazi experience, and renamed this section "Totalitarianism." And in contrast to those who used this newly fashionable term — originally employed by Mussolini, but given a pejorative connotation during the war — to encompass a variety of dictatorial regimes (e.g., Fascist Italy, Falangist Spain, Peron's Argentina, Savonarola's Florence), Arendt insisted that totalitarianism was a uniquely modern phenomenon, of which there were only two examples: Hitler's Germany and Stalin's Russia. Moreover, she argued that given their use of terror, secret police, ideological control, and other such instruments, there was no hope of revolution or reform from within a totalitarian state. The only possibility of change for the better lay in outside intervention.

Initially conceived as the autopsy of a slain monster, Arendt's manuscript thus became — or, at a minimum, became readily readable as — a clarion warning about the beast's surviving twin. When the book finally appeared (1951), the Korean War was just breaking and Joseph McCarthy, fresh from his electoral victory of the preceding year, was raising the anti-Communist fervor to an ever higher pitch. In this overheated atmosphere, *The Origins of Totalitarianism* proved a sensation and was quickly enshrined as a central text of the Cold War, taking its place alongside Orwell's *1984*, Huxley's *Brave New World*, and Koestler's *Darkness at Noon*. Unlike these works of fiction, however, Arendt's claimed the status of scholarship, while its author commanded a respect that was doubly grounded in her impeccable academic training and her harrowing life experiences.

RIGHT TIME AND PLACE

There are some indications that the ways in which her book was read and discussed were not entirely to Arendt's liking, however much she was gratified by its success. Clearly, she was troubled by McCarthy and by 1953 she had begun to distance herself from those of the New York group whose enthusiasm for the red hunt led them to abandon concern for issues of civil liberties. Also, *The Origins of Totalitarianism* had established her as a celebrity and given her the means of moving on to larger stages: In the wake of its publication, she was invited to lecture at Princeton, Notre Dame, and Berkeley, and received a Guggenheim grant to study "Totalitarian Elements of Marxism."

In 1953 Arendt was asked to participate in a conference sponsored by the American Academy of Arts and Sciences, the governing council of which, in the spirit of the times, had identified "Totalitarianism" as a topic of the most urgent national concern. Organization of the meetings fell to a six-member steering committee, which was dominated by political scientists and scholars with strong connections to Harvard: people no less solidly anti-Communist than Arendt's New York associates, but much more likely to publish in Henry Kissinger's *Confluence* than in Philip Rahv's *Partisan Review* or Elliot Cohen's *Commentary*. Significantly, three of the six were active in Harvard's Russian Research Center (RRC), an institution that we now know—thanks to Sigmund Diamond's painstaking efforts—from its very inception (1948) had extremely close, but often covert, dealings with the Department of State, the FBI, and the CIA, and received substantial funding from the last agency, channeled through the Carnegie Corporation.

Not surprisingly, more than a third of those who participated in the conference (17/47) had taught at the RRC in the preceding years, as had a similar proportion of those presenting papers (7/20). Six who served on the Center's eleven-member executive committee were also present, along with a number of eminent scholars (David Riesman, Erik Erikson, Harold Lasswell; Nobel laureate H. J. Muller), three high-ranking State Department officials (George Kennan, chief architect of the "Containment" policy; Bertram Wolfe, director of the department's ideological advisory staff; and Ivo Duchacek, editor-in-chief of the USIA), the editors of the *Wall Street Journal* and *Christian Science Monitor,* some obscure refugees from Eastern Europe, and others who were connected in one way or another to the RAND Corporation, the United States National War College, Radio Free Europe, and the wartime Office of Strategic Service. The relations among the various institutions involved in staging this conference, and in publishing a book based on its proceedings, are diagrammed in figure 8.1

In general, participants took three items almost for granted, but stressed them repeatedly in their presentations and discussions. First was the view that Nazi Germany and Soviet Russia ought be grouped together within the encapsulating term "totalitarianism"; second, that this category should be restricted to these examples only; and third, the judgment that the entity constructed in this fashion was a very bad and a very dangerous thing that ought to be vigorously opposed. In essence, all were consistent with Arendt's *Origins of Totalitarianism,* and over the

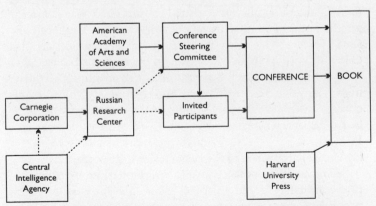

Figure 8.1 Relations among institutions that contributed to the 1953 Boston conference on "Totalitarianism." Solid arrows indicate support or involvement that was openly acknowledged; dotted arrows, that which remained covert.

course of the conference, no one was cited more often or more favorably than she.

In the wake of these meetings, Arendt came to have further dealings with members of the Harvard group, who were concerned, not only to establish "totalitarianism" as the lens through which recent history and the contemporary moment would be perceived, but also to rebut a rival discourse: that of T. W. Adorno and others who spoke, not of "totalitarianism," but "authoritarianism." In their most recent work, which had been widely read in the United States and enjoyed considerable influence, Adorno and his colleagues used extensive research questionnaires to show that many traits of the "authoritarian personality" that led Germans to embrace Hitler were disturbingly prevalent among Americans as well. And in earlier writings (which had not yet been translated into English, but were known to Arendt and several other participants), they had also treated Nazism as the culmination of a line of development in the West that runs from Homer through the Enlightenment into capitalism.

Beyond semantics, the two discourses — and those who employed them — thus differed in whether they focused on systems of domination or propensities for submission, whether they would associate Nazi Germany with the capitalist West or the Soviet Union, whether they employed the language and methods of social science or those of political philosophy, and whether ideologically they tended toward Cold War liberalism or the Frankfurt brand of Marxism. What is more, each discourse treated the other as dangerous, the one viewing the other as "soft" on Communism, and being viewed in turn as a demagoguery that itself bore the threat of fascism. Thus, with regard to the fierce but naive anti-Communism voiced by research subjects who scored high on the F− (for "Fascism") scale, Adorno wrote:

> The more the concept [of Communism] is emptied of any specific content, the more it is being transformed into a receptacle for all kinds of hostile projections, many of them on an infantile level somehow reminiscent of the presentation of evil forces in comic strips. . . . The complete irrationality, not to say idiocy, of the last three examples shows what vast psychological resources

fascist propaganda can rely on when denouncing a more or less imaginary communism without taking the trouble to discuss any real political or economic issues. If representatives of this attitude enter into any argumentation at all, it is, the last examples indicate, centered in the facile, though not completely spurious identification of communism and fascism which displaces hostility against the defeated enemy upon the foe to be.

To advance their views against this sort of opposition, the Harvard group organized another conference, held in 1956, on the theme "Authority." Sponsorship came from the American Society of Political and Legal Philosophy, an association some of them had helped to found in the preceding year. The proceedings were published by the Harvard University Press, and a subvention for the book was obtained from the Twentieth Century Fund, although this last item seems anomalous in ways. Normally, this foundation does not respond to others' proposals, but prefers to identify issues itself that it hopes to place on the national agenda, and then to enlist those people whom it feels are best suited to address them in concrete, practical terms. Still, it may be possible to infer the process which led to their support, for a director of the Fund had served on the steering committee for the "Totalitarianism" meetings, and the problem of how to confront the Soviet threat was one of the Fund's four chief priorities of the postwar era. Relations among the participating institutions are diagrammed in figure 8.2.

AND AN AUDIENCE THAT JUDGES JUST WHAT IS "RIGHT"

The 1956 conference on "Authority" was smaller than its predecessor on "Totalitarianism," and information is available only on those who gave papers, not those who participated in other ways. Still, it is interesting to note that three people who took part in the earlier meetings were among the thirteen who spoke at the later ones. Of these, two came from the Harvard group and the third was Hannah Arendt, whose antipathy for Adorno and the Frankfurt School went back to her years in Germany. Another eminent Harvard scholar who sat on the executive committee of the RRC joined them, but beyond these overlaps, the two conferences differed markedly. At the broadest level, the goal of the earlier meetings was to bring two despised regimes into closer association and to promote the use of a terminology that advanced this project. In contrast, those on "Authority" labored to dissociate favored regimes from despised ones and to show how misguided was the use of a language that permitted confusion of the two.

Whereas its predecessor gave pride of place to anti-Communists and anti-Communism, the 1956 conference — held after McCarthy's fall from power and Khrushchev's initial steps at de-Stalinization — was dominated by scholars less interested in decrying the Soviet bogey than in celebrating the virtues of the western democracies. In this, they took particular pains to stress the salutary role authority plays in the United States, regardless of the perversions to which it may be subjected elsewhere. Typical was the view of Charles Hendel, Clark Professor of Moral Philosophy and Metaphysics at Yale, who described how the United States Constitution broke decisively

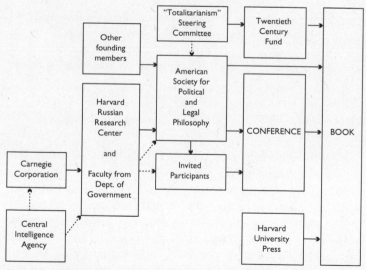

Figure 8.2 Relations among institutions that contributed to the 1956 conference on "Authority." Solid arrows indicate support or involvement that was openly acknowledged; dotted arrows, that which remained covert.

with older European notions of sovereignty, in place of which it established an authority derived from (but not vested in) the people, then went on to attribute "whatever constructive advance has been made in freedom and civilization within the past two centuries" to just this innovation.

Arendt, however, was not committed to a celebratory project, nor to the task of recuperating authority. Accordingly, she attacked the issue in quite a different fashion than did the other participants. Essentially, her argument had three parts, one of which we treated above. This, however, was only a piece in a longer line of analysis: (1) authoritarian regimes differ profoundly from those that are totalitarian; (2) authority proper no longer exists in the modern world; and (3) it is not authority that is the problem, but rather its absence, a situation the totalitarians have best been able to exploit.

> Historically, at any rate, authoritarian forms of rule did not wish to abolish, but to limit freedom, and these limitations were felt to be necessary to protect and safeguard liberty. An authoritarian structure, therefore, loses its essential substance, its *raison d'être,* if it does away with freedom altogether. Whenever this happens, it is no longer authoritarian but tyrannical. And a tyranny is no less anti-authoritarian than certain extreme types of democracy or anarchy. *There is perhaps no clearer symptom of the confusion of our vocabulary than the almost unanimous habit of calling Soviet Russia or Nazi Germany authoritarian,* while these forms of domination in fact arose out of a catastrophic breakdown of all legitimate authority. But this confusion is neither merely semantic nor theoretical; it arises directly out of the modern world, where, outside of certain islands and some circumscribed, not very important areas, it is almost impossible to have a genuine experience of what authority is, or rather was.

Toward the end of her presentation, Arendt made clear that hers was not a nostalgic lament for the loss of authority. Rather, she saw its passing, like that of tradition and religion, as something that created important opportunities as well as significant dangers. Still, others at the conference do not seem to have been particularly taken with her analysis. Although Arendt's differentiation of authoritarian and totalitarian regimes was more than welcome, as was her critique of the terminological confusion introduced by the unnamed Adorno, the others present generally ignored her idea that authority lay in the past. In contrast, they saw it as something that, although regularly embattled and occasionally abused, was still very much alive (in the West, at least), and quite a good thing at that.

Beyond this audience, however, there were others whom Arendt could reach and other channels through which she could reach them, although, as always, once her speech took the form of text, she would have even less control over the ways it would be understood and the uses to which others might put it. In 1961 she expanded her essay, incorporating material from two thematically related articles written around the same period. Under the title "What is Authority?" this composite piece appeared as a chapter in her collection, *Between Past and Future: Six Exercises in Political Thought,* where it drew the attention of Irving Kristol. His review is noteworthy, not just for the praise he lavished on Arendt, whom he hailed as "one of the most brilliant and original of living political philosophers," or on her book, which he urged "everyone to buy . . . and ponder," but for the special attention he gave this chapter.

> It is in her essay, "What is Authority?" that [Arendt's] classical perspective and her apocalyptic sensibility unite most forcefully. Beginning with the crisis of authority in the modern world — of governmental authority, religious authority, parental authority, etc. — she distinguishes between tyranny, despotism, and authority; demonstrates that the Greeks had neither the word nor the conception of it; that the Romans, with their superb piety toward the founding fathers ("authors"), invented it for the West; that Augustine formulated it for the Church; that the Church's idea of authority became the archetype for authority *per se;* that the shattering of religious authority has caused the whole edifice to crumble — but there I am trying to summarize the essay when I have already said this is impossible. A reviewer must of necessity be timid about venturing such a judgment but I do think that the future (if there is one) will very likely treasure this essay as one of the remarkable intellectual achievements of our age.

A difference in imagery merits attention: Where Arendt says flatly, in the first paragraph of her essay, that "authority has van-

ished from the modern world," Kristol speaks instead of an edifice that has crumbled, and the rubble left by the latter signals
nothing less than the difference between being and non-being.
Within it, moreover, lies the memory of what was and the
promise of what might yet be, if only there be those who are
willing and worthy to undertake the project of reconstruction.

That there are such people is made evident in a distinction
Kristol set at the beginning of his review between "political philosophers" like Arendt, who are "located at a distant remove
from mere opinion" and "political thinkers" more concerned
with "the art of the possible" and "the fusion of abstract idea
with gross circumstance . . . directed and limited by political
commitment." Implicitly, then, it falls to such practical "thinkers" and actors to take this essay and treat it not just as "A Treasure for the Future" (so the review is entitled), but as a practical
blueprint for authority's restoration.

In 1961, Kristol was not yet "godfather of the neoconservative movement," as he now likes to be styled, only one of the
more pugnacious of the New York Intellectuals and a Cold War
liberal of dubious credentials. Still, one can already see the path
of his later development in the reading he gave Arendt's essay.
Indeed, one perceives here *in nuce* the agenda that he and his
neoconservative allies — Norman Podhoretz, Jeane Kirkpatrick,
Elliot Abrams, et al. — offered to the Reagan administration for
the Cold War's final offensive. Most obviously, this included a
foreign policy of support for "authoritarian" regimes (dictators
and death squads) against their "totalitarian" rivals (Communists). Domestic concerns, however, were also shaped by the
Kristol reading of the Arendt thesis, which yielded a flood of
rhetoric and initiatives designed to shore up religion and tradition, so they could serve as the building blocks from which
the edifice of authority could be restored: restored and made
suitable for their own habitation.

PRESIDENTS AND PROTESTERS
Changes in the Mode of Authority Production

STAGES AND STAGE MANAGEMENT

Although we still have a handful of sites whose authorizing capacity is not only formidable, but ancient and abiding (the Supreme Court, the Oval Office, or the papal throne of St. Peter, for example), access to these is rigidly restricted to those who hold the offices of which they are a (perhaps *the*) prime prerogative. Others who wish to speak with authority must seek access to some other, lesser site or alternatively, they can attempt to create sites, either fabricating them *de novo* or inserting them within existing institutional structures.

Examples of such attempts were clear in the two conferences we considered in the last chapter, although it is an oversimplification to treat these as the creations of a single would-be speaker. Rather, as is usually the case in such endeavors, many actors collaborated. Some gave their time and energy; some their knowledge, connections, or names and reputations; some their cash, which tends to be the most appreciated of contributions, as its liquidity makes it convertible into all of the others. One can, however, be more precise in identifying four sorts of parties — individual and institutional — that cooperated in this undertaking. The list would include (1) intellectuals, both inside the academy and out (the learned societies that sponsored the meetings, the Harvard group that organized them, Arendt, and most of the other speakers); (2) the State, which participated both openly and covertly (the State Department representatives who spoke or attended, and the CIA, which channeled funds to the RRC); (3) the media, both public and private (the newspaper editor who helped plan and fund the meetings, representatives of other newspapers, the USIA, and Radio Liberty/Radio Free Europe, Harvard University Press, which published the proceedings); and (4) capital (the foundations which supplied funding, and most of their directors). Obviously, these groups did not all participate in equal measure, nor did each one articulate with all the others, but all had some role to play, as well as some interest in the outcome.

These same sorts of groups, and others as well, collaborate in varied combinations to produce different sorts of stages for the production and dissemination of authoritative speech: Think tanks, talk shows, newspaper columns, government bureaus, university departments, specialized journals, and professional societies and their annual meetings are a few of the many possibilities. In each specific instance, a different set of collaborators is involved, and the stage's operations can be expected to advance their interests in a manner that reflects the extent of their contributions.

Stages cannot reproduce their backers' and managers' interests in unmediated fashion, however. The interests of a stage's audience (actual or potential, real or desired) must also be taken into account, and activities on the stage are designed to attract and hold its audience, while also advancing the interests of the backers. Further, there may be disagreements among the backers and managers regarding the relative value and importance of their respective contributions, and the influence to which they are entitled. Both factors are destabilizing in different ways. In the first instance, stages are always modifying themselves in reaction to the audiences and audience responses they evoke. In the second, tensions and conflicts among collaborators often lead to changes in orientation, and also to changes of personnel.

In all cases, the production of a stage with authorizing capacity is a difficult and costly task, and production of the stage is not enough. Speakers must also be found to appear on it, and the process of their selection has its own complexities. To begin, certain kinds of credentials are conventionally sought, which involve such items as professional training, official positions, honorific titles, and institutional affiliations. In part, these help to establish speakers' qualifications and expertise, as is seen from their use in the framing devices that condition audiences' initial receptivity, such as formal introductions, certificates posted on office walls, press releases, and dust jacket blurbs. Further, the prominent display of such credentials helps constitute the stage not only as a space reserved for persons of distinction, but as a place that simultaneously derives distinction from and bestows it on those permitted to speak there.

Exclusion from this space is practiced on the basis of credentials, but the screen of credentials does not yield speakers for the stage, only the pool from which speakers are selected. A second screen, used less openly and perhaps less consciously than the first, completes the selection process. And if the screen of credentials identifies those who are qualified to speak on a given topic, the second one lifts out of this pool those who can be trusted to speak most effectively the interests of the groups and individuals who collaborate in the production and management of the stage.

To accomplish their goals, stage managers need not write speakers' lines for them, nor even coach their delivery, though at times they are tempted to do so. Least of all must they speak through their speakers in blatantly ventriloquistic fashion. Rather, they need only supply the stage and select from the pool of the qualified those who are most committed — whether sincerely or opportunistically — to saying just what the managers and backers wish to have said. Such persons they will authorize (and also pay); others, they will not. To the latter are left several alternatives: They can rest silent, revise their speeches, audition for other stages, or they can try to find backers and collaborators with whom to produce stages of their own — stages that will, of course, find themselves in competition with those from which their founders were previously excluded.

Contrasting this situation to that of antiquity, I cannot really see a loss of authority; rather, authority seems to have splintered, expanded, and multiplied. In some ways, this can be understood as a relatively straightforward consequence of demographic growth and the trend toward specialization; that is, the ongoing division of intellectual and discursive labor that lets ever more people speak with authority to ever more (but ever smaller) audiences in ever greater detail about ever more arcane topics. No doubt these are significant factors, but I do think one can take the analysis further.

SHATTERED EAGLES AND RESOURCEFUL MONKEYS

In order to illustrate these points more concretely, let me consider one last example, an incident from the spring of 1992 that the *New York Times* reported as follows (see also figure 9.1):

> LAS VEGAS, NEV. APRIL 13 [1992] (AP) — Former President Ronald Reagan was jostled but was not harmed today when a man walked onto a stage where he was speaking and smashed an honorary crystal shrine, hitting him with its shards.
>
> After smashing the statue, which had just been given to Mr. Reagan by the National Association of Broadcasters, the man tried to speak into the microphone but was grabbed by Secret

Figure 9.1 (Photo courtesy of Jim Laurie, *Las Vegas Review Journal.*)

Service agents, who threw him to the ground and then took him away.

The man in question is one Rick Paul Springer, who was most often identified in the press as a forty-one-year-old anti-nuclear activist. Over the course of his life, Mr. Springer has also worked as a carpenter, a paramedic, an able-bodied seaman, a counselor for abused children, and has spent much time backpacking through the wilderness. In 1987, standing at the Nevada Test Site, he first realized the importance of the issue to which he would devote himself thereafter, and which he believes is essential to the survival not just of humanity, but of all living creatures and the earth itself.

Since then he has committed himself to the work of organizing, raising funds, and speaking out about the danger of nuclear tests, in the belief that ending tests is the first step toward abolishing nuclear weapons altogether. The task has been difficult, and although he is convinced that most people agree with him in a general way, complacency is widespread and few share his sense of urgency. Finding effective channels though which to spread his message has also been a problem, for the antinuclear issue is hardly on the agenda of the major media. But in 1990, he had an idea.

What Springer envisioned was an event mixing music and politics in the spirit of the Woodstock and Live Aid concerts. Those attracted by the music could be educated about the issue, and the spectacle itself would be so impressive as to ensure press coverage, through which the message could be further spread. With this, he expected to constitute a breakthrough to mass awareness, after which patterns of reporting, the level of pressure on the government, and finally, policy decisions would have to change.

Rick Springer called his vision the Hundredth Monkey Project in allusion to a book by Ken Keyes, Jr. that is popular among those committed to the antinuclear cause. It tells a story that begins in 1952, when a monkey on the Pacific island of Koshima learned to wash the sweet potatoes that previously she and her fellow monkeys had eaten covered with sand. Over the next six years, according to researchers who studied these monkeys, the practice spread slowly from one monkey to another.

But in the fall of 1958, it seems that a certain critical mass was reached when roughly a hundred monkeys had learned to wash their sweet potatoes. Then, almost at once, this knowledge spread to all the other monkeys on the island, and to monkeys on other islands as well. As Keyes told the story, "The added energy of this hundredth monkey somehow created an ideological breakthrough," and he went on to draw a moral: "Your awareness is needed in saving the world from nuclear war. You may be the 'Hundredth Monkey.'"

For two years, Springer devoted his efforts (and virtually all of his personal savings) to realize his Hundredth Monkey Project. In promotional materials, he predicted that 500,000 people would attend and that "dozens of international speakers and world class musical artists" would appear. Further, he described the method he was pursuing, which he also recommended to those whose help he solicited: "To envision and believe in the event as an end to nuclear testing. To secure the involvement and support of dedicated world organizers, celebrities, inspirational leaders, indigenous peoples, world and local peace groups, and individual activists at large" (see appendix A).

Securing such support proved difficult, however. Soon he discovered that an almost unbreachable wall of agents and managers separated him from the musical artists he hoped to engage. Of the one hundred twenty performers on his original list, he managed to speak directly with no more than a handful, and only one (Ritchie Havens) agreed to appear. Established organizations, although sympathetic, would not commit themselves unless they could see that all other aspects of the project were firmly in place. Similarly, foundations were unwilling to make grants, and explained that the elements of political action in his plans could compromise their tax-exempt status. After submitting nearly a hundred applications, he received funds from only one backer: $5,000 from the Rex Foundation, which ultimately went for Porta-potties.

Choosing a location also posed problems. Although he considered Washington, DC for the visibility it would offer and San Francisco for ease in attracting a crowd, he ultimately opted for a setting as close as possible to the Nevada Test Site, where the threat of testing could be confronted directly, and where he himself had first become committed to the cause. Insurance proved expensive and permits impossible to obtain, even after prolonged negotiations in which he felt a new hurdle was added for every one he cleared. In spite of all the obstacles, Springer forged ahead and laid plans for a ten-day extravaganza with three distinct parts: "The Event," a concert in the Nevada desert (10–12 April 1992); "The Walk," a communal march to the test site, some fifty-five miles away (13–17 April); and finally, "The Action," a mass protest at government offices in Las Vegas timed for Earth Day (18 April).

Gradually, some pieces fell together. Speakers were lined up and bands were booked, although not the top talent he had sought. Important support came from Earth Day International, which named the Hundredth Monkey its official Project for 1992, and later from Greenpeace, which gave its endorsement just three weeks before the opening events. Finally, two thousand people gathered in the desert on Friday, 10 April: a respectable turnout, but far less than Rick Springer had hoped. "I was a great dreamer and visionary," he would later observe, "but I wasn't very realistic."

To be sure, lack of stars and lack of a crowd, if nothing else, kept the event from becoming news. There was no national coverage, and even the Las Vegas paper showed little interest. Other problems were also distressing. By monitoring government radio communications, Springer and his colleagues learned that a nuclear test was scheduled for Tuesday, 14 April, when their own plans called for them to be approaching the test site. It is difficult to gauge their emotions at this point: Excitement at what they had accomplished mingled with frustration at the ways they had fallen short, and there were varying measures of anger, disappointment, energy, and resolve. On Sunday night, a decision was made to travel the eleven miles from the concert grounds to Las Vegas on the following day, 13 April, and to stage a protest at the offices of the U.S. Department of Energy.

OTHER PEOPLE'S STAGES

Many of the group took part in this action, and twenty-six of them were arrested. Some five hundred others, according to plan, began their march to the test site. And, on the same day, across town at the Las Vegas Hilton, the National Association of Broadcasters convened its annual meeting, with 50,000 people from the radio and television industry in attendance. Springer had been aware of this coincidence for months, and he was also aware of the opportunities it presented. Off and on, he had thought about how he might call the antinuclear issue to the attention of the NAB, a group that, in his view, "has a deathhold on the media."

Among the ideas he entertained, his favorite scenario was one in which a hundred people in monkey costumes would enter the Hilton and scamper about, waving signs and distributing leaflets. When the day came, however, he had neither a hundred people nor the money for monkey suits. And so, he made his way to the Hilton alone, holding press credentials (obtained by a friend) that would admit him to the meeting's prime event, and he pondered just what he would do.

Arriving at the Hilton's banquet room, he found a group of three thousand top media executives listening as Eddie Fritts, president of the NAB, concluded his remarks and presented the crystal eagle and the Association's Distinguished Service Award to Mr. Reagan for his "contributions to broadcasting and the American public." Then, to warm applause, the Great Communicator himself moved to the podium. His address, included in full as appendix B, was a rambling affair, in which jokes ("It's a pleasure to be in Las Vegas, the city that never sleeps . . . I used to work in a city that never wakes up"), flattery ("Radio and television waves are the Paul Reveres of the universe . . . Before radio, most of the world was not free"), and autobiographical reminiscences ("In Hollywood if you did not sing or dance you became an after-dinner speaker. Pretty soon I did more speaking than acting and found myself running for Governor . . .") laid the ground for predictable observations on themes dear to the ex-President, his constituency, and his immediate audience: the evils of Communism and drugs, and the ways in which the Bible, the family, radio, television, and the movies can help combat them.

Meanwhile, off to the side, Rick Springer wrestled with his conscience, prayed quietly, and worked up his courage. Finally, at what seemed to him an appropriate moment, he strode forward, slowly and resolutely. Given his dress, manner, and general appearance, most people took him for a sound technician until he picked up the two-foot high crystal eagle, raised it over his head, and — in what he later described as "the clearest, most meditative moment of my life" — smashed it to bits. Then he advanced to the podium, displaced Reagan from the microphone, and spoke four words — "Excuse me, Mr. President" — before the Secret Service laid him out.

As he was dragged away, Springer was heard to shout: "Help, there's a nuclear bomb test tomorrow," and he later explained that he wished not only to publicize his cause, but to warn the broadcasters and through them the world of a pressing danger, for he views each test as nothing less than "bombing the water supply of future generations." Backstage, he was handcuffed and placed under arrest, then taken to a Las Vegas jail, where he was charged with state and federal offenses. After a minute or two, President Reagan returned and finished his speech, quipping to an appreciative crowd, "Is he a Democrat, by chance?"

So strongly does this incident resemble that of Thersites, with which we began our inquiry, it seems excessive to belabor the point. Still, it is worth specifying the areas of closest resemblance.

- Both involve an authorized and an unauthorized speaker.
- The speech of the authorized speaker, while foolish, is given a respectful, even an enthusiastic hearing.
- Conflict erupts when the unauthorized speaker enters the authorized and authorizing place.
- He does so to challenge policies associated with the authorized speaker, which, in his view, create terrible dangers that must be avoided.
- Within this arena, no one responds to the content of his speech; rather, they challenge his right to speak there.
- Before he can finish, he is violently removed.
- After this brief period of turbulence, control of the authorized and authorizing sphere reverts to the authorized speakers, and the audience on hand signals its approval.
- The possibility remains open, however, that other audi-

ences, hearing the story at second hand, may reach other conclusions.

I do not mean to underestimate the strength or importance of these similarities: Indeed, I was led to study the Las Vegas episode precisely because of them, and because they suggested to me that authority in contemporary society operates much as it did in the ancient world. Still, there is a danger in overemphasizing them, and mistaking part of a story for the whole. For however similar these incidents may be, both should be situated within longer histories, and we need to recall that Springer, like Thersites, was involved in other actions before and after these moments of highest drama.

If we shift our attention and focus on earlier phases of their activity, it rapidly becomes evident how much Thersites and Rick Springer differ from one another and, what is more, how much their differences reflect and result from other differences between their respective eras. We have seen how Springer, in all his work on the Hundredth Monkey Project, worked to orchestrate a collaboration between activists and entertainers, hoping to produce a new stage from which to authorize the speech of people he would select to advance his views. Such an option was hardly available to Thersites. Homeric society, as we have seen, had very few authorized and authorizing places, nor did it allow for the possibility of others being created, least of all through human agency. Given their normal exclusion from Assembly, those who fell outside the sceptre-bearing elite had little hope of speaking with authority. In such circumstances, one of the few bold strategies available to them is that adopted by Thersites: to master the corrosive discourses of blame and ridicule and use them to speak not with, but *against* authority.

STRUGGLES BETWEEN ACTORS AND STRUGGLES BETWEEN STAGES

Later phases of Rick Springer's activity also differ markedly from the corresponding period in the life of Thersites. Our last glimpse of the latter shows him barred from assembly, tearfully accepting the silence to which he has been condemned by Odysseus, the Achaean soldiers, and the Homeric text.

Springer, however, has managed to find other options, not necessarily because he is more clever, determined, or the like, nor because his cause is more just, but precisely because his society maintains a multitude of stages, with some degree of competition among them. Exclusions from one need not be the last word; indeed, exclusion from one stage can prompt invitations from others.

In a subsequent series of interviews, articles, and court appearances, Rick Springer has continued to speak out, and he has had opportunities, not only to speak, but to speak in privileged settings. Among the most interesting of these was his appearance on "CBS This Morning," Friday, 17 April, four days after his encounter with Mr. Reagan (see appendix C for a transcript).

This show, which is seen in two and a half million households daily, offers a mix of news, opinion, features, entertainment, and pleasant chit-chat among its regular hosts. Guests are presented for a number of reasons, and in styles that cue the audience on how each one is to be regarded. When it wishes to authorize their speech, the show is fully capable of doing so. Particularly important are formal introductions and the level of deference or courtesy shown by hosts. Consider, for instance, the way in which the day's lead guests were characterized in the first seconds of this broadcast.

> HARRY SMITH (co-host): Good morning. It is Friday. April 17th. I'm Harry Smith.

> PAULA ZAHN (co-host): Good morning, everybody. I'm Paula Zahn. Welcome to "CBS This Morning."

> SMITH: Making headlines this morning, the FDA has new rules for breast implants. We're going to talk with Commissioner David Kessler for a minute.

> ZAHN: And you'll meet the protester who crashed in on Ronald Reagan this week.

When Dr. Kessler was brought on as the show's first guest, his professional title and official position were emphasized, and Paula Zahn gave him a warm welcome. Springer was treated somewhat differently.

HARRY SMITH: Anti-nuclear activist Rick Springer says he never had any intention of hurting former President Reagan earlier this week. Springer says he just wanted to make a point. Still, the incident startled Mr. Reagan and jolted the Secret Service. Springer is with a group called The 100th Monkey, which opposes all nuclear testing. And he joins us this morning from KLAS-TV in Las Vegas. Good morning.

In these introductory remarks, Harry Smith gave basic information, while also signaling caution in three different ways: (1) his repeated use of the phrase "Springer says" to preface his guest's characterizations of the incident; (2) his adversarial juxtaposition of these to the reactions of more responsible observers ("*Still,* the incident startled Mr. Reagan and jolted the Secret Service"); and (3) his subtle suggestion that Springer's views lie outside the accepted mainstream (as one who "opposes *all* nuclear testing"). The "protester" and "activist" would be given an opportunity to speak, but the host, the show, and the network were careful not to offer anything that could be construed as an endorsement of him, his actions, or what he would have to say.

Smith's first question was reasonably open-ended: "What were you trying to accomplish earlier this week?" Seizing the opportunity, Springer began to explain how he hoped to use the NAB convention to alert the country to the realities of nuclear testing. At this, Smith rapidly changed tack, and began to treat Springer himself as the story: a curiosity or "human interest" item. His next eleven questions focused narrowly on events at the Hilton, as he tried to steer conversation away from the issue of nuclear testing.

"What was smashed when you went up onto the stage next to the former president?"

"Did you smash that intentionally?"

"What exactly happened when you got on the stage up there?"

"Did you give any consideration to what might happen to you when you went on that stage?"

"The question everybody has is how did you get so close?"

"Did you have any IDs?"

"Did you have any of the requisite, sort of, media passes?"

"What have you been charged with?"
"Are you surprised at all that they let you go?"
"What's the possibility that you will go to jail?"
"How long might you have to serve?"

In his answers, Springer struggled to introduce wherever possible items that he thought important: the bomb test at the Nevada Test Site, France's decision to discontinue its testing program, his lifetime commitment to nonviolence. Moving to wrap things up, Smith offered one last question, which was, in effect, a call to repent and show remorse.

HARRY SMITH: Do you have any regrets about what you did this week?

RICK SPRINGER: Well, I certainly must offer an apology to Mr. Reagan. I am very sorry that the Secret Service jostled him in an effort to get me off the stage. I have no regrets as to the fact that I approached the — the podium, and I think that the coverage that I have received due to this act, is an excellent example of what it takes to wake up and startle the media and, indeed, the American public, whose apathy is responsible for the continuation of nuclear testing to this day.

HARRY SMITH: Mm. Rick Springer, we thank you for joining us. Do appreciate it. Twenty two after.

When Springer's image vanished from the screen, others joined the conversation, offering their judgments, and cueing their audience on how to regard him.

PAULA ZAHN: Good morning.

HARRY SMITH: Wasn't that interesting?

PAULA ZAHN: I loved that segment.

HARRY SMITH: Springer.

MARK MCEWEN (meteorologist): He could talk. Most of the time you get people like Squeaky Fromme — you remember?

HARRY SMITH: Well, as it turns — this guy is a well-known — I don't know about well-known, but there is lots of tape of him leading nuclear — anti-nuclear demonstrations and stuff. I mean, that's really what this guy is all about. That's — because he was released so quickly and everybody said, "What? Excuse me."

MARK MCEWEN: Yeah.

HARRY SMITH: And he has a — he has a real track record of — of pacifism, so . . .

MARK MCEWEN: I thought that was great. Do you think you're going to go to jail? "No, I think they're going to drop the charges," which I thought — I don't know if I would have said that. I'd say, "Oh, please — oh, please — oh, please."

PAULA ZAHN: But he did apologize for hitting the former president with the shards of glass.

MARK MCEWEN: Absolutely.

HARRY SMITH: It's just amazing — just amazing . . .

Apparently, Rick Springer surprised his hosts and threw them off their script, as can be seen from the mangled syntax with which they offered their reactions. In effect, after initially holding him at arm's length, the authorized spokespersons of this widely-viewed show bestowed their (partial and guarded) approval on him, taking particular note of his courage, his commitment, and his powers of articulation. And this, in turn, prompted reaction from other quarters.

Four days later, on 21 April, the *Wall Street Journal* ran a particularly aggressive editorial (appendix D) that began by lamenting, "It was predictable, but a bit startling nonetheless, to find Richard Paul Springer staring out at us from our TV sets." It went on to depict him in lurid prose as "the latest entry to a special galaxy of media-produced stars — people whose aberrations, disturbances and general aggressions against society have won them fame as 'political activists,'" and to place him among the ranks of "political fanatics prepared to wreak whatever havoc necessary to advance their notions of humanity."

So hysterical is the rhetoric, and so obvious the financial interests being defended, one is tempted to think the *Journal* felt threatened by Rick Springer, and viewed the spectre of him on network TV much as Odysseus viewed Thersites in the center of the Homeric assembly: So wrong a person in so right a place as to be cause for major alarm. Such a comparison, however, here turns misleading, for Odysseus voiced no criticism of the assembly, and the *Journal* hardly views "CBS This Morning" as a (let along *the*) "right place." Witness the editorial's closing swipe.

> Since Mr. Springer used phony press credentials, the Secret Service is planning to look harder at security arrangements and, especially, at press credentials. This prospect incited alarmed responses from the usual quarters that the Secret Service might now jeopardize First Amendment rights.
>
> This isn't news, since there is hardly anything that happens, nowadays, that isn't seen as a threat to the First Amendment. What *would* be news would be if the producers of a show such as "CBS This Morning" decided that giving a character like Richard Springer a place in the media spotlight wasn't smart or healthy or in the public interest. That wouldn't simply be news, of course. That would be a miracle.

Beyond any conflict of individuals or debate on issues of policy, plainly evident here is a conflict between stages that goes well beyond the familiar rivalry of print and electronic media. Both possess some authorizing capacity, but insofar as their backers, interests, and audiences diverge, so too do the specific principles of selectivity on which they operate. Most often, these stages tolerate or ignore one another, but occasionally their differences lead to open conflict, as here, where the *Wall Street Journal,* an elite organ of and for capital, chastises "CBS This Morning," a mildly populist middlebrow show, for what it takes to be a characteristically promiscuous and irresponsible act of authorization. The point of the struggle is not just whose speech gets authorized, but more importantly, who does the authorizing and how. In its bitching about "media-created stars," one can hear the *Journal*'s displeasure with stars created by other media, and authorized speakers who speak others' interests.

One could pursue the details of this case almost indefinitely. Among issues worth pursuing further: (1) Did the *Journal* genuinely feel threatened by Springer, or did it seize on him as a club with which to beat CBS? (2) For whose eyes was the editorial written? Was its intent to wean an audience away from television, to diminish TV's authorizing capacity, to shame TV producers into better behavior, to intimidate them into sticking closer to standards the *Journal* regarded as normative (i.e., hegemonic), or something else again? (3) Why was the editorial written in a language of scorn and ridicule? Ought it be considered an instance of corrosive discourse? (4) What were the reactions to the editorial within CBS? Were there any communications between CBS executives and those at the *Journal*? Was there any public response?

The time has come, however, to return to the broader issue of whether authority in the modern world differs markedly from its ancient counterpart, an issue on which I remain frankly ambivalent. On the one hand, the materials I have considered above convince me that authority itself remains very much what it always has been: an effect characteristic of strongly asymmetric relations between speaker and audience, predisposing the latter to defer to the discourse of the former in ways that are often quite uncritical. This notwithstanding, I have come to believe that within recent history there has emerged nothing less than a new mode of authority production, the central operation of which is no longer the production of speech, nor its authorization, but rather the production of stages with authorizing capacity.

In this, we have moved from a situation of scarcity to one of abundance. Ancient Greece, Rome, and Scandinavia — to cite the examples considered in earlier chapters — had relatively few authorized and authorizing places. Consequently, each such site commanded the attention and respect of large audiences, sometimes approximating the total population, over very long periods of time. Given their obvious value, control over these sites was tightly managed, usually by an aristocratic oligarchy. Access was severely limited, and competition might be fierce, for the chief problem facing those outside the oligarchy who wished to produce an act of authoritative speech (e.g., Thersites, Cotta, Egil's witnesses) was gaining entry to these few, but extremely potent workshops of authority production.

In contrast, we now have a large and ever increasing number of stages that are organized by entrepreneurial consortiums as instruments or factories for the mass production (and ongoing reproduction) of the authority effect. With this expansion comes specialization, subdivision of markets, and competition among stages, as the controlling interests of each stage (financial, ideological, and aesthetic) not only give shape and direction to its activities, but place it in rivalry with other stages that embody and advance other interests. Success or failure in this competition — which may involve open polemic, more discreet struggles for speakers, audiences, financial backing, favorable reviews, or all the above — produces a different, and possibly volatile, history for each stage. Some stages rise and others fall, some adapt in order to survive, and whenever one rings down its final curtain, there are others waiting to take its place.

APPENDIX A

Mailing from the "Hundredth Monkey" Project

STOP NUCLEAR TESTING!
In 1963, due to international concern over fallout from atmospheric nuclear testing, the Partial Test Ban Treaty was signed. This was hopefully the first step to a total ban on nuclear testing. Since that time the radioactive poisoning of our world has continued. Over 700 underground nuclear explosions have shaken the Earth at the Nevada Test Site. For the past five years, the Soviet Union has appealed for a Comprehensive Test Ban. It is time for US to take the next step. LET'S STOP NUCLEAR TESTING!

THE EVENT ... April 12–14, 1991, 500,000 global citizens will gather in Las Vegas, Nevada, 65 miles southeast of the Nevada Test Site, to hear dozens of international speakers and world class musical artists inform, inspire, and demand an end to nuclear testing. This will be preceded on April 11 by a Comprehensive Test Ban Summit, and followed on April 15 by a five day mass walk to the Nevada Test Site.

Originally published as a leaflet, distributed in the months before April 1991. It is quoted here by permission of Rick Springer.

THE PURPOSE . . . TO STOP NUCLEAR TESTING at the Nevada test site through world awareness, political pressure, and direct action including a petition drive, and a mass walk to the test site. To educate the world through media exposure and a full length feature movie of the event. To expand the nonviolence ethic through mass nonviolence trainings in conjunction with the event. To raise funds to finish the job, clean-up the test site and return the land to its true keepers: The Western Shoshone Nation.

THE METHOD . . .   To envision and believe in the event as an end to nuclear testing. To secure the involvement and support of dedicated world organizers, celebrities, inspirational leaders, indigenous peoples, world and local peace groups, and individual activists at large.

BE THE HUNDREDTH MONKEY!

APPENDIX B

*Remarks by President Ronald Reagan at National
Association of Broadcasters' 70th Annual Convention
13 April 1992*

This is a beautiful award and a very special honor. All the more
so because it involves a business that has been my heart and
soul for so many years. As David Sarnoff, a great visionary in
broadcasting, once said, "we have 'hitched' our wagon to the
electron."

I just happened to hitch my wagon a little earlier than you
did. In fact, when I was a young lad Ben Franklin asked me to
hold his kite for him. As lightning flashed across the sky, I said,
"No, you go ahead sir."

And that was the man who wanted to be "healthy, wealthy,
and wise"!!

It's a pleasure to be in Las Vegas, the city that never sleeps.
I was telling Eddie [Fritts, President of the NAB] I used to
work in a city that never wakes up. But I didn't have to tell him
which one, because he worked there with me. He did a superb
job as Vice Chairman of my presidential board of advisors on
Private Sector Initiatives.

And of course, Washington is in the throes of a political season — angry rhetoric, intricate parliamentary maneuvers,

Courtesy of National Association of Broadcasters.

treacherous backstabbing. And that's just the debate over new broadcast licenses.

Sounds like a good pilot for the new T.V. season!

You know, one thing you can always expect in our business is the unexpected. I probably wouldn't be standing here to-day — if not for a strange twist of fate one day. When I gradua-ted from college in Illinois in 1932, the Great Depression was at gale force. I was hired as a rookie announcer at a little thousand-watt station in Iowa. The catch phrase was, "Station W.O.C., Davenport — where the West begins, in the state where the tall corn grows."

Later, I moved to W.H.O., our sister station in Des Moines. I spent four years there and they were among the most pleasant of my life. If I had stopped there, I believe I would have been happy the rest of my life.

I ended up doing play-by-play for the Chicago Cubs and even went with the Cubs for spring training in California in 1937. By the way, it was on that trip, just by chance, I met an agent who signed me up for the movies. And in Hollywood if you did not sing or dance you became an after-dinner speaker. Pretty soon I did more speaking than acting and found myself running for Governor. And not willing to leave bad enough alone, I ran for President and ended up having to leave my beloved California for eight years in public housing in Wash-ington. And now, here I am, at the prime of my life, out of work!

So I want to thank you for giving this young fellow his start and for all the other things you do for your country! You pro-vide not just news and entertainment, but wisdom about the human condition.

You save countless lives by warning about floods, hurri-canes, and other natural disasters. And charities also save lives by using your stations to raise hundreds of millions of dollars every year.

Last year broadcasters relayed video messages from soldiers in Desert Storm to the United States. The cheerful words "Hi, Mom! I'm in the desert. I miss you!" brought together not just families but our whole country.

Broadcasting has transformed our universe. Radio and television waves are a sixth human sense—the extra dimension of the twentieth century. This invisible energy inspires humans to be human—to learn, laugh, love, hate, go to war or join together in peace. Instantly.

Radio and television waves are the Paul Reveres of the universe. They are liberators undeterred by icy tundra or trackless desert. You tear down Berlin Walls, uproot bamboo curtains and destroy dictators.

Before radio, most of the world was not free. Life, to quote Hobbes, was "brutish, nasty and short." Even a century ago, our own nation was fragmented and isolated. We had over 20,000 newspapers—but almost every paper was confined to a particular city or town. Communications were so slow it took three days for Americans to learn about Dewey's landmark victory in Manila Bay in 1898.

The ancient Greeks discovered how to generate electricity—static electricity. But it was not until 1887 that a primitive radio wave was transmitted.

Heinrich Hertz sent an electric current running through a wire with a gap in it. The electricity jumped off at a gap and landed on a wire on the other side of the room. Like a bird flying from one perch to another.

In 1901, Marconi sent the "dot dash" signal, and soon after Lee De Forest added voices and music to the airwaves, including a live concert by Enrico Crauso [sic] in 1912.

Americans rushed out to buy elegant Atwater Kent radios. Or they built their own receivers with a spool of wire, a crystal, an aerial and earphones.

The high tech revolution touched every part of our lives.

Radio helped the British navy win the historic Battle of Jutland in 1916. Even so, a top naval officer wrote that "to trust . . . the wireless reports of cruisers which are out of sight is to run a needless risk." The official later got over his skepticism. He used radio to offer his fellow citizens "nothing but blood, sweat, and tears" and led Britain through its darkest and finest hour.

Back home, and a world away, I was announcing for the Chicago Cubs during their finest and not-so-finest hours.

Despite the baseball benefits, some prominent observers actually lamented the arrival of instant communications. They feared the airwaves would carry the virus of the Russian Revolution to other nations.

Even President Woodrow Wilson warned his fellow Americans: "With the tongue of the wireless and the tongue of the telegraph, all the suggestions of disorder are now spread throughout the world."

Funny how years later radio would spread "disorder" in the communist monolith itself.

Veteran newscaster Daniel Schorr tells a story about his visits to Eastern Europe. He says people didn't ask much about the President of the United States. They asked if he knew Willis Conover, the famed broadcaster for Voice of America.

In those early days, some well-meaning people also feared the rise of television. In a terrifying book called *1984*, George Orwell predicted big brother would use a "telescreen" to control his own subjects.

When *1984* was published shortly after World War II, Albania was fast becoming an Orwellian state. The tiny mountainous country was tightly controlled by the communists, impoverished, cut off from the rest of the world.

Like Big Brother, Dictator Enver Hoxha needed television for his propaganda. He also needed modern industry. So he electrified the Albanian countryside. He then lost control of his subjects. Many people—risking severe punishment—secretly switched to Yugoslavian, Greek and Italian channels.

On television, Albanians saw Eastern Europe turn toward democracy—and followed suit. Today, television is often the only electrical appliance in an Albanian home. Foreign broadcasts are so common that many people in that underdeveloped country speak at least one foreign language.

In fact, the *Los Angeles Times* recently had this headline: "Stressed Out Albanians are becoming Couch Potatoes."

George Orwell, bless his heart, was wrong about the "telescreen."

Look what happened when the long-dreaded year of 1984 finally arrived. A prominent political candidate made many public criticisms of the leader of the United States. But he was not imprisoned, because America is a great and free country.

Broadcasting now has another challenge—China.

Twenty years ago, Ted Koppel was ABC's Correspondent for China. Getting news from China was not easy in those days. He had to climb a hill in Hong Kong and try to pick up short-wave radio reports from the mainland.

But in the spring of 1989, shortly after the students rebelled in Beijing, Mr. Koppel did the impossible. He sent a live television report from one of the most tightly guarded places in the world — Tiananmen Square.

Like a spy in a movie, Mr. Koppel rode a bicycle under the noses of the Chinese authorities. A microphone was in his shirt and a miniature camera was mounted on his bicycle. A small truck behind him transmitted his commentary to a satellite many miles above. The satellite bounced Mr. Koppel's report back to New York and into the homes of millions of Americans.

No single man or group can control technology. No man can rule the satellites, transistor radios, camcorders, copy machines or notebook computers.

Technology is literally in the hands of people — and so is the power.

And more electronic marvels are coming our way.

Digital audio broadcasting — almost unheard of four years ago — brings crystal clear tones to the radio. High definition television more than doubles the number of lines on screen and creates a stunning picture.

Experts even predict that computer generated images will bring back legendary performers in entirely new roles. Including Bonzo?

Pretty soon, there could be a new device in your hand. A cellular telephone, personal computer, radio and television with an inflatable screen — all rolled into one.

You can carry the magic box to the farthest desert or the highest mountain. Bounce your signals off a satellite. Catch the 60 Minutes show on top of Mount Everest.

Rarely would a hiker get lost in a snowstorm or a driver in a dangerous part of town. Amelia Earhart — stranded on a deserted island — would reach in her pocket and ring up a rescue party.

You wouldn't have to be E.T. to phone home.

America, the Cold War victor, stands triumphant on the world stage.

Our culture is as powerful and transcendent as our military. In 1989, Americans made the top five movies in Greece, Ireland, Italy, the Netherlands, Norway, Switzerland, Hungary, Bolivia, Brazil, Australia, and Japan. In October 1991, almost half the top fifty T.V. entertainment programs in Italy and Spain were American — including programs like "Cheers" and "Golden Girls."

Your collected work has escaped the earth and is speeding across the universe. Even shows canceled after thirteen weeks. Can you imagine the reaction of aliens who pick up an episode of "Twin Peaks"?

But can our nation handle peace as well as war? Or will we become a self-absorbed nation of couch potatoes?

I may be old fashioned on this subject. But I believe the communications business has a key role in strengthening the spiritual values that knit our society together.

For centuries after the birth of Christ, bibles were copied by hand. A single bible could take a year or more to produce.

Today, the contents of the bible are relayed instantly around the world. A spiritual revival is taking place in Eastern Europe, Russia, Latin America and other areas, nourished by radio and television.

In our secular age, our children are especially malleable and curious and vulnerable. The culture of their elders has a lasting influence on their young minds.

The entertainment industry has taken commendable steps in the war against illegal drugs. As you know, my wife Nancy has worked hard on this issue. And references about drug use are far fewer these days than they were fifteen or twenty years ago. Alcohol abuse is also under sharp scrutiny — especially drinking and driving. And that's all to the good. But we must preserve and shelter and strengthen the American family. A strong family is the cradle of civilization.

As the twenty-first century comes swiftly upon us, broadcasting faces many other challenges — demographic changes, cable competition, government regulation and of course, licensing of frequencies.

Some people may fear the future, the unknown. But our broadcasting industry shouldn't. We need only recall George Orwell and his misplaced fears about the "telescreen." And I know something else from my long experience: the people in this business aren't in the habit of shying away from challenges.

Certainly not the inventor Edwin Howard Armstrong. In the 1930s Armstrong found an intriguing radio signal. But leading mathematicians and engineers scoffed at his discovery. They said the new wave was inconsequential and doomed to extinction. Armstrong didn't realize he was supposed to fail. He went back to his tiny lab and perfected his invention. The result was F.M. radio — a clean, static-free sound used not just commercially but in police and fire stations, guided missiles, even for communicating in outer space.

That's the tale of broadcasting in this century. A pioneer's epic of hard work, a lot of luck and vivid imagination — and unexpected blessings beyond our dreams.

And that will be the story of the next century as well. It is my hope that human dignity will be everywhere respected; that the free flow of people and ideas will include not only the newly freed states of Eastern Europe, but all those still struggling for their freedom.

America's solemn duty is to constantly renew its covenant with humanity to complete the grand work of human freedom that began over 200 years ago. This work, in its grandness and nobility, is not unlike the building of a magnificent cathedral. In the beginning, the progress is slow and painstaking. The laying of the foundations and the raising of the walls should be measured in decades rather than years. But as the arches and spires begin to emerge in the air, others join in, adding their faith and dedication and love to speed the work to its completion.

My friends, the world is that cathedral. And our children, if not we ourselves, will see the completed work — the worldwide triumph of human freedom, the triumph of human freedom under God.

Thank you all very much and God bless you.

APPENDIX C

Interview with Rick Springer "CBS This Morning,"
17 April 1992

HARRY SMITH (co-host): Anti-nuclear activist Rick Springer says he never had any intention of hurting former President Reagan earlier this week. Springer says he just wanted to make a point. Still, the incident startled Mr. Reagan and jolted the Secret Service. Springer is with a group called The 100th Monkey, which opposes all nuclear testing. And he joins us this morning from KLAS-TV in Las Vegas. Good morning.

RICK SPRINGER: (Anti-nuclear Activist): Good morning.

HARRY SMITH: What were you trying to accomplish earlier this week?

RICK SPRINGER: Well, I have known about the National Association of Broadcasters convention for approximately six months, and I thought that this was incredible timing as relates to our project to stop nuclear testing. I thought this was a great opportunity to address the NAB and to let them know that nuclear testing does continue just 60 miles north of Las Vegas.

HARRY SMITH: What was smashed when you went up onto the — onto the stage next to the former president?

RICK SPRINGER: That was a crystal statue of an eagle, symbol of freedom to the western Shoshone Nation, whose land nuclear testing continues on today.

HARRY SMITH: And did you smash that intentionally? What — what exactly happened when you got on the stage up there?

RICK SPRINGER: Well, you know, I stood at the side hearing Eddie Fritz's speech for approximately 10 minutes, and then Mr. Reagan was on. I was trying to get my nerve up. It was, you know, pretty scary to know I was going up there to make this announcement without permission, and as I approached the podium, I had no intention of doing anything to that statue, but I found myself turning to the statue and raising it over my head and breaking it on the pedestal.

HARRY SMITH: Did you give any consideration to what might happen to you when you went on that stage?

RICK SPRINGER: Well, actually, I did. I — I — while I was standing at the side, I had many visions, and I did consider the possibility that the Secret Service may shoot me in the process of trying to make my announcement.

HARRY SMITH: The question . . .

RICK SPRINGER: I . . .

HARRY SMITH: The question everybody has is how did you get so close?

RICK SPRINGER: Well, you know, it's a — it was a convention where you had to have passes to it. I casually walked on stage, and — and I have heard from many people that they thought that because I was moving in a confident, casual manner, that — that I must be a sound technician. And of course, when I approached the — the podium, I wanted to announce to the attendees that there is a nuclear bomb test scheduled for this week, and that France had discontinued their nuclear testing program, and it was time for us to do likewise.

HARRY SMITH: Did you have any IDs? Did you have any of the requisite, sort of, media — media passes?

RICK SPRINGER: Yes, I had been lucky, and a friend of a friend had just gotten a press packet to me two days before. I hadn't even had time to read that packet until I was en route to the conference, and it was just at that point that I read that Mr. Reagan was receiving an award. I didn't even really believe at that point that he was going to be there in person.

HARRY SMITH: Mm-hmm.

RICK SPRINGER: But when I did enter the room, I found that he was there.

HARRY SMITH: What have you been charged with?

RICK SPRINGER: I have been charged with threatening a former president.

HARRY SMITH: Are you surprised at all that they let you go?

RICK SPRINGER: No, not really. I believe that my life is an—is an indicator of my commitment to non-violence. In fact, this entire project, The 100th Monkey, is based on the non-violent teachings of Gandhi and Martin Luther King.

HARRY SMITH: Do you have any regrets about what you did this week?

RICK SPRINGER: Well, I certainly must offer an apology to Mr. Reagan. I am very sorry that the Secret Service jostled him in an effort to get me off of the stage. I have no regrets as to the fact that I approached the—the podium, and I think that the coverage that I have received due to this act, is an excellent example of what it takes to wake up and startle the media and, indeed, the American public, whose apathy is responsible for the continuation of nuclear testing to this day.

HARRY SMITH: Mm. Rick Springer, we thank you for joining us. Do appreciate it. Twenty-two after.

PAULA ZAHN: (co-host): Good morning.

HARRY SMITH: Wasn't that interesting?

PAULA ZAHN: I loved that segment.

HARRY SMITH: Springer.

MARK MCEWEN: (meteorologist): He could talk. Most of the time you get people like Squeaky Fromme—you remember?

HARRY SMITH: Well, as it turns — this guy is a well-known — I don't know about well-known, but there is lots of tape of him leading nuclear — anti-nuclear demonstrations and stuff. I mean, that's really what this guy is all about. That's — because he was released so quickly and everybody said, "What? Excuse me."

MARK MCEWEN: Yeah.

HARRY SMITH: And he has a — he has a real track record of — of pacifism, so . . .

MARK MCEWEN: I thought that was great. Do you think you're going to go to jail? "No, I think they're going to drop the charges," which I thought — I don't know if I would have said that. I'd say, "Oh, please — oh, please — oh, please."

PAULA ZAHN: But he did apologize for hitting the former president with the shards of glass.

MARK MCEWEN: Absolutely.

HARRY SMITH: It's just amazing — just amazing. . . .

APPENDIX D

"The Hundredth Monkey Speaks": Editorial from the
Wall Street Journal *21 April 1992*

It was predictable, but a bit startling nonetheless, to find Richard Paul Springer staring out at us from our TV sets Friday morning. Mr. Springer, recall, is the anti-nuclear "protester" who lurched onto a podium in full view of the Secret Service, shoved speaker Ronald Reagan and smashed a crystal statue that sent glass flying into Mr. Reagan's face. A representative of an anti-nuclear group that calls itself the Hundredth Monkey, Mr. Springer contentedly proceeded to explain his motives during an interview on "CBS This Morning."

He had plenty of reason for contentment. The precise goal of people who engage in violent zealotry is, of course, media publicity, and Mr. Springer now has had his reward. He had been given the opportunity to address a national television audience on the evils of nuclear testing. As he told CBS, "I think that the coverage that I've received due to this act is an excellent example of what it takes to wake up and startle the media . . ."

Mr. Springer looks to be the latest entry to a special galaxy of media-produced stars—people whose aberrations, disturbances and general aggressions against society have won them fame as "political activists."

Wall Street Journal, 21 April 1992, p. A16.

Billy Boggs was a mentally disturbed homeless woman in New York City, given to defecating on the streets and threatening passers-by. Then Ms. Boggs was discovered by the media (as well as by the ACLU) and her celebrity soon catapulted her to the front pages and lecture gigs at Harvard.

Another recently anointed media star went on to sue the police, the town officials and the library of Morristown, New Jersey, because the library wanted to expel him for harassing other patrons. His ambitions expanding along with the coverage, New Jersey vagrant Richard Kreimer collected a bunch of money. Though he and his ACLU attorneys lost on appeal, Mr. Kreimer cherishes plans to address the Democratic Convention this summer.

Richard Springer, in turn, belongs to the ranks of political fanatics prepared to wreak whatever havoc necessary to advance their notions of humanity. He has, as he told CBS, no regrets nor has the law given him any, at least so far. After being charged with threatening a former President, Mr. Springer was released on his own recognizance by order of U.S. Magistrate Lawrence Leavitt. The prosecutors requested that bail be imposed, but were refused. In the magistrate's view, there were no indications that the accused would flee or that he might be a danger to society.

Perhaps so, but during his televised interview Mr. Springer delivered a blow-by-blow account of his preparations to seize the podium. As he headed toward Mr. Reagan, he had, he recalled, no intention of doing anything to that statue, "but I found myself turning to the statue and raising it over my head and breaking it. . . ." It strikes us that anyone who is such a stranger to his violent and destructive impulses — and who acts on those impulses — certainly bears watching.

The Springers of the world know that they live in a society that tolerates their breaches of the peace and their threats. Mr. Springer exuded the confidence of a man who understood he would be cosseted to the full extent the law allowed. He faces up to three years, if convicted — but, as he told Harry Smith, "I personally believe the charges are going to be dropped."

Since Mr. Springer used phony press credentials, the Secret Service is planning to look harder at security arrangements and, especially, at press credentials. This prospect incited alarmed responses from the usual quarters that the Secret Service might now jeopardize First Amendment rights.

This isn't news, since there is hardly anything that happens, nowadays, that isn't seen as a threat to the First Amendment. What *would* be news would be if the producers of a show such as "CBS This Morning" decided that giving a character like Richard Springer a place in the media spotlight wasn't smart or healthy or in the public interest. That wouldn't simply be news, of course. That would be a miracle.

APPENDIX E

"Excuse Me, Mr. President": Excerpts from an article by
Rick Springer

. . . The tables around me were covered with Budweiser cans as
the crowd laughed and applauded at jokes that weren't funny.
My mind flashed on other scenes: Russian children with birth
defects, South Pacific women dying of breast cancer from the
French testing program, strange mutated wildlife in the desert
down-wind of the Nevada test site. I remembered "down-
winder" Terry Tempest Williams's essay about her cancer-
plagued Utah family, "The Clan of One-Breasted Women" . . .

As I approached the eagle statue on its pedestal — in what
seemed the clearest, most meditative moment of my life — I
grabbed the statue by its frosted base, raised it from the pedestal high over my head, and — like a nuclear weapon detonating
under Western Shoshone land — laid it to waste. I let the base
fall from my hands and proceeded to the podium. What I
hoped to say — "Emergency, there is a bomb test happening tomorrow at the test site" — fell way to the formality of etiquette,
"Excuse me, Mr. President," I said.

Next thing I knew I was being whisked backward by security. I yelled, "Help, there is a nuclear bomb test tomorrow,"

Rick Springer, "Excuse Me, Mr. President," *New Age Journal* (July/August
1992), pp. 50–53.

but a hand was at my throat and another at my mouth. I was dumped to the floor, hauled backstage, and handcuffed. The deed was done . . .

Why did you choose to make this statement?

Where do I begin? Maybe because after forty-five years of citizen opposition, after the United States' failure to follow through on the mandate of the 1963 Partial Test Ban Treaty to end testing for all time, after the failure of the January 1991 United Nations effort to end testing (opposed by only the United States and Great Britain, out of 117 nations), I believed that the media were ignoring the testing issue out of private concerns. It seemed clear to me that the major media depend a great deal upon the very corporations that control weapons manufacture and research — and in the case of General Electric, which owns NBC, the corporation *is* the media.

The agents threw a shirt over my head to escort me through the press at the Hilton. I had them take it off. I am not a criminal, I wanted to say. I am a patriot to the Earth, no less ashamed of my actions than someone who pulls a life-saving fire alarm. I agree with Martin Luther King, Jr., who once said: "I refuse to accept the cynical notion that nation after nation must spiral down the militaristic stairway into the hell of thermonuclear destruction." I'm simply ringing out a warning . . .

APPENDIX F

United States v. Springer:
Excerpt from the Federal Court Record

THE COURT: I want to make sure, Mr. Springer, that you understand that by pleading guilty you are waiving certain important Constitutional rights regarding the charges. First of all, by pleading guilty you are waiving your right to a trial by jury at which you would be presumed innocent and at which you would be represented by counsel. Do you understand that?

THE DEFENDANT: Yes, I do.

THE COURT: You're also waiving your right to cross-examine any witness called to testify against you, as well as your right to summons witnesses to testify on your own behalf. Do you understand that?

THE DEFENDANT: Yes, I do.

THE COURT: Finally, Mr. Springer, by pleading guilty you waive your right to remain silent regarding the charge. By that

United States of America v. Rick Paul Springer, heard in District Court of Nevada, Las Vegas, October 22, 1992. Docket No. CR-S-92-109-PMP(RJJ), The Honorable Philip M. Pro Presiding. Transcript by Northwest Transcripts, Inc. These proceedings were reported at some length in the *Las Vegas Review Journal* for 23 October 1992 ("Activist enters a guilty plea"), p. 1B, and received less prominent coverage elsewhere.

I mean, if you went to trial you could not be forced to testify if you did not want to at your own trial. Do you understand that?

THE DEFENDANT: Uh-huh, yes.

THE COURT: But you're waiving that right today and you're agreeing to tell me here in open court under oath what you did that violated the law in this case. Do you understand that?

THE DEFENDANT: Yes, I do . . .

THE COURT: Would you just tell me in your own words what you did on or about April 13, 1992 that causes you to plead guilty at this time; what conduct did you engage in at that time?

THE DEFENDANT: Well, I attended the National Association of Broadcasters Convention, without a concrete plan, but the plan formulated as I was there; and I made a decision that I was willing to take the stage in order to make an announcement about an upcoming nuclear bomb test. And in the process of taking the stage I was inspired to destroy this crystal eagle, sacred symbol of freedom for our nation and indigenous people as well, and some of the glass shards inadvertently flew through the air and hit Mr. Reagan.

I'm definitely guilty of not having thought out what was going to happen with those shards, and I'm also guilty of neglecting to consider that the Secret Service would be prompted to respond. I was so overtaken by the issue of nuclear testing. I believe that each nuclear bomb test is actually polluting present and future generations, and I believe that it is — it is the same as calling out to the world that we are about to have a bomb dropped on us, because in essence we are.

So with that information I approached the podium to announce to this broadcasters convention. And because Mr. Reagan was on stage at this time the Secret Service of course was forced to respond, justifiably, and so therefore I feel that I'm guilty of having interfered with their duty to protect the President.

NOTES

EPIGRAPHS

"All authority": Carl J. Friedrich, "Loyalty and Authority," *Confluence* 3 (1954), p. 312.

"It is the access": Pierre Bourdieu, *Language and Symbolic Power* (Cambridge, Mass.: Harvard University Press, 1991), p. 109.

CHAPTER ONE

Buyers, Sellers, and Authorities

Works in political philosophy: See, inter alia, David V. J. Bell, *Power, Influence, and Authority: An Essay in Political Linguistics* (New York: Oxford University Press, 1975); R. Blaine Harris, ed., *Authority: A Philosophical Analysis* (University, Ala.: University of Alabama Press, 1976); Richard E. Flathman, *The Practice of Political Authority: Authority and the Authoritative* (Chicago: University of Chicago Press, 1980); E. D. Watt, *Authority* (New York: St. Martin's Press, 1982); Richard T. DeGeorge, *The Nature and Limits of Authority* (Lawrence: University Press of Kansas, 1985); J. Roland Pennock and John W. Chapman, eds., *Authority Revisited* (New York: New York University Press, 1987); and Joseph Raz, ed., *Authority* (New York: New York University Press, 1990). DeGeorge, Harris, and Watt all have extensive bibliographies. An earlier collection in the same vein is Carl J. Friedrich, ed., *Authority* (Cambridge, Mass.: Harvard University Press, 1958).

Works in social psychology: The most important are: T. W. Adorno, Else Frenkel-Brunswik, Daniel J. Levinson, and R. Nevitt Sanford, *The Authoritarian Personality* (New York: Harper and Row, 1950); Richard Christie and Marie Jahoda, eds., *Studies in the Scope and Method of 'The Authoritarian Personality'* (Glencoe, Ill.: Free Press, 1954); Milton Rokeach et al., *The Open and Closed Mind: Investigations into the Nature of Belief Systems and Personality Systems* (New York: Basic Books, 1960); and Stanley Milgram, *Obedience to Authority* (New York: Harper and Row, 1974). Rather anomalous is the approach of Richard Sennett, *Authority* (New York: Alfred A. Knopf, 1980).

Works in sociology: For Weber's position, see G. Roth and C. Wittich, eds., *Economy and Society* (New York: Bedminster Press, 1968), pp. 212–300 and 941–54. Among those who take this as their point of departure are Jeremiah F. Wolpert, "Toward a Sociology of Authority," in *Studies in Leadership*, ed. Alvin W. Gouldner (New York: Russell, 1965), pp. 679–702; Robert A. Nisbet, *Tradition and Revolt: Historical and Sociological Essays* (New York: Random House, 1968); *Idem, The Twilight of Authority* (London: Heinemann, 1976); Edward Shils, *Tradition* (Chicago: University of Chicago Press, 1981); *Idem, The Constitution of Society* (Chicago: University of Chicago Press, 1981); Talcott Parsons, *Politics and Social Structure* (New York: Free Press, 1969).

Recent works: See, in particular, Pierre Bourdieu, *Language and Symbolic Power* (Cambridge, Mass.: Harvard University Press, 1991); *Idem, Outline of a Theory of Practice* (Cambridge: Cambridge University Press, 1977); Michel Foucault, *The Archaeology of Knowledge* (New York: Pantheon Books, 1972); *Idem, Power/Knowledge: Selected Interviews and Other Writings* (New York: Pantheon Books, 1980); Mikhail Bakhtin, *Rabelais and his World* (Bloomington: Indiana University Press, 1984); Idem, "From Notes Made in 1970–71," in *Speech Genres and Other Late Essays* (Austin: University of Texas Press, 1986), pp. 132–58; Maurice Bloch, *Ritual, History and Power: Selected Papers in Anthropology* (London: Athlone Press, 1989); Idem, ed., *Political Language and Oratory in Traditional Society* (New York: Academic Press, 1975); James C. Scott, *Domination and the Arts of Resistance: Hidden Transcripts* (New Haven: Yale University Press, 1990); *Idem, Weapons of the Weak: Everyday Forms of Peasant Resistance* (New Haven: Yale University Press, 1985). More specialized, but extremely helpful works include Andrew Apter, *Black Critics and Kings: The Hermeneutics of Power in Yoruba Society* (Chicago: University of Chicago Press, 1992); Lamont Lindstrom, *Knowledge and Power in a South Pacific Society* (Washington: Smithsonian Institution Press, 1990); Joel Kuipers,

Power in Performance: The Creation of Textual Authority in Weyewa Ritual Speech (Philadelphia: University of Pennsylvania Press, 1990); Sophia Menache, *Vox Dei: Communication in the Middle Ages* (New York: Oxford University Press, 1990); Donald Brenneis and Fred Myers, eds., *Dangerous Words: Language and Politics in the Pacific* (Prospect Heights, Ill.: Waveland Press, 1991); Richard Terdiman, *Discourse/Counter-Discourse: The Theory and Practice of Symbolic Resistance in Nineteenth Century France* (Ithaca, N.Y.: Cornell University Press, 1985); and Marcel Detienne, *Les maîtres de vérité dans la grèce archaïque,* 3d ed. (Paris: François Maspero, 1979).

Latin *auctoritas:* The classic discussion remains R. Heinze, "Auctoritas," *Hermes* 60 (1925): 348–66. See also, more recently, K. Lütcke, *'Auctoritas' bei Augustin, mit einer Einleitung zur römischen Vorgeschichte des Begriffs* (Stuttgart: W. Kohlhammer, 1968), pp. 13–46. For a full listing of the term's occurrence within legal contexts, see the Savigny Institute's *Vocabularium Iurisprudentiae Romanae, Vol. 1* (Berlin: Georg Reimer, 1903), pp. 513–17.

Greater than influence, less than command: In Rome, a distinction was made between *auctoritas* and *imperium.* Only high-ranking magistrates and military commanders could speak with *imperium* while acting within their official capacities, and when they did so their words were legally binding. The speech of those entitled to speak with *auctoritas* but not *imperium* (e.g., senators or priests) was not enforceable in the same way, but exerted considerable moral pressure on the hearer.

Auctoritas venditoris and *mancipatio:* For the earliest attestations, see P. R. Coleman-Norton, trans., *The Twelve Tables* (Princeton: Princeton University Dept. of Classics, 1950), pp. 11 and 13 ($5.2 and 6.3–4, respectively). For some of the more recent discussions, see Alan Watson, *Rome of the XII Tables* (Princeton: Princeton University Press, 1975), pp. 134–56; Hans Julius Wolff, "Ein Vorschlag zum Verständnis des Manzipationsrituals," in Fritz Baur et al., eds., *Beiträge zur europäischen Rechtsgeschichte und zum geltenden Zivilrecht: Festgabe für Johannes Sontis* (Munich: C. H. Beck, 1977), pp. 1–9; O. Behrends, "La mancipatio nelle XII Tavole," *Iura* 33 (1982): 46–103; J. G. Wolf, "Die Mancipatio: Roms älteste Rechtsgeschaft," in *Jahrbuch der Heidelberger Akademie der Wissenschaft* (1984); M. Lemosse, "La mise en cause judiciare de l'auctor," *Labeo* 30 (1984): 163–70; Max Kaser, "Altrömisches Eigentum und 'usucapio,'" *Zeitschrift der Savigny-Stiftung für Rechtgeschichte* 105 (1988): 122–64; and André Magdelain, "Auctoritas rerum," in *Jus Imperium Auctoritas: Études de droit romain* (Rome: École française de Rome, 1990), pp. 685–705. Beyond this, there is a large literature dating back to the 1930s.

Authority and Authorities

Executive and epistemic authority, "in authority" and "an authority": Particularly insightful on this point is R. B. Friedman, "On the Concept of Authority in Political Philosophy," in *Authority*, pp. 56–91. Regarding the kinds of authority based upon and operative through claims to specialized knowledge, see Thomas Haskell, ed., *The Authority of Experts: Studies in History and Theory* (Bloomington: Indiana University Press, 1984) and Stanley Aronowitz, *Science as Power: Discourse and Ideology in Modern Society* (Minneapolis: University of Minnesota Press, 1988). Epistemic and executive authority are not necessarily opposed to one another, but can be complementary. Often the two articulate in hierarchic fashion, such that epistemic authority supplies advice, expertise, and the like to executive authority, while the latter retains final decision-making power.

Command and obedience: For Weber, authority is *Herrschaft* ("domination") that has been legitimized, and results in the ability to issue commands that will be obeyed. I am inclined to think that such a model impoverishes our understanding of authority, and privileges the position of military officers and factory bosses, while obscuring the equally real (if less blunt) authority of others who do not deal in commands: poets, philosophers, scientists, etc. Weber seems to have toyed with a broader notion of authority and domination, but tossed it aside in the following passage: "A position ordinarily designated as "dominating" can emerge from the social relations in a drawing room as well as in the market, from the rostrum of a lecture-hall as well as from the command post of a regiment, from an erotic or charitable relationship as well as from scholarly discussion or athletics. Such a broad definition would, however, render the term "domination" scientifically useless" (*Economy and Society*, pp. 942–43).

Between Coercion and Persuasion

Persuasion and coercion: The discussion of Hannah Arendt, *Between Past and Future* (New York: Penguin Books, 1977), pp. 92–93, is most helpful on this point.

Anarchist critiques: See, for example, the essays on "Authority and Anarchism" that appeared in J. Roland Pennock and John Chapman, eds., *Anarchism* (New York: New York University Press, 1978), or Robert Paul Wolff, *In Defense of Anarchism* (New York: Harper and Row, 1970).

"Capacity for reasoned elaboration": See Carl J. Friedrich, "Power and Authority," in *An Introduction to Political Theory* (New York:

Harper and Row, 1967), pp. 121–32; Idem, *Tradition and Authority* (London: Macmillan, 1972).

Authorized and Authorizing Objects, Times, and Places

Uniforms and insignia: Alongside Charles Merriam's old idea of *miranda* ("things to be admired") and *credenda* ("things to be believed") as the instruments through which authority is constructed and maintained (*Political Power* [New York: McGraw Hill, 1934], pp. 102–32), one should note Stanley J. Tambiah's attention to "*palladia* and *regalia*, which are enduring sedimentations and objectifications of power and virtue, the possession of which is a guarantee of legitimacy" (*The Buddhist Saints of the Forest and the Cult of the Amulets* [Cambridge: Cambridge University Press, 1984], p. 241 [slightly altered]); Clifford Geertz, "Centers, kings, and charisma: Reflections on the symbolics of power," in *Local Knowledge: Further Essays in Interpretive Anthropology* (New York: Basic Books, 1983), pp. 121–46 is also useful. Recent studies of such items are many and varied, although Ernst Kantorowicz, *The King's Two Bodies: A Study in Medieval Political Theology* (Princeton: Princeton University Press, 1957) remains fundamental. See, inter alia: Rudolf H. Wackernagel, *Die französische Kronungswagen von 1696–1825: Ein Beitrag zur Geschichte des representativen Zeremonienwagen* (Berlin: Walter de Gruyter, 1966); Ole Wanscher, *Sella Curulis: The Folding Stool, An Ancient Symbol of Dignity* (Copenhagen: Rosenkilde & Bagger, 1980); Joseph Cornet, *Art royal kuba* (Milan: Edizioni Sipiel, 1982); Martin Metzger, *Königsthron und Gottesthron: Thronformen und Throndarstellungen in Ägypten und im vorderen Orient in Zweiten und Dritten Jahrtausend vor Christus* (Neukirchen: Neukirchener Verlag, 1985); Nathan Joseph, *Uniforms and Nonuniforms: Communication through Clothing* (New York: Greenwood Press, 1986); Ilse Hayden, *Symbol and Privilege: The Ritual Context of British Royalty* (Tucson: University of Arizona Press, 1987); Claes Arvidsson and Erik Blomquist, *Symbols of Power: The Esthetics of Political Legitimation in the Soviet Union and Eastern Europe* (Stockholm: Almquist & Wiksells, 1987); Valery M. Garrett, *Mandarin Squares: Mandarins and their Insignia* (Hong Kong: Oxford University Press, 1990); Asa Boholm, *The Doge of Venice: The Symbolism of State Power in the Renaissance* (Gothenburg: Institute for Advanced Studies in Anthropology, 1990); and Reinhart Staats, *Die Reichskröne: Geschichte und Bedeutung eines europaischen Symbols* (Göttingen: Vandenhoeck & Ruprechts, 1991). Most broadly on the significance and efficacy of fetishized objects, see Pierre Bourdieu, *Distinction: A Social Critique of the Judgement of Taste* (Cambridge, Mass.: Harvard University Press, 1984) and Arjun Appadurai, ed., *The Social Life of Things* (Cambridge: Cambridge University Press, 1986).

Rituals of coronation: Numerous detailed studies are available. See, inter alia: Richard Jackson, *Vive le roi! A History of the French Coronation from Charles V to Charles X* (Chapel Hill: University of North Carolina Press, 1984); Sean Wilentz, ed., *Rites of Power: Symbolism, Ritual and Politics since the Middle Ages* (Philadelphia: University of Pennsylvania Press, 1985); David Cannadine and Simon Price, eds., *Rituals of Royalty: Power and Ceremonial in Traditional Societies* (Cambridge: Cambridge University Press, 1987); Janos M. Bok, ed., *Coronations: Medieval and Early Modern Monarchic Ritual* (Berkeley and Los Angeles: University of California Press, 1990).

Defrocking: I have been unable to find any serious analyses of the procedures of ritual defrocking. Examples of annual ceremonies in which rulers are stripped of their insignia and then subjected to abuse and humiliation in order to dramatize the fact that their authority derives from their office and not their person are well-known, however, and offer some important similarities. See, for example, the Swazi Ncwala ritual as described by Hilda Kuper, *An African Aristocracy: Rank among the Swazi* (London: Oxford University Press, 1947), pp. 197–225, or the texts describing the fifth day of the Babylonian Akitu festival, which are available in James Pritchard, *Ancient Near Eastern Texts*, 3d ed. (Princeton: Princeton University Press, 1969), p. 334. For a challenging alternative interpretation of the latter, see Jonathan Z. Smith, *Imagining Religion: From Babylon to Jonestown* (Chicago: University of Chicago Press, 1982), pp. 90–96.

The emperor's new clothes: See Norbert Elias, *The Court Society* (New York: Pantheon Books, 1983), p. 86 for an amusing and instructive historic episode in which the authority of the naked Marie Antoinette was temporarily eclipsed by the high symbolic value members of her court accorded to her royal garments.

Authorized Speech and Significant Silence

The silence of the audience: I am grateful to Pier Giorgio Solinas for having first suggested this line of inquiry to me in a branch office of the Monte dei Paschi di Siena, where he observed that one habitually and almost automatically drops one's voice upon entering only a very few sorts of establishment: churches, banks, and museums, where one feels oneself to be in the presence of the traditionally sacred or that of its modern correlatives, art and money. On silence as a signifying practice, see Bernard Dauenhafer, *Silence: The Phenomenon and its Ontological Significance* (Bloomington: Indiana University Press, 1980), Deborah Tannen and Muriel Saville-Troike, eds., *Perspectives on Silence* (Norwood, N.J.: Ablex, 1985), and Maria Grazia Ciani, ed., *The Regions of Silence* (Amsterdam: J. C. Gieben, 1987).

Conjunctions and Disruptions

Textual authority: The one point I would make begins with the observation that whereas speech acts exist in the moment, texts endure over time. As a result, it is not sufficient to *establish* the authority of a text, one must also insure the text's transmission and the reproduction of its authority over successive generations. Such tasks are best accomplished by large, powerful, and enduring institutions: states, churches, schools, and the like. For treatment of the differences and relations between discursive and textual authority, with specific reference to those texts most properly called canonic, see F. F. Bruce and E. G. Rupp, eds., *Holy Book and Holy Tradition* (Manchester: Manchester University Press, 1968); Frederick Denny and Roderick Taylor, eds., *The Holy Book in Comparative Perspective* (Columbia: University of South Carolina Press, 1985); Miriam Levering, ed., *Rethinking Scripture: Essays from a Comparative Perspective* (Albany: State University of New York Press, 1987); and William A. Graham, *Beyond the Written Word: Oral Aspects of Scripture in the History of Religion* (Cambridge: Cambridge University Press, 1987). More broadly, see Stanley Fish, *Is There a Text in this Class? The Authority of Interpretive Communities* (Cambridge, Mass.: Harvard University Press, 1980); Robert von Hallberg, ed., *Canons* (Chicago: University of Chicago Press, 1984); Michel Foucault, "What is an Author?" in Paul Rabinow, ed., *The Foucault Reader* (New York: Pantheon Books, 1984), pp. 101–20; Richard Ohmann, *Politics of Letters* (Middletown, Conn.: Wesleyan University Press, 1987); and Walter Ong, *Orality and Literacy: The Technologizing of the Word* (New York: Methuen, 1982).

Authority at second hand: I do not mean that, like Kierkegaard's "disciple at second hand," I believe these accounts because they are transmitted to me by others who believed them and whom I believe. Rather, I believe they gave a sufficiently accurate picture of their society to be found credible by their primary audience, regardless of whether I believe them or whether from some unobtainably objective vantage point they "ought" to be believed.

CHAPTER TWO

The Homeric Assembly: Forms and Procedures

Homeric *agorē:* see Richard John Cunliffe, *A Lexicon of the Homeric Dialect* (Norman: University of Oklahoma Press, 1963), p. 4. The term is derived from a verb "to gather, assemble" (*agō*).

Assemblies are described at *Iliad* 1.53–303, 2.86–398, 2.788–808, 4.1–72, 7.345–79, 8.1–40, 8.4898–542, 9.9–79, 18.243–313, 19.40–276, 20.4–32, and at *Odyssey* 2.1–259, 8.1–47, 16.361–408, and 24.413–66. The best descriptions of its physical space are found at *Iliad* 18.503–504, and *Odyssey* 6.266–67. With regard to the etiquette of sitting, standing, speaking, and remaining silent, note especially *Iliad* 2.95–100, 19.78–82, *Odyssey* 1.372–73, and the formulaic line *Iliad* 1.68 (=1.101, 7.354, 7.365, *Odyssey* 2.224). The procedural forms which I have described reflect the recurrent patterns evident in these texts. Deviations from those patterns are also instructive; for instance, when the Trojans remain standing in assembly due to their terror at Achilles' return to battle (*Iliad* 18.245–48); when Hector holds a spear as he speaks, no sceptre being available (*Iliad* 8.493–96); or when Telemachus takes the seat normally assigned to his father (*Odyssey* 2.14). See further the discussions of Georges C. Vlachos, *Les sociétés politiques homériques* (Paris: Presses universitaires de France, 1974), pp. 171–206; M. I. Finley, *The World of Odysseus,* 2d ed. (Harmondsworth, England: Penguin Books, 1979), pp. 78–82; Walter Donlan, "The Structure of Authority in the Iliad," *Arethusa* 12 (1979), pp. 51–70; Jurij V. Andreev, "Die politischen Funktionen der Volksversammlung im homerischen Zeitalter: Zur Frage der 'militärischen Demokratie'," *Klio* 61 (1979), pp. 385–405; and Marcel Detienne, *Les maitres de vérité dans la grèce archaïque* (Paris: Maspero, 1979), pp. 81–103.

A Jointly Hosted Assembly

Rumor: Capitalization in the Greek text indicates that Rumor (*Ossa,* singular feminine) is to be understood as a personified abstraction. Rumors are generally taken to originate from Zeus (cf. *Odyssey* 1.282–83, 2.216–17), and at the conclusion of the *Odyssey* she appears once more in personified form, bearing the news of the suitors' fate to their relatives, whom she leads to an assembly that is potentially quite explosive, in part because no human leader has called it (*Odyssey* 24.413–20).

"Let us flee with the ships . . .": Agamemnon speaks these same lines in earnest at a later assembly (9.27–28), only to have Diomedes conclusively argue in favor of staying at Troy to continue the war (9.32–49). Diomedes' speech is thus established as the properly heroic response to Agamemnon's suggestion of flight, and it thus contrasts markedly with that of Thersites. But Diomedes is also similar to Thersites (and to Achilles, whom Thersites resembles) in ways, for he also speaks in strenuous opposition to Agamemnon, and prefaces his speech with explicit assertions that it is right to fight with foolish kings, that the assembly is the proper place in which to do this, and that kings so challenged ought not respond with anger (9.32–33).

The Flight to the Ships

A favorite in antiquity: The scene was often cited by those with aristocratic sympathies and became quite controversial among those of more democratic bent. For instance, Socrates' fondness for this passage was introduced as evidence in his trial to the effect "that he selected the very worst passages from the most respected poets, and he used these as evidence to teach his followers to be evildoers and supporters of tyranny . . ." Xenophon, *Memorabilia* 1.2.56–59.

The sceptre as a prod: When humans appear as the object of the verb *elaunō,* usually reserved for the driving of cattle and horses, such a usage carries the implication that they are being treated like animals. Cf. *Iliad* 7.158, 24.532, and esp. 4.299.

Dirt and disorder: Within book 2 alone, cf. 2.93–98, 2.142–51, 2.198.

"Kings nurtured by Zeus": This formula appears frequently in Homer (*Iliad* 1.176, 2.660, 5.463, 7.109) and once in Hesiod (*Theogony* 82). Its significance has been briefly considered by Vlachos, *Les sociétés politiques homériques,* pp. 119–20 and 124–25.

The only non-noble character: Thersites' social identity is established by five separate factors: (1) the recurrent contrast of nobles and commoners which dominates the beginning of book 2 and culminates in the encounter of Odysseus and Thersites; (2) Odysseus strikes him with the sceptre, treatment previously reserved for commoners (2.199); (3) the authorial voice calls him "most base" (*aiskhistos,* 2.216) of all the Greek army; (4) Odysseus tells him "there is no other man who is lowlier (*kherioteros*) than you among those who came with Atreides to Troy" (2.248–49); and (5) no genealogy is provided for him, something unthinkable for a noble. Of these arguments, I consider the first, second and fifth to be most important, although the fourth is often taken to be conclusive. *Kherioteros,* however, may be used with reference to qualities of person (thus 4.400, *Odyssey* 14.176, and 10.237–39), as well as those of birth (thus 1.80, 20.106, and *Odyssey* 11.621). Still, nowhere else is this term ever used in an insult made to a person's face. This highly marked usage indicates just how lowly Odysseus takes Thersites to be — on all possible grounds — and how utterly secure he feels in attacking him.

The Basest, Most Hated of Men

The etymology of his name: See, most extensively, Pierre Chantraine, "A propos de Thersite," *L'Antiquité classique* 32 (1963), pp. 18–27. Essentially, *thersos* is the Aeolian form of the Homeric *tharsos,* which denotes a boldness or daring that is positively valued when the hero in question has a deity's backing (*Iliad* 5.2, 7.153, 17.570, 21.547; *Odyssey* 1.321, 3.76, 6.140, 9.381, 14.216), but is condemned as foolhardy audacity when this is not the case (*Iliad* 21.395).

Thersites: Recent secondary literature includes Eddie R. Lowry, Jr., *Thersites: A Study in Comic Shame* (New York: Garland Publishing Co., 1991); N. Postlethwaite, "Thersites in the *Iliad*," *Greece and Rome* 35 (1988), pp. 126–33; Peter W. Rose, "Thersites and the Plural Voices of Homer," *Arethusa* 21 (1988), pp. 5–25; W. G. Thalmann, "Thersites: Comedy, Scapegoats, and Heroic Ideology in the *Iliad*," *Transactions of the American Philological Association* 118 (1988), pp. 1–28; Øivind Andersen, "Thersites und Thoas vor Troia," *Symbolae Osloenses* 57 (1982), pp. 7–34; H. D. Rankin, "Thersites the Malcontent, A Discussion," *Symbolae Osloenses* 47 (1972), pp. 36–60; and Joachim Ebert, "Die Gestalt des Thersites in der Ilias," *Philologus* 113 (1969), 159–75. See also the discussions of Gregory Nagy, *The Best of the Achaeans: Concepts of the Hero in Archaic Greek Poetry* (Baltimore: Johns Hopkins University Press, 1979), pp. 259–64; and James Redfield, "Drama and Community: Aristophanes and Some of his Rivals," in *Nothing to Do with Dionysos? Athenian Drama in its Social Context*, ed. J. J. Winkler and F. I. Zeitlin (Princeton: Princeton University Press, 1990), pp. 314–35, esp. 332–34.

This singular fellow: As a measure of just how unusual Thersites is, note that his ten-line description includes two superlatives (*aiskhistos*, 2.216; *ekhthistos*, 2.220) and seven terms unattested elsewhere in the epic (*ametroepos*, 2.212; *kalōaō*, 2.212; *akosmos*, 2.213; *aiskhistos*, 2.216; *pholkos*, 2.217; *phoxos*, 2.219; *psednē*, 2.219).

Blame poetry: On the nature and importance of blame and shame in Homeric society, see Nagy, *Best of the Achaeans*, pp. 211–75 (the passage quoted is at pp. 262–63); Arthur H. Adkins, "Threatening, Abusing and Feeling Angry in the Homeric Poems," *Journal of Hellenic Studies* 89 (1969), pp. 7–21; and James M. Redfield, *Nature and Culture in the Iliad: The Tragedy of Hector* (Chicago: University of Chicago Press, 1975), pp. 115–19.

"Most hated": The term *ekhthistos* is used three other times in the *Iliad*, and two of these occurrences run parallel to that we are considering. Thus, Agamemnon tells Achilles, "To me you are the most hated of the kings reared by Zeus" (1.176), just as Zeus tells Ares, "To me you are the most hated of the gods who dwell on Olympus" (5.890). Here, as in Achilles' and Odysseus's attitude toward Thersites, superiors regard a subaltern who is given to insubordination and disruptive violence (whether of speech or of action) as "most hateful." These passages complement one another to produce the following distribution:

Most hated among	By
Ares gods	Zeus, the paramount god
Achilles kings	Agamemnon, the paramount king
Thersites men	Achilles and Odysseus, the paramount heroes

It is also said that Hades is the most hated of gods to men (9.159), but this is a markedly different situation, insofar as it involves the judgment passed on a superior by his subordinates, rather than vice versa. Accordingly, an entirely different set of values is called into play, in which lack of forgiveness replaces insubordination as the cardinal offense.

The Taming of the Scold

Comparison of Thersites' speech and that of Achilles: The quotation is from Francis Cairns, "Cleon and Pericles: A Suggestion," *Journal of Hellenic Studies* 102 (1982), p. 203, slightly modified.

Just a short while earlier: The difference is actually two weeks, as consideration of *Iliad* 1.425 and 1.493 makes clear.

"Had he been Diomedes . . .": The opinion is that of Quintilian 11.1.37.

"Looking darkly": James P. Holoka, "'Looking Darkly' (ὑπόδρα ἰδών): Reflections on Status and Decorum in Homer," *Transactions of the American Philological Association* 113 (1983), pp. 1–16. The passages quoted are at p. 16.

"To speak in assembly": The verb *agoreuein* is used at 2.250 and 2.256, the adverbial form *agorēthen* at 2.264. Also significant is the way in which the crowd's approval for Odysseus's action is voiced at 2.274–75: "the greatest deed he has accomplished among the Argives is keeping this outrageous hurler of words *out of the assembly*" (*eskh' agoraōn*).

The Sweetness of Laughter

Laughter: Redfield, *Nature and Culture in the Iliad,* pp. 261–62. Note also G. S. Kirk's observation that "misfortune and undignified appearance are the two things that normally seem to cause heroic — and divine — amusement in the *Iliad*" in *The Iliad: A Commentary* (Cambridge: Cambridge University Press, 1985) 1:144. Cf. the remarks of Robert Darnton, *The Great Cat Massacre* (New York: Basic

Books, 1984), pp. 77–78 regarding the significance of situations which are regarded as funny by members of societies from which we are temporally or spatially removed, but which "strike the modern reader as unfunny, if not downright repulsive."

Walking stick: The emblem of royal authority here appears in disguise, just as Odysseus, the rightful king, is himself disguised as a beggar. The sceptre cum walking stick thus reveals to the audience what is hidden from Irus and the suitors: It is a king who acts and speaks in this episode. Further, it is subtly established that the words with which Odysseus dismisses Irus carry full and proper authority, just as do those he addresses to Thersites before striking him with the sceptre.

Public degradation: We should also note that in two of the five cases of "sweet" laughter, the threat of sexual violence and consequent humiliation also appears. For not only does Odysseus threaten to strip Thersites naked and expose his genitals (2.262), but one of the suitors tells Irus that if he loses his fight:

> "I will throw you into a black ship and send you to the mainland,
> To King Echetus, the bane of all mortals,
> Who will cut off your nose and ears with merciless bronze,
> And having pulled off your testicles, he will give them to the dogs to eat
>   raw."
>
> (*Odyssey* 18.83–87)

Honor: I here make use of the formulations offered by Michael Herzfeld, *The Poetics of Manhood: Contest and Identity in a Cretan Mountain Village* (Princeton: Princeton University Press, 1985). See also the essays in J. B. Peristiany, ed., *Honour and Shame: The Values of Mediterranean Society* (Chicago: University of Chicago Press, 1966).

The Halt and the Lame

Limping as cause of laughter: Scholium A to *Iliad* 2.217 states that it is his limp which made Thersites laughable, while Scholium bT to 2.212 compares him to Hephaestus, with explicit reference to *Iliad* 1.599–600. These texts are found in Hartmut Erbse, ed., *Scholia Graeca in Homeri Iliadem (Scholia Vetera),* 7 vols. (Berlin: Walter de Gruyter, 1969–88) 2:230 and 2.228, respectively.

Hephaestus: For differing accounts of the fall which made him lame, see *Iliad* 15.18–24, 18.395–97, *Odyssey* 8.311–12, and the discussion of Marie Delcourt, *Héphaistos ou la légende du magicien* (Paris: Société "Les Belles Lettres," 1957), pp. 115–16. Delcourt also treats the common association of lameness with artisans and those of the lower social orders in pp. 121–122, on which see also my treatment in *Death, War, and Sacrifice: Studies in Ideology and Practice* (Chicago:

University of Chicago Press, 1991), pp. 244–58, esp. 247–48 and the literature cited therein.

Hephaestus, Aphrodite, and Ares: As is well known, Hephaestus wrought revenge on his faithless wife and her sure-footed lover by entrapping them and putting them on public display while they were making love, at which point the divine company broke once more into "unquenchable" laughter, as much at the cuckolded husband as the discomfitted couple (*Odyssey* 8.326 and 8.343).

Silenced Speakers and Erased Traditions

Death of Thersites: The fragment from Arctinus is found in Albertus Bernabé, *Poetarum Epicorum Graecorum: Testimonia et Fragmenta*, Part I (Leipzig: B. G. Teubner, 1987), pp. 67–68. A play on the same theme, entitled "Achilles, the Killer of Thersites," is attributed to Chaeremon. Proclus's and Eustathius's summaries of that work are available in August Nauck, *Tragicorum Graecorum Fragmenta*, 2d ed. (Göttingen: Vandenhoeck & Ruprecht, 1985), 1:217–18. Other sources include Lycophron, *Alexandra* 999–1000 and scholia, Quintus of Smyrna 1.722–81, and Apollodorus, *Epitome* 5.1.

Thersites' birth and early exploits: The scholium citing Pherecydes appears in Erbse, 1:228. Other sources that preserve these stories are treated in Gebhard's article on Thersites in the *Pauly-Wissowa Realencyclopadie der classischen Altertumswissenschaft* (Munich: A. Druckenmüller, 1980), Vol. V/A, cols. 2455–71, esp. 2460–61.

"Experts have debated . . .": Those who view later sources as filling in Homeric lacunae include Gebhard, pp. 2458–60, and Andersen, "Thersites und Thoas vor Troia." Those who view them as preserving traditions omitted from the *Iliad* include W. Kullmann, "Die Probe des Achaierheeres in der Ilias," *Museum Helveticum* 12 (1955), pp. 254–73, esp. 270–71; *Idem, Die Quellen der Ilias* (Wiesbaden: Hermes Einzelschriften, 1960), pp. 102–3, 146–48, 225, 303–6; Ebert, "Die Gestalt des Thersites"; and H. D. Rankin, "Thersites the Malcontent." Chantraine, "A propos de Thersite," takes an inconclusive position.

A person bereft of social standing: On the importance of patrilineal descent for establishing social identity and status, see Finley, *World of Odysseus,* pp. 77–78. The dread of having no known patrilineal ancestry—that is, of belonging to "a lineage without name" (*geneēn . . . nōnymnon*)—is voiced at *Odyssey* 1.222.

"Odysseus struck only plebeians": Quoted from the scholium that appears in Erbse, 1:228.

Odysseus's Weapon and the Legitimacy of Kings

The sceptre: For the fullest discussions of the sceptre, see P. E. Easterling, "Agamemnon's *skēptron* in the *Iliad*," in *Images of Authority: Papers presented to Joyce Reynolds,* ed. Mary MacKenzie and Charlotte Roneché (Cambridge: Cambridge Philological Society, 1989), pp. 104–21; Robert Mondi, "Σκηπτοῦχοι βασιλῆες: An Argument for Divine Kingship in Early Greece," *Arethusa* 13 (1980), 203–16; and J. L. Melena, "En torno al σκῆπτρου homérico," *Cuadernos de Filología Classica* 3 (1972), 321–56

Gold: The sceptre is said to be golden at *Iliad* 2.268, although the description of 1.234–37 and 1.245–46 makes clear that it is a wooden branch studded with golden nails. That it is called "undecaying" (*aphthitos,* 2.46) is also significant, for when used of material objects, this adjective almost invariably refers to items made of gold (a metal not subject to rust) by Hephaestus for the gods (cf. 5.724, 13.22, 14.238, and 18.370). Given that the sceptre is, essentially, a gold-covered club, it is tempting to see in this image a line of indigenous analysis and criticism that shows authority ultimately to rest on force beneath the divine mystifications in which it cloaks itself.

Pelops: He is named as Zeus's son by Calyce, daughter of King Aethlios of Elis, in Scholium T to *Iliad* 2.104b.

The passage is a subtle one: A further distinction is made between those kings who rule by right of inheritance (Pelops, Atreus) and those who took power from their predecessors by force or guile (Thyestes, Agamemnon), different verbs being used to describe the way they came to possess the sceptre.

With sceptres in hand: *Iliad* 2.206, in which the sceptre is associated with law and with speech in assembly, is formulaic, being repeated at 9.99. Those who pass judgments elsewhere appear with sceptres in hand (*Iliad* 9.156=9.298, 18.505–6, *Odyssey* 11.569), as do those who speak in assembly and other privileged spheres (*Iliad* 1.234, 3.218, 7.412, 23.568; *Odyssey* 2.37). That judgments were regularly pronounced within the assembly-place is suggested by *Iliad* 11.806–8, 16.387–88, 18.497–508, and *Odyssey* 12.439–41.

CHAPTER THREE

Power and Authority in the Making of Kings

Roman kingship: The best study to date is Paul M. Martin, *L'idée de royauté à Rome: De la Rome royale au consensus républicain* (Clermont-Ferrand, France: Adosa, 1982). Also useful, but dated (and tendentious) in certain respects is Ugo Coli, *Regnum* (Rome: Apollinaris, 1951).

The crisis of the first century B.C.: The standard work on the period is Sir Ronald Syme, *The Roman Revolution* (London: Oxford University Press, 1960). Also useful are Mary Beard and Michael Crawford, *Rome in the Late Republic* (Ithaca, N.Y.: Cornell University Press, 1985); E. S. Gruen, *The Last Generation of the Roman Republic* (Berkeley and Los Angeles: University of California Press, 1974); R. Seager, ed., *The Crisis of the Roman Republic* (Cambridge: Cambridge University Press, 1969); and a host of more specialized studies.

Structure of the conjuncture: The term and concept are taken from Marshall Sahlins, *Islands of History* (Chicago: University of Chicago Press, 1985).

Selection of the ancient Roman kings: The fullest treatment is Martin, *L'idée de royauté à Rome,* pp. 41–73, which is preferable to Coli, *Regnum,* pp. 79–98, where the selection of a king is treated as a divine, and not a human process, and accordingly the importance of augury is emphasized to the exclusion of all else, notwithstanding the fact that Livy mentions election by people and Senate for all of the post-Romulan kings and augury for one only (Numa, 1.18.6–10).

Power of the people and authority of the Senate: This contrast is explicitly drawn in Livy's account of the first royal election (1.17.8–9) and in Cicero *Laws* 3.28.

Popular assembly or acclamation: Acclamation is attested for the election of Numitor (Livy 1.6.2) and Romulus (1.7.1), but in no other cases is acclamation by the people mentioned (unless one takes note of the fact that Servius [1.47.3] and Tarquin the Proud [1.48.5] were hailed as king by their wives). In discussing the selection of Numa, Livy makes mention of a popular vote (*suffragium,* 1.17.9), but this may be an anachronism, since he makes an explicit comparison to the votes taken in the comitial assembly in his day. Uncertain also is the question of whether all senators were eligible to participate in the selection of a king, or only those of patrician families. On this, see André Magdelain, "De l'auctoritas patrum à l'auctoritas senatus," in *Jus Imperium Auctoritas: Études de droit romain* (Rome: École Française de Rome, 1990), pp. 385–403.

Ratification by the Senate: Cicero *Laws* 3.27–28, specifies that the authority of the Senate consisted above all in its capacity to turn proposals into laws by making them *ratus,* i.e., by ratifying them. Significantly, *ratus* is a term that was used in mathematic, scientific, and legal discourses to designate something that had been definitively fixed through proper reasoning (*ratiō,* from the same root as *ratus*): "laws" of celestial motion, for instance, as well as senatorial decrees or legal decisions. As a result, anything that a qualified—i.e., authorized and authorizing—person or group pronounced to be *ratus* was thereafter accepted as absolutely valid and utterly binding. See further Albert Yon, *Ratiō et les mots de la famille de reor: Contribution à l'étude historique du vocabulaire latin* (Paris: H. Champion, 1933).

"Power should be in the people . . .": Cicero *Laws* 3.28: "*potestas in populo, auctoritas in senatu sit.*"

Etymology of *auctoritas:* For detailed linguistic discussions of the derivation and significance of *auctoritas,* see R. Heinze, "Auctoritas," *Hermes* (1925), pp. 348–66 and Émile Benveniste, *Vocabulaire des institutions indo-européennes* (Paris: Editions de Minuit, 1969), 2: 148–51.

Voice of consequentiality: Senatorial ratification augmented the status of any proposal by imbuing it with the Senate's *auctoritas.* Technically, such ratification transformed a proposal into a resolution (a *Senatusconsultum*) through which the Senate gave its authoritative counsel—something which was considerably more than advice, but still rather less than a command—to the relevant magistrates. A vote of the Senate did not establish law, however, for it was only when the magistrates (who, in their official capacity, held *imperium,* the right of command, as well as *auctoritas*) took action upon this counsel that it acquired the full and compelling force of law. See the classic discussion of Theodor Mommsen, *Römisches Staatsrecht,* Vol. 3 (Basel: Julius Schwabe, 1952), pp. 1033–34, conveniently summarized in E. D. Watt, *Authority,* pp. 12–13.

Attempts at Prompting the Voice of the People

Caesar and the kingship: For convenient reviews of the large and ever-growing literature, see Dietrich Felber, "Caesars Streben nach der Königswürde," in *Untersuchungen zur römischen Geschichte,* Band I, ed. Franz Altheim (Frankfurt am Main: Vittorio Klostermann, 1961), pp. 259–73; and Zwi Yavetz, *Julius Caesar and his Public Image* (Ithaca, N.Y.: Cornell University Press, 1983), pp. 10–57. For a variety of opinions regarding Caesar's desires and maneuvers, see Andreas Alföldi, *Caesar in 44 v. Chr.: I. Studien zu Caesars Monarchie und ihren Wurzeln* (Bonn: Rudolf Habelt, 1985); Idem, *Caesariana: Gesammelte Aufsätze zur Geschichte Caesars und seiner Zeit* (Bonn: Rudolf Habelt, 1984); Christian Meier, *Caesar* (Berlin: Severin und Siedler, 1982), esp. pp. 564–68; Stefan Weinstock, *Divus Julius* (Oxford: Clarendon

Press, 1971); Matthias Gelzer, *Caesar: Politician and Statesman,* trans. Peter Needham (Oxford: Basil Blackwell, 1968), esp. pp. 317–18.

The wreathed statues: Dio Cassius 44.9.2–3 maintains that Caesar's enemies planted the diadems; Appian *Civil War* 2.108 is slightly more ambiguous, saying it was someone who wanted to spread talk of Caesar's wish to become king; Nicolaus of Damascus *Life of Augustus* 20.4–10 takes no position himself, but has Caesar accuse the tribunes of the deed; Suetonius *The Deified Julius* 79.1, attributes it to "someone from the crowd"; and Plutarch *Caesar* 61.8, *Antony* 12.4 leaves responsibility entirely unclear. The sources also differ on whether this incident preceded, followed, or was concurrent with Caesar's return from the Alban Mount on 26 January. The fullest study of this incident is Hans Kloft, "Caesar und die Amtentsetzung der Volkstribunen im Jahre 44 v. Chr.," *Historia* 29 (1980), pp. 315–34. On the significance of the diadem, see Alföldi, *Caesar in 44 v. Chr.,* pp. 105–60; Hans W. Ritter, *Diadem und Königsherrschaft* (Munich: C. H. Beck, 1965); and Weinstock, *Divus Julius,* pp. 148–52, 319–20, and 333–36.

"A symbol of slavery": The quotations come from Nicolaus of Damascus *Life of Augustus* 20.5.

Feriae Latinae: For descriptions of the ritual, see H. H. Scullard, *Festivals and Ceremonies of the Roman Republic* (Ithaca, N.Y.: Cornell University Press, 1981), pp. 111–15; Pierangelo Catalano, *Linee del sistema sovrannazionale romano* (Turin: G. Giappichelli, 1965), pp. 168–73; and F. Münzer, "Feriae Latinae," in *Realenzyklopaedie der klassisches Altertumswissenschaft,* vol. 6/2, ed. Pauly and Wissowa, pp. 2213–16. Caesar presided over celebration of the Feriae Latinae on three different occasions: 59 B.C. (in his capacity as consul), 49 B.C. (as dictator), and 44 B.C., a year in which he was consul and dictator, and conceivably would-be king.

Red sandals: The quotation is taken from Dio Cassius 43.43.2, who also specifies that Caesar adopted this footgear sometime during the year of 45 B.C.

Entry on horseback: The Senate granted special permission for such an entry, according to Dio Cassius 44.4.3. This episode has often been compared to Jesus's entry into Jerusalem on the back of a colt (or ass) which, according to the Biblical sources, plainly involved a claim of royal status. See *Matthew* 21.5, *John* 12.13–15 (both of which make reference to *Zechariah* 9.9), and *Luke* 19.38.

The *ovatio* and the people's response: The text cited is Plutarch *Caesar* 60.2, and the incident is similarly described in Dio Cassius 44.10.1; Appian *Civil War* 2.108; Suetonius *The Deified Julius* 79.1;

Nicolaus of Damascus *Life of Augustus* 20.9–10. See further the discussion of Weinstock, *Divus Julius,* pp. 320–25.

The Marcii Reges: Caesar claimed descent from this royal lineage at the time of his debut into political life. See Suetonius *The Deified Julius* 6.1 and my discussion in "La politica di mito e rito nel funerale di Giulia: Cesare debutta nella sua carriera," in *La cultura in Cesare,* ed. Diego Poli (Rome: Il Calamo, 1993), pp. 387–96.

Ouster of the tribunes: The sources differ as to whether Caesar had the tribunes removed at this time or after the episode of the wreathed statues. Suetonius *The Deified Julius* 79.1 conflates the two episodes.

Purple robes and golden throne: Descriptions are found in Cicero *Philippic* 2.85; Dio Cassius 44.11.2; and Nicolaus of Damascus *Life of Augustus* 21.4; cf. Livy 1.8.3. The granting of these honors is described by Dio Cassius 44.6.1, Appian *Civil War* 2.106, and Suetonius *The Deified Julius* 76.1, the last of whom lists them at the head of those honors he judged to be "greater than human rank." Dio 44.7.2–3 and Plutarch *Caesar* 57.2–3 take them to have been offered disingenuously by senators who sought to render Caesar hateful.

Lupercalia: Within a rich secondary literature, the following are particularly useful: Robert Schilling, "Romulus l'élu et Remus le reprouvé," *Revue des études latines* 38 (1960), pp. 182–99; Giulia Piccaluga, "L'aspetto antagonistico dei Lupercalia," *Studi e Materiali di Storia delle Religioni* 33 (1962), pp. 51–62; Angelo Brelich, *Tre variazioni romane sul tema delle origini,* 2d ed. (Rome: Edizioni dell' Ateneo, 1976), pp. 72–82, 119–22; Marinella Corsano, "'Sodalitas' et gentilité dans l'ensemble lupercal," *Revue de l'histoire des religions* 191 (1977), pp. 137–58; and Dominique Briquel, "Trois études sur Romulus," in *Recherches sur les religions de l'antiquité classique,* ed. Raymond Bloch (Paris: Librairie H. Champion, 1980), pp. 267–346, esp. 267–300. Less useful is the German literature, which includes Christoph Ulf, *Das römische Lupercalienfest: Ein Modellfall für Methodenprobleme in der Altertumswissenschaft* (Darmstadt: Wissenschaftliche Buchgesellschaft, 1982) and Walter Pötscher, "Die Lupercalia — Eine Strukturanalyse," *Grazer Beiträge* 11 (1984), pp. 221–49.

Luperci Julii: The founding of this troop is noted by Dio Cassius 44.6.2 and Suetonius *The Deified Julius* 76.1, the latter of whom groups it among the honors "greater than human rank." Antony appears as its leader at Dio Cassius 45.30.2 and Nicolaus of Damascus *Life of Augustus* 21.4. After 43 B.C. celebration of the Lupercalia was discontinued, and when it resumed under Augustus, the Luperci Julii had disappeared, never to return.

A new Romulus: For Caesar's attempts to associate himself with Rome's first king, see Weinstock, *Divus Julius,* pp. 175–84; Walter Burkert, "Caesar und Romulus-Quirinus," *Historia* 11 (1962), pp. 356–76; and Andreas Alföldi, "Die Geburt der kaiserlichen Bildsymbolik: Kleine Beiträge zu ihrer Entstehungsgeschichte," *Museum Helveticum* 8 (1951), pp. 190–215.

"On the Lupercal": The lines quoted are from Antony's funeral oration, *Julius Caesar* Act III, Scene ii.

"By order of the people": Cicero *Philippic* 2.87 records the official statement which Antony and Caesar, the co-consuls for the year, had inserted in the public *Fasti:* "At the Lupercalia, Marc Antony, consul, offered the kingship to Caesar, dictator for life, by order of the people; Caesar was unwilling." Cf. Dio Cassius 44.11.3.

The people's reaction: The passages cited are Cicero *Philippic* 2.85; Plutarch *Antony* 12.3; and Appian *Civil War* 2.109. The scene of the Lupercalia is most fully described in Cicero *Philippic* 2.85–87 and 3.12; Appian *Civil War* 2.109; Plutarch *Caesar* 61.3–5 and *Antony* 12.1–4; Dio Cassius 44.11.1–3. The accounts of Suetonius *The Deified Julius* 79.2; Livy *Periochae* 116; and Velleius Paterculus 2.56.4 are extremely brief, while that of Nicolaus of Damascus *Life of Augustus* 21.1–11 deviates significantly and tendentiously from all the others. Among an extensive secondary literature, see Weinstock, *Divus Julius,* pp. 331–40; Ernst Hohl, "Das Angebot des Diadems an Cäsar," *Klio* 34 (1941), pp. 92–117; Ugo Bianchi, "Cesare e i Lupercali del 44 A.C.," *Studi Romani* 6 (1958), pp. 253–59; Karl-Wilhelm Welwei, "Das Angebot des Diadems an Caesar und das Luperkalienproblem," *Historia* 16 (1967), pp. 44–69; Konrad Kraft, *Der goldene Kranz Caesars und der Kampf um die Entlarvung des "Tyrannen"* (Darmstadt: Wissenschaftliche Buchgesellschaft, 1969); and A. Fraschetti, "Cesare e Antonio ai Lupercalia," in *Soprannaturale e potere nel mondo antico e nelle società tradizionali,* eds. F. M. Fales and C. Grottanelli (Milan: Franco Angeli, 1985), pp. 165–86.

Strategic Maneuvers: Military and Political

The Parthian campaign: Descriptions of the military preparations and the question of Caesar's kingship are found in Appian *Civil War* 2.110. Dio Cassius 43.51.1–2 also gives information on the relevant military matters and describes the political appointments made in anticipation of the campaign at 43.51.3–9 (cf. 44.1.1). Also significant is a letter that Cicero wrote in May 45 B.C., stating that Caesar had decided against embarking on a Parthian campaign for the moment, and would wait until things had been settled in Rome (*Letters to Atticus* 13.31). See further William C. McDermott, "Caesar's Projected

Dacian-Parthian Expedition," *Ancient Society* 13–14 (1982–83), pp. 223–31; and Jürgen Malitz, "Caesars Partherkrieg," *Historia* 33 (1984), pp. 21–59.

The Ides of March and senatorial consideration of military matters: See Marianne Bonnefond-Coudry, *Le Sénat de la république romaine de la guerre d'Hannibal à Auguste: Pratiques délibératives et prise de décision* (Rome: École Française de Rome, 1989), pp. 262–68.

Curia of Pompey: No special place was established for meetings of the Roman Senate, nor were there any special dates, in recognition of the fact that the Senate's authority permeated all time and space (thus Bonnefond-Coudry). Still, it was very unusual for a meeting to be held in this particular building, which was completed in 55 B.C. and had only once before served this purpose. Several theories have been advanced for why Caesar chose this site, none of them fully convincing.

The rumor of Cotta's prophecy: This rumor is reported in Suetonius *The Deified Julius* 79.3; Dio Cassius 44.15.3–4; Plutarch *Caesar* 60.1; Appian *Civil War* 2.110; and Cicero *On Divination* 2.110. It has been discussed by Felber, "Caesars Streben nach der Königswürde," pp. 254–58; Weinstock, *Divus Julius,* pp. 340–41; J. Gagé, *Apollon romain* (Paris: E. de Boccard, 1955), pp. 471–73; and Nicholas Horsfall, "The Ides of March: Some New Problems," *Greece and Rome* 21 (1974), pp. 191–99.

Enlisting the Voice of the Gods

Voice of the gods: For descriptions of the divine *afflatus* — the dramatic process through which a deity took possession of a sibyl's body and spoke through her mouth, see Vergil *Aeneid* 6.47–51 and 77–80; Lucan *Pharsalia* 5.169–224; and Seneca *Agamemnon* 710 ff.

Sibyls and Sibylline books: See Jacqueline Champeaux, "Les oracles de l'Italie antique: hellénisme et italicité," *Kernos* 3 (1990), pp. 103–11; H. W. Parke, *Sibyls and Sibylline Prophecy in Classical Antiquity* (London: Routledge, 1988); Raymond Bloch, "L'origine des livres sibyllins à Rome," *Neue Beiträge zur Geschichte der alten Welt* 11 (1965), pp. 281–92; and Henri Jeanmaire, *La sibylle et le retour de l'âge d'or* (Paris: E. Leroux, 1939).

Exploitation of prophecy: On these attempts, see Plutarch *Cicero* 17.4; Sallust *Catiline* 47.2; and Cicero *Regarding Catiline* 3.9 and 11.

Quindecemviri: The relation of these priests to the Sibylline books and to the Senate are described in Cicero *Laws* 2.20 and 2.30. Note also *On Divination* 1.4 and 2.112: the latter passage makes reference to the events treated in this chapter. See further, Gunter Wesener, "Quindecemviri" in *Realenzyklopaedie der klassisches Altertumswis-*

senschaft, vol. 24, ed. Pauly and Wissowa, pp. 1114–48; and Parke, *Sibyls and Sibylline Prophecy,* pp. 136–51.

Prophecy: For the best recent discussions, see Edwin A. Ardener, *The Voice of Prophecy and Other Essays* (New York: Blackwell, 1989), and Marilyn Waldman and Robert Baum, "Innovation as Renovation: The 'Prophet' as Agent of Change," in *Innovation in Religious Traditions,* ed. Michael Williams et al. (Berlin: De Gruyter, 1992). Within the older literature, see, inter alia, E. E. Evans-Pritchard, *Nuer Religion* (Oxford: Clarendon Press, 1956), pp. 287–310; Johannes Lindblom, *Prophecy in Ancient Israel* (Philadelphia: Muhlenburg Press, 1962); Max Weber, *The Sociology of Religion* (Boston: Beacon Press, 1963), pp. 46–59; James Mooney, *The Ghost-Dance Religion and the Sioux Outbreak of 1890,* ed. Anthony F. C. Wallace (Chicago: University of Chicago Press, 1965); Peter Worsley, *The Trumpet Shall Sound,* 2d ed. (New York: Schocken Books, 1968); Thomas Overholt, "The Ghost Dance of 1890 and the Nature of the Prophetic Process," *Ethnohistory* 21 (1974), pp. 37–63; Hélène Clastres, *La terre sans mal* (Paris: Editions du Seuil, 1975); Robert Wilson, *Prophecy and Society in Ancient Israel* (Philadelphia: Fortress Press, 1980); David Aune, *Prophecy in Early Christianity and the Ancient Mediterranean World* (Grand Rapids, Mich.: Eerdmans, 1983); Morris Silver, *Prophets and Markets: The Political Economy of Ancient Israel* (Boston: Kluwer-Nijhoff, 1983); I. M. Lewis, *Ecstatic Religion: A Study of Shamanism and Spirit Possession,* 2d ed. (London: Routledge, 1988).

The Sixteenth Quindecemvir and the Asian King

Cotta as Quindecemvir: For a summary of Cotta's career, see T. Robert S. Broughton, *The Magistrates of the Roman Republic,* 3 vols. (New York: American Philological Association, 1951–86), 2:536. What is known regarding the membership of the Quindecemviri in 44 B.C. is given in G. J. Szemler, *The Priests of the Roman Republic* (Brussels: Collection Latomus, 1972), p. 166.

Expansion of the Quindecemviri: Dio Cassius 43.51.9 (cf. 42.51.4). In packing this priestly body, Caesar was only following the lead of others, for it began with just two members, was increased to ten at an early date and then to fifteen under Sulla, with appropriate changes of name along the way (see Servius's commentary on *Aeneid* 6.73). Caesar's habit of conferring priestly office upon his relatives is mentioned by Dio Cassius 44.39.2, and his practice of placing his appointees under personal obligation to him is similarly noted in Suetonius *The Deified Julius* 23.2.

Caesar's relation to the Aurelii Cottae: The fullest discussion is the extremely useful Ph.D. dissertation of Stephen Halpern, *Caesar and the Aurelii Cottae* (Philadelphia: University of Pennsylvania, Dept. of Ancient History, 1964). Regrettably, the sole passage that makes direct reference to the relation of Caesar's mother, Aurelia, to the three brothers of similar name does so in terms sufficiently ambiguous to obscure the precise nature of that relation (Suetonius *The Deified Julius* 1.2). As a result, Friedrich Münzer, *Römische Adelsparteien und Adelsfamilien* (Stuttgart: Metzler, 1920), pp. 324 ff., concluded that the Aurelii Cottae were Caesar's first cousins once removed (as shown in the diagram below) rather than his maternal uncles. More convincing is the argument for the latter relation, as advanced by Halpern, pp. 18–22. What can be said with certainty is that the attitude of the three brothers toward Caesar, as manifested in the interventions they repeatedly made on his behalf, were avuncular in the most meaningful sense of the term, whatever their literal relation might have been. Regarding the support the Aurelii Cottae gave Caesar, see Halpern, *Caesar and the Aurelii Cottae*, pp. 40–106, and for a somewhat different view, Jean-Louis Ferrary, "A Roman Non-entity: Aurelius Cotta, tribun de la plèbe en 49 av. J.-C.," in *L'Italie préromaine et la Rome républicaine: Mélanges offerts à Jacques Heurgons* (Rome: Collection de l'école française de Rome, 1976), pp. 285–92.

Father's brother and mother's brother: See the excellent discussion of Maurizio Bettini, *Anthropology and Roman Culture: Kinship, Time, Images of the Soul,* trans. John van Sickle (Baltimore: Johns Hopkins University Press, 1991), pp. 14–66.

"A king out of Asia": On this theme, see G. Amiotti, "Gli oracoli sibillini e il motivo del re d'Asia nella lotta contro Roma," *Contributi dell' Istituto di Storia antica dell' Università del Sacro Cuore (Milano)* 8 (1982), pp. 18–26; Samuel K. Eddy, *The King Is Dead: Studies in the Near Eastern Resistance to Hellenism:* (Lincoln: University of Nebraska

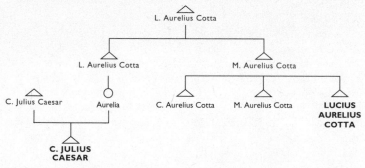

The relations of Caesar and the Aurelii Cottae, as understood by Friedrich Münzer. Cf. figure 3.3 above.

Press, 1961); Harald Fuchs, *Der geistige Widerstand gegen Rom in der antiken Welt* (Berlin: Walter de Gruyter, 1938); H. Windisch, "Die Orakel des Hystaspes," *Verhandelingen der koninklijke Akademie van Wetenschappen te Amsterdam,* Afdeeling Letterkunde, Nieuwe Reeks 28/3 (1929). On the political significance of Jewish and early Christian messianic prophecies and expectations, see Richard A. Horsley and John S. Hanson, *Bandits, Prophets, and Messiahs: Popular Movements at the Time of Jesus* (San Francisco: Harper & Row, 1985).

Prophecies and Rumors

A widespread rumor: All of the primary sources use the term rumor (Lt. *fama,* Gk. *logos*), and most of them discreetly reserve judgment as to whether it was true or false: thus Suetonius *The Deified Julius* 79.3; Dio Cassius 44.15.3–4; Plutarch *Caesar* 60.1; and Appian *Civil War* 2.110. Cicero alone asserts that the rumor was false (*On Divination* 2.110), yet he may well have done so for strategic reasons or simply to protect the reputation of his close friend Cotta (cf. Cicero *Philippic* 2.13, 14.24; *Oration on his Own House* 84; *Letters to Friends* 12.2.3). On the place of rumor in Roman politics, with direct reference to some of the events we are considering, see Zwi Yavetz, *Plebs and Princeps* (Oxford: Clarendon Press, 1969); idem, "*Existimatio, Fama,* and the Ides of March," *Harvard Studies in Classical Philology* 78 (1974), pp. 35–65; idem, *Julius Caesar and his Public Image* (Ithaca, N.Y.: Cornell University Press, 1983), esp. pp. 185–213. Also useful on this and the other means through which struggles were waged to influence popular opinion is P. A. Brunt, *The Fall of the Roman Republic* (Oxford: Clarendon Press, 1988), pp. 45–56.

Catcalls and graffiti: These are mentioned by Dio Cassius 44.12.1–3; Suetonius *The Deified Julius* 80.3; Plutarch *Caesar* 62.4; and *Brutus* 9.3.

"Cotta to silence": According to a letter that Cicero wrote in September of 44 B.C., Cotta had completely withdrawn from public life, "yielding in this to a sort of irresistible despair" (*Letters to Friends* 12.2.3).

Things Said and Unsaid

The assassination: For a thorough and highly readable account, see Paul M. Martin, *Tuer César!* (Brussels: Editions Complexe, 1988). Also useful are David F. Epstein, "Caesar's Personal Enemies on the Ides of March," *Latomus* 46 (1987), pp. 566–70; Nicholas Horsfall, "The Ides of March: Some New Problems," *Greece and Rome* 21 (1974), pp. 191–199; and J. P. V. D. Balsdon, "The Ides of March," *Historia* 7 (1958), pp. 80–94.

CHAPTER FOUR

Violence and the Voice of the Law

The Old Norse *Thing:* See the summary discussion by Reinhard Wenskus, "Ding," in *Reallexikon der germanischen Altertumskunde,* vol. 5, ed. H. Beck, H. Jankuhn, and R. Wenskus (Berlin: Walter de Gruyter, 1982), pp. 443–55. The fullest information is available for the nature and workings of the Icelandic *Thing,* on which see Kirsten Hastrup, *Culture and History in Medieval Iceland: An Anthropological Analysis of Structure and Change* (Oxford: Clarendon Press, 1985), pp. 121–30; Jesse L. Byock, *Medieval Iceland: Society, Sagas, and Power* (Berkeley and Los Angeles: University of California Press, 1988), pp. 57–71; and William Ian Miller, *Bloodtaking and Peacemaking: Feud, Law, and Society in Saga Iceland* (Chicago: University of Chicago Press, 1990), pp. 221–57. On the Norwegian *Thing,* see "Ting: Norge," in *Kulturhistoriskt lexikon för nordisk medeltid,* Vol. 18 (Malmö: Allhems förlag, 1974), pp. 346–59; Birgit and Peter Sawyer, *Medieval Scandinavia* (Minneapolis: University of Minnesota Press, 1993), pp. 80–99; and the discussion of Laurence M. Larson, trans., *The Earliest Norwegian Laws: Being the Gulathing Law and the Frostathing Law* (New York: Columbia University Press, 1935), pp. 3–31.

The Disputed Inheritance of Bjorn Brynjolfsson

Egil's Saga: The standard edition of the Icelandic text is Sigurdar Nordal, ed., *Egils saga Skalla-Grímssonar* (Reykjavik, Iceland: Islenzka Fornritafelag, 1933). As is true of all the family sagas, the work is anonymous, but most specialists now identify Snorri Sturluson (1178–1241) as its probable author. See, inter alia, M. C. van den Toorn, *Zur Verfasserfrage der Egilssaga Skallagrímssonar* (Cologne: Böhlau Verlag, 1959); Ralph Allen West, *Egil's Saga and Snorri Sturluson: A Statistical Authorship Attribution Study* (unpublished Ph.D. dissertation, University of North Carolina, Chapel Hill, Dept. of Germanic Languages, 1974); *Idem,* "Snorri Sturluson and Egil's Saga: Statistics of Style," *Scandinavian Studies* 52 (1980), 163–93.

Inheritance law: The laws cited here reflect very ancient Scandinavian patterns, as is reflected in the parallel specifications found in the *Frostathing Law* 8.1–2, *Konungsbók* sec. 118, and *Stadarhólsbók* sec. 56. For the best discussion of the way in which categories of kinship gave structure to and found expression within inheritance law, see Torben Anders Vestergaard, "The System of Kinship in Early Norwegian Law," *Medieval Scandinavia* 12 (1988), pp. 160–93. With regard to the legal intricacies of the inheritance case in *Egil's Saga,* see Konrad Maurer, *Zwei Rechtsfälle in der Eigla* (Munich: F. Straub, 1895), pp. 92–124.

Property rights of married women: See the *Gulathing Law* sec. 52, *Frostathing Law* 11.5, and the discussions of Roberta Frank, "Marriage in Twelfth- and Thirteenth-Century Iceland," *Viator* 4 (1973), pp. 473–84; Hedda Gunneng and Birgit Strand, eds., *Kvinnans Ekonomiska Ställning under Nordisk Medeltid* (Lindome: Kompendiet, 1981); J. M. Jochens, "Consent in Marriage: Old Norse Law, Life, and Literature," *Scandinavian Studies* 58 (1986), pp. 142–76; *Idem*, "En islande médiévale: A la recherche de la famille nucléaire," *Annales ESC* (1985), 95–112.

Struggles over inheritance: These feature prominently in a great many of the Old Norse sagas and have been studied by Jesse Byock, *Feud in the Icelandic Saga* (Berkeley and Los Angeles: University of California Press, 1982), esp. pp. 143–60. On the multivalent significance of familial land, see Aaron Gurevich, "Semantics of the Medieval Community: 'Farmstead', 'Land", 'World"," in *Historical Anthropology of the Middle Ages* (Chicago: University of Chicago Press, 1992), pp. 200–209.

The Raw, the Cooked, and the Royal

Bifurcation in the lineage of Kveld-Ulf: Among those who have noted and commented on this structural pattern are Preben Meulengracht Sørensen, "Starkaðr, Loki and Egill Skallagrimsson," in *Sagas of the Icelanders*, ed. John Tucker (New York: Garland Publishing Co., 1989), pp. 146–59, esp. 154–59; Kaaren Grimstad, "The Giant as a Heroic Model: The Case of Egill and Starkadr," *Scandinavian Studies* 48 (1976), pp. 284–98, esp. pp. 284–85; and Christine Fell, trans. *Egil's saga* (Toronto: University of Toronto Press, 1975), pp. xii–xiv.

Difficulties with Harald Fairhair: These turn on an inheritance dispute in which Thorolf Kveldulfsson became entangled that is, in all its particulars, the logical inversion of the later dispute between Egil and Berg-Onund. Thus, the story's protagonist appears as the defendant in the case, not its plaintiff; half brothers are the principal claimants to the inheritance, not half sisters; the second union which the deceased contracted late in his life is contested, not the first one he made in his youth; the legally correct judgment is to define the contested union as concubinage and not marriage, etc. (*Egil's Saga*, chs. 6–22). Although they are so strongly contrasted, the two cases are identical in one crucial way, for in both the king intervenes on that side which the text judges to be wrong and the person who has staked his future on the king's favor is destroyed as a result.

The king and the law: See Fritz Kern's classic discussion of "The Limitation of the Monarch by Law" in *Kingship and Law in the Middle Ages*, trans. S. B. Chrimes (Oxford: Basil Blackwell, 1956), pp. 69–79.

Also relevant are Ernst Kantorowicz, *The King's Two Bodies* (Princeton: Princeton University Press, 1957), and Sophia Menache, "The Foundations of the Medieval Monarchy," in *Vox Dei: Communication in the Middle Ages* (New York: Oxford University Press, 1990), pp. 127–49. Similar locutions to the formula employed by Egil and Arinbjorn are found at *Fornalda Saga* 47, *Bishop's Saga* i.201, and *Erybyggja Saga* 226. It is also directly echoed at *Egil's Saga* 56.68 in Arinbjorn's statement of disappointment and outrage: "We have not obtained law." Note that Egil demands "law and justice" (*logum ok réttendum*), a pair that is broken down in Arinbjorn's request for "law" (*logum*) only, and Berg-Onund's later statement that the king and queen have promised him "right" (*rétt*) in all cases under their jurisdiction (*Egil's Saga* 56.49). There is a certain irony in this pattern of distribution, for not only is the term which Berg-Onund employs less solemn than that used by his adversaries, it can also be taken to mean no more than that he will get what is due him, as in the course of things he surely does!

In the Sacred Sphere of the Law

Law, territory, and community: See Larson, *The Earliest Norwegian Laws*, pp. 3–11; Hastrup, *Culture and History in Medieval Iceland*, pp. 205–13; and A. J. Gurevich, *Categories of Medieval Culture* (London: Routledge & Kegan Paul, 1985), pp. 153–209.

Court-circle: See the discussion of Jan de Vries, *Altgermanische Religionsgeschichte* (Berlin: Walter de Gruyter, 1957), pp. 342–43, 373–75; Klaus von See, *Altnordische Rechtswörter* (Tübingen: Max Niemeyer, 1964), pp. 129–30; Walter Baetke, *Kleine Schriften* (Weimar: Hermann Böhlaus Nachfolger, 1973), p. 31; and the discussion of the term *dóm-hringr* in Richard Cleasby and Gudbrand Vigfusson, *An Icelandic-English Dictionary* (Oxford: Clarendon Press, 1957), p. 101. Some Icelandic sources (e.g., *Eyrbyggja Saga* 10 and *Landnamabók* 98) specify that a sacrificial altar stood at the center of the *Thing*-place. With regard to the significance of the hazel, see E. Hoffman-Krayer and H. Bächtold-Stäubli, *Handwörterbuch des deutschen Aberglaubens* (Berlin: Walter de Gruyter, 1930–1931), 3:1527–30, and note that in *Egil's Saga* 52.15, hazel staffs were used to mark off another solemn arena for conflict and judgment: the battlefield on which the English King Aethelstan proposed to meet King Olaf of the Scots, with the stipulation that the victor would rule over England.

Old Norse *vé* and cognates: For philological analysis, see Hermann Güntert, *Der arische Weltkönig und Heiland* (Halle, Germany: Max Niemeyer, 1923), pp. 128–29; Walter Baetke, *Das Heilige im Germanischen* (Tübingen: J. C. B. Mohr, 1942), pp. 80–90; Idem, *Kleine*

Schriften, pp. 85–86; Jan de Vries, *Altnordisches etymologisches Wörterbuch* (Leiden: E. J. Brill, 1962), p. 648–49; Emile Benveniste, *Le vocabulaire des institutions indo-européennes* (Paris: Éditions de Minuit, 1969) 2:184–86; and Winfred P. Lehmann, *A Gothic Etymological Dictionary* (Leiden: E. J. Brill, 1986), pp. 398–99. For a more phenomenological approach to such sacred circles, see Jost Trier, "Zaun und Mannring," *Beiträge zur Geschichte der deutschen Sprache und Literatur* 66 (1942): pp. 232–64.

Inviolability: Cf. *Frostathing Law* 4.58: "In three places all men are consecrated to peace (*friðhelgir*). The three places are in church, at the *Thing,* and at banquets. There all shall be inviolable [or sacrosanct, *iamhelger*]."

The Contested Marriage of Thora Lace-Sleeve

Affinal kin-relations: Note that Bjorn and Thorir are said to have established *tengðir* with one another, this being the legal term for the relations of those connected through marriage, as in *tengða-faðir,* "father-in-law," *tengða-móðir* "mother-in-law," etc. It is thus subtly implied that Thorir had accepted the legitimacy of the marriage, as well as the various kinship ties and obligations that were established through it.

Marriage practices: These are treated in the *Gulathing Law* secs. 25, 27, 51, 54; cf. *Frostathing Law* sec. 3.22, *Konungsbók* 144. See further Maurer, *Zwei Rechtsfälle,* pp. 101–2; Hastrup, *Culture and History in Medieval Iceland,* pp. 89–97; Frank, "Marriage in Twelfth- and Thirteenth-Century Iceland"; Jochens, "Consent in Marriage"; and Peter Buchholz, "Die Ehe in germanischen, besonders altnordischen Literaturdenkmälern," in *Il matrimonio nella società altomedievale* (Spoleto, Italy: Presso della sede del Centro italiano di studi sull' alto medioevo, 1977), pp. 887–900.

Witnesses: Laurence M. Larson, "Witnesses and Oath Helpers in Old Norwegian Law," in *Anniversary Essays in Mediaeval History* (Boston: Houghton Mifflin, 1929), pp. 133–56. The passage cited appears at p. 135.

King, Queen, Knave

Alf Shipman: He is named as Gunnhild's brother at *Egil's Saga* 49.1, where he is described as large, strong, violent, and a great favorite of the king and queen.

Harald Fairhair: Harald's deeds are described in the first historical section of the *Heimskringla,* entitled *Harald Fairhair's Saga,* and in *Ágrip* 1–2. See Jan de Vries, "Harald Schönhaar in Sage und Geschichte," *Beiträge zur Geschichte der deutschen Sprache und Literatur* 66

(1942), pp. 55–117, and on the nature of the early Norwegian king-ship more broadly, see Otto Koefoed-Petersen, "La royauté dans les pays scandinaves aux époques des sagas et des Vikings," in *La mono-cratie,* 2 vols. (Brussels: Recueils de la Société Jean Bodin, 1969), 2:109–18.

Toward the Fifth Voice

"So shall the gods repay . . .": This poem and others related to it have been studied in depth by Magnus Olsen, "Egils Viser om Eirik Blodøks og Dronning Gunnhild," *Maal og Minne* (1944), pp. 180–200; and Bo Almqvist, *Norrön Niddiktning: Traditionshistoriska Studier i Versmagi* (Uppsala, Sweden: Almquist & Wiksell, 1965), pp. 89–118 (with English summary at pp. 215–21). Based on details of its metric structure, Magnus Olsen, "Om Trollruner," in *Norrøne Studier* (Oslo: H. Aschehoug, 1938), pp. 12–16, argued that this poem was a magic curse, and further, that Egil inscribed it in runes on the "staff of mock-ery" discussed below. This theory has been much debated, and for a contrary view, see W. Morgenroth, "Zahlenmagie in Runeninschrif-ten: Kritische Bemerkungen zu einigen Interpretationensmethoden," *Zeitschrift der Ernst-Moritz-Arndt Universität Greifswald* 10 (1961), pp. 279–83.

Rebellions against King Eirik: These are described at *Egil's Saga* 57.4; cf. the account given at *Harald Fairhair's Saga,* chap. 43.

The staff of mockery: Made from hazel wood, the "staff of mock-ery" (*níð-stǫng*) thus not only recalls, but in a certain sense replaces and compensates for the shattered hazel staffs of the "bonds of conse-cration." That this method of ridicule was widely practiced is estab-lished by an English legal case of the thirteenth century, kindly called to my attention by William Marvin, which establishes that such prac-tices were no mere literary convention, for it is recounted that a group of poachers who had taken three deer ". . . cut off the head of a buck and put it on a stake in the middle of a certain clearing, placing in the mouth of the aforesaid head a certain spindle; and they made the mouth gape towards the sun, in great contempt of the lord king and of his foresters" (G. J. Turner, ed., *Select Pleas of the Forest* [London: Selden Society, 1901], pp. 38–40). Two other pieces of comparative evidence are also worth citing: (a) Saxo Grammaticus 3.7, where a horse's head is placed on a staff, with the mouth similarly agape, in semblance of derisive laughter; and (b) *Vatnsdœla Saga,* chap. 34, where a mare's body is sexually impaled on a staff, to imply that the man against whom this mockery is directed has been similarly pene-trated.

Mockery and the law: See, inter alia, Almqvist, *Norrön Niddiktning;* T. L. Markey, "Nordic níðvísur: An Instance of Ritual Inversion?" *Medieval Scandinavia* 5 (1972), pp. 7–118; Preben Meulengracht Sørensen, *The Unmanly Man: Concepts of Sexual Defamation in Early Northern Society* (Odense, Denmark: Odense University Press, 1983); and Folke Ström, *Níð, ergi and Old Norse Moral Attitudes* (London: The Dorothea Coke Memorial Lecture in Northern Studies, 1974). Further literature is listed in Sørensen, pp. 92–94.

Epilogue

History of the reign of Eirik Bloodaxe: The events leading up to Eirik's accession are treated in *Harald Fairhair's Saga,* chapters 32–41 (cf. *Ágrip* 5); the events of his reign, particularly his struggles with the peoples of the Trondheim and Vík shires (which go back to earlier events recounted in chapters 33, 35, and 41) in chapters 41–43; and his overthrow by Hakon the Good in *The Saga of Hakon the Good* 1–3. The relation between the *Heimskringla* and *Egil's Saga,* the former of which was certainly and the latter probably written by Snorri Sturluson, is discussed by Melissa A. Berman, "Egil's Saga and Heimskringla," *Scandinavian Studies* 54 (1982), pp. 21–50. As a king who ruled only briefly and was overthrown by his own people, Eirik offered an easy target, while Gunnhild appears throughout Icelandic literature as a witch and a troublemaker. All things considered, it seems most likely that the author of *Egil's Saga* took an extant Norwegian tradition of polemic against Eirik and Gunnhild (probably first propagated by Eirik's half brother, rival, and successor, Hakon the Good), and transformed it into an Icelandic polemic against Norwegian kingship in general. See also Preben Meulengracht Sørensen, *Fortælling og ære* (Aarhus, Denmark: Aarhus University Press, 1992), pp. 59–62.

Society against the king: On the nature of the Icelandic Commonwealth, its stand on kingship, its valuation of law, and its relations with the Norwegian throne, see, inter alia, Hastrup, *Culture and History in Medieval Iceland,* esp. pp. 7–13, 205–37; Byock, *Medieval Iceland,* esp. pp. 51–76; and Richard Tomasson, *Iceland: The First New Society* (Minneapolis: University of Minnesota Press, 1980). See also the discussion of Fell, *Egil's saga,* pp. xi–xiii. For primary sources that emphasize the *landnámsmenn's* opposition to Harald Fairhair, see, e.g., *Islendingabók* chap. 1, *Egil's Saga* chaps. 4 and 25–27, *Laxdaela Saga* chap. 2, *Eyrbyggja Saga* chaps. 1–2, *Kormak's Saga* chap. 2, *Hrafnkel's Saga* chap. 1, and *Harald Fairhair's Saga,* chap. 6. Cf. the discussion of Pierre Clastres, *Society against the State: Essays in Political Anthropology* (New York: Zone Books, 1987).

CHAPTER FIVE

Challenges to Authority and Violent Ripostes

Subtle processes of intimidation: This point is already present in Alexis de Toqueville, *Democracy in America,* and has been developed with considerable power and sophistication within feminist theory. See also such varied discussions as Pierre Bourdieu, *Language and Symbolic Power* (Cambridge, Mass.: Harvard University Press, 1991); James C. Scott, *Domination and the Arts of Resistance: Hidden Transcripts* (New Haven: Yale University Press, 1990); Robin Lakoff, *Language and Women's Place* (New York: Harper Colophon, 1975); Basil Bernstein, *Class, Codes, and Control* (London: Routledge & Kegan Paul, 1971); Erving Goffman, *Interaction Ritual* (Chicago: Aldine, 1967).

The "speech" of the slain and disappeared: Compare the discussion of Allen Feldman, *Formations of Violence: The Narrative of the Body and Political Terror in Northern Ireland* (Chicago: University of Chicago Press, 1991); Page Dubois, *Torture and Truth* (New York: Routledge, 1991); Elaine Scarry, *The Body in Pain: The Making and Unmaking of the World* (New York: Oxford University Press, 1985); Jacobo Timerman, *Prisoner without a Name, Cell without a Number* (New York: Knopf, 1981).

Attack and Counterattack: Authority and its Corrosion

Their actions differed significantly: Note also that in two of the cases we have studied, a well-established elite — the Homeric kings and the Roman Senate — reacted violently against those who threatened their power (Thersites on the one hand, Caesar on the other, albeit in a very different fashion). In the third instance we are dealing with a situation in which a new group — the royal line founded by Harald Fairhair and now headed by Eirik Bloodaxe — had recently taken power by force and was in the process of consolidating its power in institutional forms. In this attempt, they faced threats from members of the fading elite (leaders of noble families, like Egil) who could make use of their access to traditional sites of authority to contest the emergent royal rule. In such moments as Egil's lawsuit, religion and tradition were mobilized against the king's power, with the result that power set out to destroy them. Thersites' initiative thus has something potentially revolutionary about it, Caesar's looks more like a coup d'état, and Egil's is an act of resistance.

"A certain fatal despair": This phrase is quoted in Cicero *Ad Familiaris* 12.2.3, a letter written in September of 44 B.C.

Corrosive discourses: There is no systematic study that covers the myriad phenomena that one could group within this category, but one might begin with Mikhail Bakhtin's classic, *Rabelais and his World* (Bloomington: Indiana University Press, 1984); Robert M. Adams, *Bad Mouth: Fugitive Papers on the Dark Side* (Berkeley and Los Angeles: University of California Press, 1977); and Jorg Bergmann, *Klatsch: Zur Socialform der diskreten Indiskretion* (Berlin: Walter de Gruyter, 1987), the last of which contains an extremely thorough bibliography. For a variety of more specialized studies, see Karen Brison, *Just Talk: Gossip, Meetings, and Power in a Papua New Guinea Village* (Berkeley and Los Angeles: University of California Press, 1992); Lindsay Watson, *Arae: The Curse Poetry of Antiquity* (Leeds, England: Cairns, 1991); Jean-Noel Kapferer, *Rumors: Uses, Interpretations, and Images* (New Brunswick, N.J.: Transaction Publishers, 1990); Bob Black and Adam Parfrey, eds., *Rants and Incendiary Tracts: Voices of Desperate Illumination, 1558 to Present* (New York: Amok Press, 1989); Geert van Gelder, *The Bad and the Ugly: Attitudes toward Invective Poetry in Classical Arabic Literature* (Leiden, The Netherlands: E. J. Brill, 1989); David Gilmore, *Aggression and Community: Paradoxes of Andalusian Culture* (New Haven: Yale University Press, 1987); Patricia Meyer Spacks, *Gossip* (Chicago: University of Chicago Press, 1986); Michael Herzfeld, *The Poetics of Manhood: Contest and Identity in a Cretan Mountain Village* (Princeton: Princeton University Press, 1985); Jeanne Favret-Saada, *Deadly Words: Witchcraft in the Bocage* (Cambridge: Cambridge University Press, 1980); John Haviland, *Gossip, Reputation, and Knowledge in Zinacantán* (Chicago: University of Chicago Press, 1977); Mary Douglas, "Jokes," in *Implicit Meanings* (London: Routledge & Kegan Paul, 1975), pp. 90–114; P. A. Lienhardt, "The Interpretation of Rumour," in *Studies in Social Anthropology: Essays in Memory of E. E. Evans-Pritchard,* ed. J. H. M. Beattie & R. G. Lienhardt (Oxford: Clarendon Press, 1975), pp. 105–31; Frederick G. Bailey, ed., *Gifts and Poison: The Politics of Reputation* (New York: Schocken Books, 1971); *Chaos* 16 (1991), special issue on blasphemy.

Not to Praise, but to Bury

Emancipatory potential: Given the early association of *auctoritas* with the ritual of mancipation, it is tempting — if overly simplistic — to suggest that corrosive discourses stand in relation to authority much as the process of emancipation relates to mancipation. Thus, if the speech of *auctoritas venditoris* has as its essence the capacity to establish proprietary control over goods and people (who are thereby defined and treated as slaves), the essence of corrosive speech is its capacity to discredit such claims, as well as those who make and profit from them, and to liberate those who had fallen under their sway.

After Caesar's assassination: The actions of the conspirators and others in the period of complex maneuvering between the assassination and the funeral are described in Appian *Civil Wars* 2.118–43; Dio Cassius 44.20.1–35.3; Plutarch *Caesar* 67, *Antony* 14.1–2; *Brutus* 18.1–20.2; Nicolaus of Damascus 26a–27. For discussion, see Pio Grattarola, *I cesariani dalle idi di marzo alla costituzione del secondo triumvirato* (Turin: Tirrenia, 1990); Ursula Ortmann, *Cicero, Brutus, und Octavian: Republikaner und Caesarianer. Ihr gegenseitiges Verhältnis im Krisenjahr 44/43 v. Chr.* (Bonn: Habelt, 1988); Erik Wistrand, *The Policy of Brutus the Tyrannicide* (Göteborg, Sweden: Kunglige Vetenskaps-och Vitterhets-Samhället, 1981); Helga Botermann, *Die Soldaten und die römische Politik in der Zeit von Caesars Tod bis zur Begründung des zweiten Triumvirats* (Munich: C. H. Beck, 1968); and D. W. Knight, "The Political Acumen of Cicero after the Death of Caesar," *Latomus* 27 (1968), pp. 157–64.

Brutus's and Cinna's speeches in the forum: The passage quoted is Plutarch *Brutus* 18.4–6. Cf. Appian *Civil War* 2.121–23.

The funeral and the oration: Descriptions are given by Appian *Civil Wars* 2.143–47; Dio Cassius 44.35.4–49.4; Suetonius *The Deified Julius* 84; Plutarch *Caesar* 68.1, *Cicero* 42.3, *Brutus* 20.3, *Antony* 14.3–4; Cicero *Philippic* 2.90–91, *Letter to Atticus* 14.10.1. Partial accounts are also found in Nicolaus of Damascus 17 and Quintilian 6.1.3.1. It is generally accepted that Appian drew much of his information on the funeral from C. Asinius Pollio's now lost history of the civil wars, a source that seems to have treated Antony in considerably more sympathetic fashion than did most later works, which were influenced by the propaganda of Octavian (later Augustus), Antony's final and most bitter rival. On the evaluation and interpretation of these sources, see Weinstock, *Divus Julius,* pp. 346–63; Andreas Alföldi, *Studien über Caesars Monarchie* (Lund, Sweden: Lund University, 1955), pp. 63–65; Emilio Gabba, *Appiano e la storia delle guerre civili* (Florence: La Nuova Italia, 1956), pp. 119–51; Wilhelm Kierdorf, *Laudatio Funebris: Interpretationen und Untersuchungen zur Entwicklung der römischen Leichenrede* (Meisenheim am Glan, Germany: Anton Hain, 1980), pp. 150–54; G. Kennedy, "Antony's Speech at Caesar's Funeral," *Quarterly Journal of Speech* 54 (1968), pp. 99–106. Alternatively, Monroe E. Deutsch, "Antony's Funeral Speech," *University of California Publications in Classical Philology* 9 (1928), pp. 127–48 has argued for the greater reliability of Suetonius's account.

Irony and subverbal cues: In Shakespeare's version of Antony's address, a similar tension exists between the denotative value of certain words and the attitude of the speaker toward these words and toward those with whom they are associated. Inevitably, this finds expression in the precise intonation and gestures with which these lines are delivered: "For Brutus is an honorable man, / So are they all, all honorable men" (*Julius Caesar,* act III, scene ii).

Displaying the toga: The text quoted is Appian *Civil Wars* 2.146. Cf. *ibid.* 2.147; Dio Cassius 44.35.4; Suetonius *The Deified Julius* 84; Plutarch *Antony* 14.4, *Brutus* 20.3, *Caesar* 58.1.

Contemporary judgments of the oration: The sources quoted are Dio Cassius 45.35.4 and Cicero *Philippic* 2.90–91. The most important guides to normal practice in eulogies are Cicero *De Oratore* 2.45–46, 3.41–48; and Polybius 6.53–54. While the latter text admits the possibility of arousing sympathy (*sympatheia* 6.53.3), appeals to pity (Greek *oiktos* or *pathos,* Latin *miseratio*) are not condoned, nor is anything even vaguely related to anger (Greek *orgē* or *deinōsis*). Most fully, see the discussion of Kierdorf, *Laudatio Funebris;* for a convenient summary of funeral practices, J. M. C. Toynbee, *Death and Burial in the Roman World* (London: Thames & Hudson, 1971), pp. 43–50.

Fire, Sword, and Invective

Antony's intentions for the body: Suetonius *The Deified Julius* 84. Burial in the Field of Mars was itself a signal honor, previously accorded only to the ancient kings, Sulla, and Julia, the wife of Marius, whom Caesar himself had buried there, thus establishing a new and highly distinguished location for the tomb of the Julian *gens.*

Caesar's cremation and the assault on the conspirators' homes: These events are described in Suetonius *The Deified Julius* 84–85; Appian 2.147–48; Dio Cassius 44.50.2–4; Plutarch *Antony* 14.4, *Brutus* 20.4, *Caesar* 58.1; Livy *Periochae* 116. In order to avoid the dangers of a funeral (which the shrewdest among them clearly foresaw), the conspirators originally intended to fling Caesar's body into the Tiber (Suetonius *The Deified Julius* 82.4; Dio Cassius 44.35.1; cf. Appian *Civil Wars* 2.135; Cicero *Letter to Atticus* 14.10.1). On the crowd's action and its importance, see B. Liou-Gille, "Funérailles *in urbe* et divinisation, les funérailles de César," in *Res Sacrae: Hommages à Henri Le Bonniec,* eds. D. Porte and J.-P. Néraudan (Brussels: Latomus, 1988), pp. 288–93; Alföldi, *Studien über Caesars Monarchie,* pp. 53–82, esp. pp. 65–70; Z. Yavetz, *Plebs and Princeps* (Oxford: Clarendon Press, 1969), pp. 63–70; and Guy Achard, "«Ratio Popularis» et funérailles," *Études classiques* 93 (1975), pp. 166–78, esp. pp. 173–75.

The fate of Helvius Cinna: Valerius Maximus 9.9.1; Suetonius *The Deified Julius* 85; Dio Cassius 44.50.4; Appian *Civil Wars* 2.147; Plutarch *Caesar* 58.2–3, *Brutus* 20.5–6; Valerius Maximus 9.9.1.

Amatius (pseudo-Marius) and the altar to Caesar: These events are described in Appian *Civil Wars* 3.2–3, 16, and 36; Dio Cassius 44.51.1, Suetonius *The Deified Julius* 85; Livy *Periochae* 116. On the significance of these events (with some disagreement as to their details), see Weinstock, *Divus Julius,* pp. 364–67; Alföldi, *Studien über Caesars Monarchie,* pp. 70–76; Yavetz, *Plebs and Princeps,* pp. 58–62, 70–74; Helga Gesche, *Die Vergottung Caesars* (Frankfurt: Michael Lassleben Kallmünz, 1968), pp. 64–67; M. Montagna Pasquinucci, "L' 'altare' del tempio del divo Giulio," *Athenaeum* 62 (1974), pp. 144–55; and Cornelia Cogrossi, "Pietà popolare e divinizzazione nel culto di Cesare del 44 a.C.," *Contributi dell' Istituto di Storia Antica* 7 (1981), pp. 141–60.

Caesar's cousin: Most have rejected Amatius's claims to descend from Marius, but the opposite view has been forcefully argued by F. J. Meijer, "Marius' Grandson," *Mnemosyne* 39 (1986), pp. 112–21. If the claims are taken as valid, one could understand why Amatius was able to establish himself as the head of the most ardent Caesarophiles, why he was able to rally a large following among the Roman populus, and why Antony treated him as a serious threat. The family relations between Caesar and Amatius would be as in the accompanying chart.

A new piece of sacred space: If the place of Caesar's cremation was thus sacralized, it is also worth noting that the time and the place of his death were correspondingly profaned, for the Senate decided never again to meet on the Ides of March, which it designated the "Day of Parricide," while the Curia of Pompey, where the assassination occurred, was burnt, walled up, and finally converted to a public lavatory (cf. Suetonius *The Deified Julius* 88.3; Appian *Civil Wars* 2.147; Dio Cassius 47.19.1).

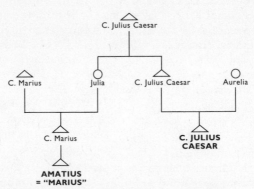

Family connections between Caesar and Amatius ("Marius").

Rich ensemble of practices: Plutarch *Brutus* 20.4 explicitly compares aspects of Caesar's tumultuous funeral to that celebrated for Clodius some eight years earlier. On the latter, see Dio Cassius 40.49.1–3; Appian *Civil Wars* 2.21; and Cicero *Pro Milone* 33 and 86. The discussion of Guy Achard, "«Ratio Popularis» et funérailles," *Études classiques* 93 (1975), pp. 166–78 is fundamental. Caesar himself was part of this tradition, for in 69 B.C., he transformed the funeral of his aunt into a highly charged demonstration on behalf of Marius, her husband, whom the senatorial oligarchy had consigned to disgrace. On these and related events, see my article, "La politica di mito e rito nel funerale di Giulia: Cesare debutta nella sua carriera," in *La cultura in Cesare,* ed. Diego Poli (Rome: Il Calamo, 1993), pp. 387–96.

Amatius's death and subsequent events: Appian *Civil Wars* 3.3; Cicero *Philippic* 1.5; Livy *Periochae* 116. Dating is based on Cicero's *Letter to Atticus* 14.8. Regarding the army as Antony's base of support, see Rita Scuderi, "Marco Antonio nell' opinione pubblica dei militari," *Scienze storiche* 17 (1978), pp. 117–37.

Crime and Punishment

Rituals of execution: For a variety of views, see the essays collected in *Du châtiment dans la cité: Supplices corporels et peine de mort dans le monde antique* (Rome: École française de Rome, 1984), esp. Jean-Michel David, "Du *Comitium* à la roche Tarpéienne. Sur certains rituels d'exécution capitale sous la République, les règnes d'Auguste et de Tibère" (pp. 131–76) and Dominique Briquel, "Formes de mise à mort dans la Rome primitive: quelques remarques sur une approche comparative du problème" (pp. 225–40).

Reactions to Amatius's execution: The fullest description is in Appian *Civil Wars* 3.3, from which the quoted phrase is taken. See also Cicero *Philippic* 1.5; Dio Cassius 44.51.1–2. Note that the victims of Antony's repression were also treated to ritual degradation: the slaves among them were crucified, and freed men were flung from the Tarpeian Rock.

The Tears of a Clown

Profound disorder: Thersites' speech is said to be *a-kosmos* ("acosmic") at *Iliad* 2.214 and *ou kata kosmon* ("not in accord with order") in the following line. The order in question may simply be that of social rectitude and propriety, but it may also be the very order of the cosmos, as is indicated when the latter phrase is used to describe the actions of those gods who would go so far as to defy Zeus's will (Cf. *Iliad* 5.759 and 8.12).

Other audiences: Throughout antiquity opinions are almost universally hostile. Change comes rather gradually, as when Shakespeare gave his thoroughly unpleasant Thersites some credit for intellect and wit, in contrast to the other, more brawny Greeks(e.g. *Troilus and Cressida,* act II, scenes i and iii), or when Lessing, while generally approving of Homer's portrayal, reacted thus to the extra-Homeric descriptions of Thersites' death at the hands of Achilles:

> The irascible and murderous Achilles becomes more hateful to me than the malicious, snarling Thersites; and I am offended by the cheers of the Greeks at this deed. My sympathies are with Diomedes, who draws his sword to avenge the murder of his kinsman, for I feel that Thersites as a human is my kinsman too. (*Laocoon,* chap. 23; trans. E. A. McCormick)

Nineteenth- and twentieth-century liberals have often adopted Thersites as a hero, following J. P. Mahaffy's depiction of him as one of "the first critics that rose up among the people and questioned the divine right of kings to do wrong" (*Social Life in Greece* (New York: Macmillan, 1898), p. 13. Others, however, have taken a different stance, as witness the attempt of some Nazi ideologists to see in him the prototype of an older, "Asiatic" population (i.e. Semitic), in contrast to the *Iliad*'s other, more Aryan heroes: thus, e.g., Hans F. K. Günther, *Rassengeschichte des hellenischen und römischen Volkes* (Munich: J. F. Lehmann, 1929), pp. 20–21. For the history of various interpretations, see Gebhard's article in the Pauly-Wissowa *Realencyklopädie der classischen Altertumswissenschaft,* vol. 5 A/2, pp. 2455–71; Abraham Feldman, "The Apotheosis of Thersites," *Classical Journal* 42 (1946–47): 219–221; H. D. Rankin, "Thersites the Malcontent: A Discussion," *Symbolae Osloenses* 47 (1972): 36–60; Peter Rose, "Thersites and the Plural Voices of Homer," *Arethusa* 21 (1988): 5–25; and Antonio La Penna, *Tersite censurato e altri studi di letteratura fra antico e moderno* (Pisa: Nistri-Lischi, 1991).

CHAPTER SIX

Queens and Lovers

"A small woman to look at, but large in her voice": *lítil kona synom en mikil rǫþom (Ágrip* 5.5).

Queenship acquired by marriage: Obviously, queens regnant are an exception, but even where a woman can inherit the throne (e.g., England, Denmark), this happens only in the absence of male heirs. The overwhelming majority of queens still acquire their royal status through marriage, and women born in a royal line remain princesses, unless they happen to marry kings.

The text has prepared us: The homonymy between the queen and Berg-Onund's wife (Gunnhild Bjornsdaughter) also serves to arouse suspicion. At the very least, it introduces a useful ambiguity, for the audience always knows that Berg-Onund is sleeping with Gunnhild, but is never quite sure which Gunnhild it is. Covert connections are established among these characters from the very outset. Thus, for reasons that are absolutely nonexistent at the surface level of the narrative, but are immediately evident to anyone familiar with the saga, Berg-Onund and the two Gunnhilds all make their first appearance in the very same chapter (chap. 37).

"To Gunnhild he was quite dear": *við Gunnhildi þó miklu kærra, Egil's Saga* 56.22. Regarding Old Norse *kærr*, "dear, beloved, intimate," see Richard Cleasby and Gudbrand Vigfusson, *An Icelandic-English Dictionary* (Oxford: Clarendon Press, 1957), p. 368.

Gunnhild as a stock character: Her role in the death of Halfdan the Black is described in *Harald Fairhair's Saga* 41; her cruelty and influence over Eirik in *Ágrip* 5.5 (cf. 7.2 and *Fagrskinna* 24); over Harald Graycloak in *Theodricus*, pp. 10–11; her seduction of various Icelanders in *Njal's Saga* 3–6, *Laxdæla Saga* 19 and 21–22. Extensive discussions of Gunnhild may be found in Sigurðar Nordal, "Gunnhildur konungamóðir," *Samtíð og Saga* 1 (1940), pp. 135–55; Magnus Olsen, "Hild Rolvsdatter vise om Gange-Rolv og Harald Hårfagre," *Maal og Minne* (1942), pp. 1–70; Halvdan Koht, "Dronning Gunnhild — motparten til Egil Skallagrimsson," *Norsk Historisk Tidsskrift* 34 (1946–48), pp. 509–17. Briefer discussions (in more accessible languages) are available in Rolf Heller, *Die literarische Darstellung der Frau in den Isländersagas* (Halle, Germany: Max Niemeyer, 1958), pp. 133–36; and Jenny M. Jochens, "The Female Inciter in the Kings' Sagas," *Arkiv for Norsk Filologi* 102 (1987), pp. 100–42, esp. pp. 116–19.

Gunnhild's marriage: These events are described in chapter 32 of *Harald Fairhair's Saga*.

The Wise Woman and the Dummy

Cicero on Cotta's prophecy: See Jerzy Linderski, "Cicero and Roman Divination," *Parola del Passato* 37 (1982), pp. 12–38 esp. pp. 37–38. The arguments for dating final revision of Cicero's text between 16 March and 22 April of 44 B.C. were first advanced by R. Durand, "La date du *De Divinatione*," in *Mélanges Boissier* (Paris: A. Fontemoing, 1903), pp. 173–83, and have been accepted by most scholars. An exception is J. Boes, "A propos du *De Divinatione*, ironie de Cicéron sur le *nomen* et l'*omen* de Brutus," *Revue des études latines* 59 (1981), pp. 164–76, who suggests a date in June of the same year.

Cicero's discretion: It is possible that Cicero withheld Cotta's name out of consideration for a man he considered a close personal friend, and to whom he was deeply indebted. Although he objected to Cotta's support for Caesar (see his *Letter to Atticus* 13.44.1), still he recalled that Cotta had secured signal honors for him in 63 B.C. and four years later had played a crucial role in bringing him back from exile. See Cicero *Letters to Friends* 12.2.3, *Philippic* 2.13, and *On his own house* 2.13. Family considerations may also have weighed heavily: Cicero held Cotta's older brother, Gaius Aurelius Cotta, in such esteem that he placed the culminating argument of his treatise *On the Nature of the Gods* in this man's mouth.

Augustus and the Sibylline texts: See Suetonius *The Deified Augustus* 31.1 (cf. Tacitus *Annals* 6.12) and the discussion of Jean Gagé, *Apollon romain* (Paris: E de Boccard, 1955), pp 542–55, or H. W. Parke, *Sibyls and Sibylline Prophecy in Classical Antiquity* (London: Routledge, 1988), p. 141, both of whom would date Augustus's intervention rather earlier than attested in the Suetonian text.

Dreams and Nightmares

Taxonomy of divination: This system is most fully articulated at *On Divination* 2.26–27, but pieces of it are spelled out elsewhere, with occasional variations in terminology (cf. 1.4, 12, 34, 109–10, 113, 127–30, and 2.42). It is also attested in Quintillian *Oratorical Institutions* 5.11.42. Recent discussions of Cicero's attitude toward divination include Linderski, "Cicero and Roman Divination"; François Guillaumont, *Philosophe et augure: Recherches sur la théorie Cicéronienne de la divination* (Brussels: Collection Latomus, 1984); Nicholas Denyer, "The Case against Divination: An Examination of Cicero's *De Divinatione*," *Proceedings of the Cambridge Philosophical Society* 31 (1985), pp. 1–10; Mary Beard, "Cicero and Divination: The Formation of a Latin Discourse," *Journal of Roman Studies* 76 (1986), pp. 33–46; and Malcolm Schofield, "Cicero for and against Divination," *Journal of Roman Studies* 76 (1986), pp. 47–65.

Complex techniques: The most extensive study of divination in Greece and Rome is still A. Bouché-Leclercq's four-volume *Histoire de la divination dans l'antiquité* (Paris: E. Leroux 1879–82). More recently, see Jean-Pierre Vernant, ed., *Divination et rationalité* (Paris: Éditions du Seuil, 1974); Friedrich Pfeffer, *Studien zur Mantik in der Philosophie der Antike* (Meisenheim am Glan, Germany: Anton Hain, 1976); and the three volumes of studies on "La divination dans le monde étrusco-italique" that were published as Supplements No. 52, 54, and 56 of *Caesarodunum* (1985–86).

Taxonomy as a logical and social system: See my discussion in *Discourse and the Construction of Society* (New York: Oxford University Press, 1991), pp. 131–41.

The sibyl's madness: Cicero *On Divination* 1.4. Cf. 2.110 and the discussion in the following chapter.

The soul in sleep: Cicero *On Divination* 1.63–64. Cf. 1.129.

Priam's household: Helenus as augur and Cassandra as sibyl are mentioned at *On Divination* 1.89.

Women as dreamers: In *On Divination,* Cicero discusses twenty-seven famous dreams, which because of their historic import are more likely to be associated with men than are ordinary dreams. Even so, the first four he mentions all belong to women, and women account for more than a quarter of the total (7/27). The women in question are Caecilia (1.4), the mother of Dionysius, tyrant of Syracuse (1.39), Rhea Silvia (1.40), Hecuba (1.42), Phalaris's mother (1.46), and two unnamed women (1.121 and 2.145).

Calpurnia's dreams: Plutarch *Caesar* 63.5–6. Cf. Appian *Civil Wars* 2.115; Dio Cassius 44.17.1; Suetonius *The Deified Julius* 81.3. The latter two sources report that Caesar also had premonitory dreams of his death and apotheosis, in which he ascended to heaven and grasped Jupiter's hand.

The meaning of these dreams: See Artemidorus *The Interpretation of Dreams* 4.30. It is also worth noting the special significance of the pediment which, by vote of the Senate, was permitted to crown Caesar's house. No other Roman dwelling possessed such adornment, which was otherwise reserved for temples and the Regia, i.e., the dwellings of gods and kings. See further, Weinstock, *Divus Julius,* pp. 280–81.

Dismissal of dreams as old-womanish: Cicero, *On Divination* 2.125. Cf. 2.129 and 2.141. A different, but no less gendered argument was offered by Epicurean philosophers, who maintained that in sleep the soul is not liberated from the body. Rather, when the body is exhausted, the (female) imagination overpowers the (male) intellect and produces the worthless visions of dreams. Thus, e.g., Plutarch *Brutus* 37.2–3.

Caesar, Calpurnia, and divinations on the morning of the Ides: Plutarch *Caesar* 63.6–7. Cf. Appian *Civil Wars* 2.115 and Dio Cassius 44.17.3, who states that in addition to extispicy, Caesar employed another "rational" form (divination by birds), with equally inauspicious results.

Decimus Brutus's intervention: Plutarch *Caesar* 64.1–3. Cf. Appian *Civil Wars* 2.115; Dio Cassius 44.18.1–2; Suetonius *The Deified Julius* 81.4.

Corrosive Discourses Again

Women and gossip: The pattern is also common in contemporary society. See, for example, A. Rysman, "How the 'Gossip' Became a Woman," *Journal of Communication* 27 (1977), pp. 176–80; V. Aebischer, "Chit-chat: Women in interaction," *Osnabrücker Beiträge zur Sprachtheorie* 9 (1979), pp. 96–108; D. Jones, "Gossip: Notes on Women's Oral Culture," in *The Voices of Women and Men,* ed. Ch. Kramarae (Oxford: Pergamon Press, 1980), pp. 193–98; B. Althans, "Halte dich fern von den klatschenden Weibern . . .": Zur Phänomenologie des Klatsches," *Feministische Studien* 2 (1985), pp. 46–53; J. Levin and A. Arluke, "An Exploratory Analysis of Sex Differences in Gossip," *Sex Roles* 12 (1985), pp. 281–86.

Rumor personified: Regarding the appearance of this goddess in Homer, see chapter 2 and the accompanying note. Hesiod uses a more condemnatory terminology than does Homer, speaking of "False Stories" (*Pseudea*), rather than Rumor (*Ossa*). He also provides her with a singularly unattractive genealogy, making her the daughter of Strife and granddaughter of Night (*Theogony* 229). Elsewhere, he treats "false stories" as an inanimate entity, and describes how Zeus placed these, along with "a treacherous nature," inside Pandora, the first and prototypical woman (*Works and Days* 78; cf. *Theogony* 27, where it is told that the Muses, being women, know how to tell false, as well as true stories). The most striking personification of Rumor, however, is that of Vergil, who tells how fear of this monster drove the noble Aeneas to abandon his love.

Rumor [*Fama*] runs swiftly through the great cities of Libya:
Rumor, who is faster than any other evil.
She thrives on her speed, and as she moves, she gathers strength.
Small at first due to fear, soon she lifts herself up to the skies.
She strides across the earth and puts her head in the clouds.
Mother Earth bore her last, as sister to Coeus and Enceladus,
Out of anger at the gods.
She is fleet of foot and swift of wing,
A huge, horrendous monster. As many feathers as she has on her body,
She has just as many watchful eyes (wondrous it is to tell!),
And just as many tongues; just as many mouths make noise, and she perks
    up just as many ears.
By night, she flies in the darkness between heaven and earth,
Shrieking, nor do her eyes droop in sweet sleep.
By day she sits guard on rooftops

Or high towers, and terrifies great cities,
She is a messenger who clings as tenaciously to the false and the twisted as
    she does to the true.
Delighting, she filled up the people with multifaceted gossip,
And sang truths and falsehoods alike
Of how Aeneas came, born of Trojan blood,
He with whom fair Dido thinks it worthy to join herself;
How they kept warm together in dissolute comfort, all through the
    winter,
Forgetful of their realms, and prisoners of a disgraceful passion.

                                          (*Aeneid* 4.173–94)

CHAPTER SEVEN

Gods and Gold

Agamemnon's sceptre and the line of Argive kings: The sceptre's divine origin and history are recounted at *Iliad* 2.101–8. Note that the passage uses different verbs (*didomai* and *leipō*) to distinguish between kings who gained the throne by hereditary succession (Atreus), and those who took it by force (Thyestes, Agamemnon). It does not, however, make much of this difference, since those whom others might conceivably call "usurpers" hold the sceptre no less than do dynastic heirs. In both cases, royal authority comes with and depends on possession of the sceptre.

Physical construction of the sceptre: Transformation of branch into sceptre is described at *Iliad* 1.234–37; its adornment with gold nails or studs is noted a few lines later at 1.245–46. Golden sceptres are also mentioned at *Iliad* 1.15, 1.28, 1.374, 2.268, 11.30 and *Odyssey* 11.91 and 11.569.

Golden objects in Homer: Of the 58 golden objects mentioned in the *Iliad,* 33 belong to gods. Of the 36 types of objects (cups, armor, gear for horses and chariots, etc.) 23 have exemplars belonging to gods. To cite but one example of the symbolic significance attached to gold, we are told that the shield which Hephaestus made for Achilles had five layers: two of bronze, two of tin, and one of gold. And when Achilles expected a powerful spear-thrust of Aineias to break through his shield, the golden layer protected him where no other would have sufficed, since "it is difficult for the glorious gifts of the gods to be pierced or broken" (*Iliad* 20.259–72).

Priests, seers, poets: For Chryses' sceptre, see *Iliad* 1.14–15, 1.28, and 1.373–74; Teiresias's, *Odyssey* 11.91; Hesiod's, *Theogony* 22–34. Kings described as bearing a sceptre include Agamemnon, Achilles, Odysseus, Menelaus, Nestor, Proetus, and Minos.

The Chaeroneans and the sceptre: Pausanias 9.40.11–41.1. For discussion of this fascinating passage, see Paul Veyne, *Did the Greeks Believe their Myths?* (Chicago: University of Chicago Press, 1988), pp. 100–101, and P. E. Easterling, "Agamemnon's *skēptron* in the *Iliad*," in *Images of Authority: Papers presented to Joyce Reynolds*, ed. Mary MacKenzie and Charlotte Roueché (Cambridge: Cambridge Philological Society, 1989), pp. 116–17.

Rape, Inspiration, and Effluvial Fumes

Tortured chain of meditations: See further H. W. Parke, *Sibyls and Sibylline Prophecy in Classical Antiquity* (London: Routledge, 1988), esp. pp. 71–99 and 136–51; Raymond Bloch, "L'origine des livres sibyllins à Rome," *Neue Beiträge zur Geschichte der alten Welt* 11 (1965), pp. 281–92.

Tarquin's purchase of the scrolls: The story is told by several authors, among them Aulus Gellius *Attic Nights* 1.19.1, who cites "ancient annals" as his source. For the fullest discussion, see J. Gagé, *Apollon romain* (Paris: E. de Boccard, 1955), pp. 24–38.

Virgil on the Cumaean Sibyl: The passage quoted is *Aeneid* 6.47–80, on which see the commentary of R. G. Austin, *P. Vergili Maronis, Aeneidos Liber Sextus* (Oxford: Clarendon Press, 1977), pp. 48–68. The description of Apollo "tiring" (*fatigat*) the Sibyl's mouth refers to the practices of breaking wild horses, as is made explicit by Lucan *Pharsalia* 5.176: "She also receives the bit and bridle" (*accipit et frenos*). The image is rich, but profoundly disturbing. It mixes violence, eroticism, and the domestication of women and animals, while also specifying the Sibyl's mouth as the site through which the god takes possession of her and through which he will ultimately speak.

Lucan's accounts: See Lucan *Pharsalia* 5.86–101, 5.116–20, and 5.161–82. Compare also Seneca *Agamemnon* 710–25.

Delphi and effluvial vapors: For a convenient discussion of the rationalizing tradition that explained the Pythia's experience of inspiration as the result of exposure to intoxicating fumes, and the archaeological evidence that indicates the improbability of any such phenomenon, see H. W. Parke, *Greek Oracles* (London: Hutchinson, 1967), pp. 77–80.

Gods, Oaths, Bluffs, and Curses

Homeric assembly as "sacred circle": The phrase occurs only this one time, with reference to the assembly depicted on Achilles' shield, which is atypical in other respects. Conceivably, characters in the text were meant to regard it as an idealized version of their own practices or as a memory of their ancestors' more archaic practices.

Kings claim divine favor: Thus, for example, Homeric kings were said to be "nurtured by Zeus" (*diotrephēs, Iliad* 1.176, 2.98, 5.463), while their Norwegian counterparts were "known to the gods" (*goð-kynning, Ynglingatál* 25).

Agamemnon's oath: The passage cited is *Iliad* 19.258–65. Compare the oath Agamemnon swears by Zeus, Sun, rivers, earth, and the powers below just before the duel of Paris and Menelaus (3.276–80), and that Hector swears by Zeus at Dolon's insistence, while holding the sceptre (10.329–31). The program Telemachus announces for his assembly is also relevant: "Proclaim the story to all, and let the gods be witnesses" (*mython pephrade pasi, theoi d' epi martyroi estōn, Odyssey* 1.273).

Implausible assertions: As one gauge of audience reactions, consider the suggestion of an ancient scholium that Agamemnon's claim not to have desired Briseis in bed is meant "hyperbolically." See Erbse, ed., *Scholia Graeca in Homeri Iliadem*, 5:624.

Ring-oaths: The description of procedures for consecrating the ring and the wording of the oath witnesses swore by it is taken from *Landnamabók* 268. A virtually identical passage is found at *Flateyjarbók* 1.249.14ff. See also *Viga-Glum's Saga* 25; *Eyrbyggja Saga* 4.7 and 16.8; *Hávamál* 110; and the *Anglo Saxon Chronicle* 876.

Symbolism of rings: Hermann Güntert, *Der arische Weltkönig und Heiland* (Halle, Germany: Max Niemeyer, 1923), p. 71.

Egil's curse: *Egil's Saga* 56.91.

Where oaths become curses: Note the ambiguity of the English expression "to swear an oath," which can denote both solemn and obscene speech acts. Similar data within the Indo-European family of languages have been collected by Otto Schrader, *Reallexikon der indogermanischen Altertumskunde*, ed. A. Nehring (Berlin: Walter de Gruyter, 1929), pp. 226–30; Carl Darling Buck, *A Dictionary of Selected Synonyms in the Principal Indo-European Languages* (Chicago: University of Chicago Press, 1948), p. 1437; and Émile Benveniste, *Le vocabulaire des institutions indo-européennes* (Paris: Éditions de Minuit, 1969), 2:163–75, who argue that "oaths" were originally self-activating "curses" that rebounded on the speaker in the event of their violation.

Negation of religion and negation of authority: Wherever authority rests on religion, any slip in authority can be interpreted as a withdrawal of divine favor, and the charge of religious failing can be strategically used in a campaign of de-authorization. The varying uses to which the traditional Chinese ideology of the "Mandate of Heaven" was put offers an excellent case in point.

CHAPTER EIGHT

A Woman Speaks with Authority Regarding its Disappearance

Arendt on authority: "What was Authority?" was first published in Carl J. Friedrich, ed., *Authority,* Nomos, vol. 1 (Cambridge, Mass.: Harvard University Press, 1958), pp. 81–112.

"Authority as we once knew it . . .": Arendt, "What was Authority?" pp. 110–11.

Sleight of hand and the etymology of *religio:* Two rival etymologies were current in antiquity and experts remain undecided between them. One posits derivation from *re-ligare* ("to reconnect") and the other from *re-legere* ("to reread, relate again"). Arendt lists only the former and cites Cicero as her source, without mentioning any specific text ("What was Authority?" p. 99). The one passage where Cicero discusses this etymology, however, is *On the Nature of the Gods* 2.72, where he weighs in heavily on the opposite side. While this detail has little importance for Arendt's argument, one cannot help wondering if she made an innocent mistake or carried out a successful bluff, appropriating Cicero's prestige (his "authority," if you will) to support a view antithetical to his own.

Changes in warrants for authority: See, inter alia, Reinhard Bendix, *Kings or People? Power and the Mandate to Rule* (Berkeley and Los Angeles: University of California Press, 1978); and Thomas Haskell, ed., *The Authority of Experts: Studies in History and Theory* (Bloomington: Indiana University Press, 1984).

Right Speech and Speaker

Hannah Arendt: Biographical information is taken from Elisabeth Young-Bruehl, *Hannah Arendt: For Love of the World* (New Haven: Yale University Press, 1982). Within a large and growing literature, I have found the following particularly helpful: S. J. Whitfield, *Into the Dark: Hannah Arendt and Totalitarianism* (Philadelphia: Temple University Press, 1980); George Kateb, *Hannah Arendt: Politics, Conscience, Evil* (Totowa, N.J.: Rowman & Allanheld, 1983); Christopher Lasch, Introduction to a special issue on Arendt, *Salmagundi* 60 (1983), pp. iv–xvi; George McKenna, "Bannisterless Politics: Hannah Arendt and her Children," *History of Political Thought* 5 (1984), pp. 333–60; Robert Mayer, "Hannah Arendt, Leninism, and the Disappearance of Authority," *Polity* 24 (1992), pp. 399–416; and Margaret Canovan, *Hannah Arendt: A Reinterpretation of her Political Thought* (Cambridge: Cambridge University Press, 1992).

Taken for a "liberal" by "conservatives" and vice versa: See her observations: Hannah Arendt, "On Hannah Arendt," in *Hannah Arendt:
The Recovery of the Public World,* ed. Melvyn Hill (New York: St. Martin's Press, 1979), pp. 333–34. Bernard Crick's assessment (in the
same volume, p. 32) that she was a conservative with an anarchist twist
("a marriage, as it were, of Tocqueville and Prudhomme") seems to
me particularly apt. One should also note that the Hungarian Revolt
of 1956 had a profound effect on Arendt, and after that date her anarchist strain became more pronounced.

New York Intellectuals: For the best general discussions, see Alexander Bloom, *Prodigal Sons: The New York Intellectuals and their World*
(New York: Oxford University Press, 1986); and Alan M. Wald, *The
New York Intellectuals: The Rise and Decline of the Anti-Stalinist Left from
the 1930s to the 1980s* (Chapel Hill: University of North Carolina Press,
1987). According to Young-Bruehl, p. 196, Arendt made the acquain-
tance of this group through Irving Howe, Nathan Glazer, and Martin
Greenberg, her colleagues at Schocken. Mary McCarthy, Dwight
Macdonald, and Alfred Kazin became her close friends; Kazin aided
in the final corrections to *The Origins of Totalitarianism* and arranged
for its publication.

Totalitarianism: An instructive discussion of this term's history and
its place in Cold War discourse was touched off when, in the midst of
the Vietnam conflict, new editions appeared almost simultaneously of
Arendt's *Origins of Totalitarianism* (3d ed., 1966) and Carl J. Friedrich
and Zbigniew Brzezinski, *Totalitarian Dictatorship and Autocracy,* 2d
ed. (Cambridge, Mass.: Harvard University Press, 1965). See Robert
Burrowes, "Totalitarianism: The Revised Standard Version," *World
Politics* 21 (1969), pp. 272–94; Carl J. Friedrich, Michael Curtis, and
Benjamin R. Barber, *Totalitarianism in Perspective: Three Views* (New
York: Praeger, 1969); Les K. Adler and Thomas G. Paterson, "Red
Fascism: The Merger of Nazi Germany and Soviet Russia in the Amer-
ican Image of Totalitarianism, 1930's–1950's," *American Historical Re-
view* 75 (1970), pp. 1046–64; and Herbert J. Spiro and Benjamin R.
Barber, "Counter-Ideological Uses of 'Totalitarianism'," *Politics and So-
ciety* 1 (1970), pp. 3–21.

The Origins of Totalitarianism: The English edition was published
by Secker and Warburg in 1951 under the title *The Burden of Our Time.*
The first American edition followed in the same year and was brought
out by Harcourt, Brace & Co. Revised editions followed in 1958,
1966, and 1968. For a summary of the book's contents, descriptions
of the process through which it was written, and critical commentary,
see Young-Bruehl, pp. 199–211; Canovan, pp. 17–62; Wald, 269.

Reactions to *The Origins of Totalitarianism:* Reviewers opined that Arendt had "given scholarly support to the increasingly widely held dictum that Soviet communism is nothing but Red fascism" (J. F. Brown in *Annals of the American Academy of Political and Social Science* 277 [Spring 1951], p. 272). Michael Bittman's summary of the book's impact is useful: "[Arendt's] analysis justified, after the event, the inescapable logical necessity of fighting Hitler. At the same time it acted as a giant conducting rod, capturing this lightning flash of militance and directing it against the political system of the USSR, The limitless dread aroused by the evidence of Nazi atrocities passed from Hitler's now defunct regime to the United States' newly emerging rival in world affairs" ("Totalitarianism: The Career of a Concept," in *Hannah Arendt: Thinking, Judging, Freedom,* eds. Gisele Kaplan and Clive Kessler [Sydney: Allen and Unwin, 1989], p. 58). Similar assessments are offered by Bloom, pp. 218–20 and Wald, pp. 268–70. The discussion of Young-Bruehl, pp. 256–58 seems to me misleading in its emphases.

Right Time and Place

Distancing herself from the New York group: The clearest sign of this is Arendt's article entitled "The Ex-Communists," *Commonweal* 57 (20 March 1953), pp. 595–99. According to Young-Bruehl, pp. 273–75, both Arendt and her husband (Herman Blücher, who had himself been a member of the German Communist party) were distressed by the excesses of McCarthyism and the role played by former Marxists turned informers and denouncers. Although Arendt focused on Whittaker Chambers, Irving Kristol's strident article "Civil Liberties, 1952 — A Study in Confusion," *Commentary* (1952), pp. 228–36 is said to have particularly offended her, and prompted her decision to speak out. Still, the closing paragraph of her article reveals the profound ambivalence with which she regarded those whom she addressed there. "Much as we desire to establish friendship with you, much as we are in sympathy with your experiences and frequently with your personalities, as long as you insist on your role as ex-Communists, we must warn against you. In this role, you can only strengthen those dangerous elements which are present in all free societies today and which we do not want to crystallize into a totalitarian movement or a totalitarian form of domination, no matter what its cause and ideological content."

"Totalitarianism" conference: A description of how these meetings were organized is given in Carl J. Friedrich's preface to the volume that appeared under his editorship as *Totalitarianism* (Cambridge, Mass.:

Harvard University Press, 1954; reprinted by Grosset & Dunlap, 1964), pp. vii–viii: A full list of participants appears at p. v.

Steering committee: The members were Erwin D. Canham, Karl Deutsch, Merle Fainsod, Carl Friedrich, Alexander Gerschenkron, and Harold Lasswell. Deutsch took his Ph.D from Harvard in 1949; Fainsod, Friedrich, and Gerschenkron were long-time faculty members. Canham, Deutsch, and Friedrich published in *Confluence* (as did several other conference participants, Arendt included), and Lasswell served on its advisory board. Both Gerschenkron and Fainsod sat on the executive committee of the RRC, for which they were also project directors (Fainsod would later serve as its director from 1959 to 1964). Friedrich's relations to the RRC were less intense, and were mediated through the colleagues with whom he offered a seminar on "Totalitarian Dictatorship": Fainsod and Zbigniew Brzezinski. On the relations among this course, these people, and the RRC, see the preface to Friedrich and Brzezinski's *Totalitarian Dictatorship and Autocracy*, pp. vii–ix. Brzezinski participated in the "Totalitarianism" meetings, and worked on the team that transcribed discussion sessions.

Russian Research Center and its sponsors: See Russian Research Center, Harvard University, *Ten-Year Report and Current Projects: 1948–1958* (privately published, January 1958); idem, *The Second Decade: A Progress Report, 1958–1968* (June 1968); Ellen Condliffe Lagemann, *The Politics of Knowledge: The Carnegie Corporation, Philanthropy, and Public Policy* (Middletown, Conn.: Wesleyan University Press, 1989), pp. 172–75; and, above all, Sigmund Diamond, *Compromised Campus: The Collaboration of Universities with the Intelligence Community, 1945–1955* (New York: Oxford University Press, 1992), esp. pp. 50–110.

References to Arendt at the "Totalitarianism" conference: Thus, for instance, Arendt was the only scholar cited by name in George Kennan's keynote address, "Totalitarianism in the Modern World," in *Totalitarianism*, ed. Carl J. Friedrich pp. 17–31, esp. p. 25; Kennan also went out of his way to refer to her favorably in the course of discussion (pp. 82–83). She was also cited in highly respectful fashion by others, including Carl Friedrich, N. S. Timasheff, Waldemar Gurian, Bertram D. Wolfe, Albert Lauterbach, and Karl Deutsch.

Further dealings with the Harvard group: According to Friedrich and Brzezinski, p. ix, Arendt became one of five "consultants" to the Fainsod-Friedrich-Brzezinski course on totalitarian dictatorship. Fainsod is also cited prominently in the "Preface to Part Three" Arendt added to the 1956 edition of *The Origins of Totalitarianism*.

Adorno and the discourse of "authoritarianism": Most immediately on the mind of conference participants was T. W. Adorno, Else Frenkel-Brunswik, Daniel J. Levinson, and R. Nevitt Sanford, *The Authoritarian Personality* (New York: Harper, 1950), which was mentioned dismissively in several papers (Friedrich, ed., *Authority,* pp. 35, 127). Deeper in the background was Max Horkheimer and T. W. Adorno, *Dialectic of Enlightenment* (1947; reprint, New York: Herder and Herder, 1972). See further Susan Buck-Morss, *The Origin of Negative Dialectics: Theodor W. Adorno, Walter Benjamin, and the Frankfurt Institute* (New York: Free Press, 1977) and Martin Jay, *Adorno* (Cambridge, Mass: Harvard University Press, 1984).

"The more the concept is emptied of any specific content": Adorno, *The Authoritarian Personality,* pp. 723–74.

"Authority" conference: Proceedings of the 1956 meetings were published under the editorship of Carl J. Friedrich as *Authority,* Nomos, vol. 1 (Cambridge, Mass.: Harvard University Press, 1958). Details regarding organization and funding of the meetings is given by Friedrich in his preface to the volume, pp. v–vi.

Twentieth Century Fund: See Adolf A. Berle, *Leaning Against the Dawn: An Appreciation of the Twentieth Century Fund . . . 1919–1969* (New York: The Twentieth Century Fund, 1969), for a description of this foundation's self-understanding and characteristic mode of operation. The Fund's interests after the close of the Second World War are summarized at pp. 43–45. Erwin D. Canham, editor of the *Christian Science Monitor* and author of *New Frontiers for Freedom* (New York: Longmans Green, 1954) was the trustee who also served on the steering committee that organized the "Totalitarianism" meetings.

And an Audience that Judges Just What is "Right"

Participants in the "Authority" conference: A much broader range of disciplines was represented than in the earlier meetings (political science, philosophy, law, sociology, economics, history, and anthropology), and with only a few exceptions, all those who took part were highly accomplished scholars. Distribution according to national origin also contrasts with the "Totalitarianism" meetings. Whereas participants from eastern Europe were well represented at the latter (seven Russians, plus two each from Poland, Czechoslovakia, Austria, and Hungary), they were absent at the "Authority" conference, where those who were not American by birth came from the western democracies (England, France, Canada, and Germany, which by 1956 was grouped firmly with the west).

Participants from the Harvard group: Carryovers from the "Totalitarianism" meetings were Carl Friedrich and Herbert Spiro, who were joined by Talcott Parsons. The presence of Spiro is interesting, for he was one of the very few members of the Harvard group who was *not* active in the RRC; moreover, he would later have some sharply critical things to say about the concept of "totalitarianism," both in his article on "Counter-Ideological Uses of 'Totalitarianism'" cited above, and in the entry on "Totalitarianism" he contributed to the *International Encyclopedia of the Social Sciences* (1968). On the important role played by Parsons within the RRC, see Diamond, pp. 88–95 passim.

Antipathy to Adorno: Arendt reacted violently to Adorno when he rejected her first husband's *Habilitationschrift* in 1929, and in 1933 she was distressed by what she considered his attempts to cooperate with the Nazi regime and to hide his Jewish ancestry. Later, she resented the way Adorno dealt with Walter Benjamin, and feared he was suppressing the latter's posthumous writings, which she herself had delivered to him on Benjamin's instructions. See Young-Bruehl, pp. 80, 109, 166–67. As late as 1972, Arendt could still state: "I hate to use the word ['critical'] because of the Frankfurt School." Hannah Arendt, "On Hannah Arendt," p. 309.

"Whatever constructive advance has been made in freedom": Charles Hendel, "An Exploration of the Nature of Authority," in *Authority*, ed. Carl J. Friedrich pp. 3–27. The quote is taken from pp. 24–25.

"Historically, at any rate": Arendt, "What was Authority?" pp. 83–84 (emphasis added).

Critique of Adorno: Compare a related essay in which Arendt emphasized the importance of terminological distinctions in general, and more specifically insisted—against Adorno—on the need to distinguish between tyranny, authoritarianism, and totalitarianism ("Authority in the Twentieth Century," *Review of Politics* 18 [1956], pp. 403–17, esp. pp. 405–7 and 413–14. Similar views were also voiced by Carl J. Friedrich, "Loyalty and Authority," *Confluence* 3 (1954), pp. 307–16, esp. p. 308.

Expansion of the essay: Hannah Arendt, "What is Authority?" in *Between Past and Future* (New York: Viking Press, 1961), pp. 91–141, which incorporates the text of "What was Authority?" along with selected paragraphs from "Authority in the Twentieth Century," *Review of Politics* 18 (1956), pp. 403–17 and "Religion and Politics," *Confluence* 3 (1953), pp. 105–26.

"It is in her essay . . .": Irving Kristol, "A Treasure for the Future," *New Republic* 145/19 (10 July 1961), pp. 19–20.

Irving Kristol: Kristol began his political evolution as a Trotskyist in the 1930s, and—like others in the New York circle—became an anti-Stalinist in the 1940s and a Cold War liberal in the 1950s. In 1951 he was the first executive director of the American Committee for Cultural Freedom (ACCF), an organization designed to rally intellectuals to the anti-Communist cause. In 1953, he left New York for England to found *Encounter,* the flagship journal of the ACCF's European counterpart, the Congress for Cultural Freedom (CCF). Returning to the United States in 1959, he moved further to the right in subsequent years, a move that accelerated after 1966, when it was revealed that *Encounter* and the CCF had been covertly funded by the CIA, a blow that destroyed his reputation in liberal circles. Continuing his rightward migration in later years, he served as the Henry R. Luce Professor of Urban Values at New York University (1969), an advisor to the Nixon administration, a member of the *Wall Street Journal's* board of contributors, a founding director of the Committee for the Free World (1981), a Senior Fellow of the American Enterprise Institute, and one of the foremost theoreticians, publicists, and fundraisers for the "neoconservative" movement. See further Wald, pp. 350–54; Bloom, pp. 369–74; Irving Kristol, *Reflections of a Neoconservative* (New York: Basic Books, 1983); David Burner, *Column Right: Conservative Journalists in the Service of Nationalism* (New York: New York University Press, 1988). On Kristol's involvement with *Encounter,* the CCF, and the CIA, see Peter Coleman, *The Liberal Conspiracy: The Congress for Cultural Freedom and the Struggle for the Mind of Postwar Europe* (New York: Free Press, 1989), pp. 61–63.

"Authority has vanished from the modern world": Arendt, "What was Authority?" p. 81; "What is Authority?" p. 91.

Neoconservatives: On this group, see Peter Steinfels, *The Neoconservatives* (New York: Simon and Schuster, 1979); David Edgar, "The Free or the Good," in *The Ideology of the New Right,* ed. Ruth Levitas (Cambridge: Polity Press, 1986), pp. 55–79, esp. 63–69; Christopher Hitchens, "A Modern Medieval Family," *Mother Jones* (July–August 1986), pp. 52–56, 74–76; Sidney Blumenthal, *The Rise of the Counter-Establishment: From Conservative Ideology to Political Power* (New York: Times Books, 1986); Paul Gottfried and Thomas Fleming, *The Conservative Movement* (Boston: Twayne, 1988), pp. 59–76; and J. David Hoeveler, *Watch on the Right: Conservative Intellectuals in the Reagan Era* (Madison: University of Wisconsin Press, 1991). Norman Podhoretz acknowledged the extent to which he was influenced by Arendt in *Making It* (New York: Random House, 1967), pp. 89, 179, and 289 and *Breaking Ranks* (New York: Harper & Row, 1979), p. 39. A similar, but more scholarly acknowledgment is made by Jeanne Kirkpatrick in *Dictatorships and Double Standards* (New York: American Enterprise Institute, 1982), p. 98. The abiding importance of Arendt for neoconservatives has been noted by Isidore Silver, "What Flows from Neoconservatism," *The Nation* (9 July 1977), pp. 44–51, esp. 49–50.

CHAPTER NINE

Stages and Stage Management

Throne of St. Peter: It is probably worth noting that only pronouncements made from this exalted seat are regarded as infallible, and are said to be made *ex cathedra* ("from the chair").

Shattered Eagles and Resourceful Monkeys

New York Times' account: "Reagan Unhurt After Man Smashes 30-Pound Statue," 14 April 1992, p. A16. See also the *Times'* follow-up stories: "Protester Who Accosted Reagan is Released on Own Recognizance," 15 April 1992, p. A16; and "Protester at Reagan Speech Had Press Credentials," 16 April 1992, p. A8. Most major dailies included similar stories, following Associated Press coverage. Jim Laurie's photograph (figure 9.1) was usually included, and a videotape of the incident made by the NAB was shown on most television news broadcasts.

Rick Paul Springer: Most of the information included here is taken from interviews with Mr. Springer (25 January 1993), correspondence with him (16 September and 13 October 1993), as well as discussions with several of his colleagues in the Hundredth Monkey Project and his attorneys, William Carrico (10 December 1992) and Susan Quig-Terry (26 January 1994). I have also made use of biographical materials included in the Hundredth Monkey grant proposal, a copy of which Mr. Springer kindly sent to me. I am also grateful to him for having corrected several minor errors of fact in an earlier draft of this chapter.

Complacency is widespread: At times, Mr. Springer speaks very harshly on this, as when he explained to me his view "The U.S. is largely a nation of spoiled brats, seduced into a stupor of complacency through comfort, convenience, materialism and entertainment." Interview, 25 January 1993.

The Hundredth Monkey: Ken Keyes, Jr., *The Hundredth Monkey* (Coos Bay, Ore.: Vision Books, 1982). The sentences quoted come from pp. 15 and 19. According to Keyes (interview, 26 August 1993), he was not connected with Springer or the Hundredth Monkey Project, but had no objections to his use of the name. Keyes' book itself has a fascinating history. Some 1.1 million copies have been distributed in the United States, and it has been translated into a dozen foreign languages. About a quarter of these copies Keyes donated to people or groups who promised to make good use of them; the rest were priced cheaply so they could circulate widely, but still yield some profit, and with the income he has funded a center, foundation, publishing house, and training institute devoted to the antinuclear cause. On page 2 of *The Hundredth Monkey* appears the following notice: **"This book is not copyrighted.** You are asked to reproduce it in whole or in part, to distribute it with or without charge, in as many languages as possible, to as many people as possible. The rapid alerting of all humankind to nuclear realities is supremely urgent. If we are wiped out by nuclear destruction in the next few years, how important are the things we are doing today."

Promotional materials: Mailing distributed by the Hundredth Monkey Project, courtesy of Rick Springer.

"I was a great dreamer": Interview, 25 January 1993. Reflecting on this statement later (private correspondence, 16 Sept. 1993), Springer stated: "Perhaps I said 'I was a great dreamer,' but what I really believe is that 'I *am* a great dreamer.'"

Other People's Stages

National Association of Broadcasters: It is worth underscoring the size and importance of the NAB. According to the *Encyclopedia of Associations,* 28th ed. (1994) p. 88, it has some 17 million members and a professional staff of 165. It publishes two annuals and two weeklies, maintains 28 standing committees, and has an annual budget of $17 million. Moreover, as the trade association for the radio/television industry, it is, in effect, that stage whose audience consists of the people who manage the most popular stages of all others.

"A deathhold on the media": Interview, 25 January 1993. Mr. Springer further argued that a small number of large corporations control communications in the United States and that, in general, the media support the nuclear industry, citing Ben H. Bagdikian, *The Media Monopoly,* 4th ed. (Boston: Beacon Press, 1992) in support of his views.

Eddie Fritts: According to Mr. Reagan's remarks, prior to becoming executive director of the NAB, Fritts had served in his administration as vice chairman of the Presidential Board of Advisors on Private Sector Initiatives.

"The clearest, most meditative moment": Rick Springer, "Excuse Me, Mr. President," *New Age Journal* (July/August 1992), p. 50.

"Bombing the water supply": Interview, 25 January 1993. See also the testimony Mr. Springer gave in court, quoted in appendix F.

State and federal offenses: Springer was initially charged with interfering with the work of the Secret Service and destroying private property (the crystal eagle) and was released on his own recognizance. In October 1992, he pled guilty to the former charge in federal court, and was sentenced to four months in prison. For a complex set of reasons, he elected not to report as scheduled in June 1993, but to continue his work against nuclear testing. He was apprehended two months later, while doing media interviews in connection with commemorations of the bombing of Hiroshima and Nagasaki. Charged with failure to surrender, Mr. Springer pled not guilty and argued that a higher moral law compelled him to continue his work against nuclear testing. His first trial on these charges ended with a hung jury (27 October 1993), and in the wake of this, state charges against him were dropped. Federal prosecutors elected to retry his case, however, and won conviction in a second trial (24 January 1994). As I write, Mr. Springer is in the North Las Vegas Detention Center, where he awaits sentencing on these charges.

"Is he a Democrat, by chance?": Peter Viles, "Reagan's Shattering Moment," *Broadcasting* 122/17 (20 April 1992), p. 5.

Struggles between Actors and Struggles between Stages

Interviews: Most notable is Springer's appearance on "CBS This Morning," quoted in appendix C. He also appeared on a local broadcast in Los Angeles (Channel 9, "Cross-Talk"). According to the May 1992 edition of "Monkey Business" (the newsletter of the Hundredth Monkey Project): "Rick has been doing innumerable TV and radio interviews in order to bring the nuclear testing issue to light, and challenge the media to do responsible reporting." The newsletter also announces a lecture tour and the production of a documentary film covering the full ten days of Project events.

Articles: Mr. Springer published an account of his April actions, in — significantly — a counter-cultural journal: "Excuse Me, Mr. President," *New Age Journal* (July/August 1992), pp. 50–53 (for excerpts, see appendix E). He has been working on a book of the same title.

Court appearances: Gaining use of these stages proved both more costly and more difficult than Springer anticipated. When he pled guilty to federal charges, he was allowed to make a statement of his views that was reported in the press (U.S. vs. Rick Paul Springer, Docket No. CR-S-92-109-PMP[RJJ], heard 22 October 1992, Las Vegas District Court; appendix F). Springer pled not guilty to state charges, and hoped to focus this trial squarely on the issue of nuclear testing.

"CBS This Morning": Quotations are taken from the transcript for the 17 April 1992 "CBS This Morning" show, produced by Burrelle's Information Services, Livingston, New Jersey.

Introductions: One gets some idea of the various shades of authorization that are extended simply from considering the way guests were introduced on the 17 April show. In order, they were as follows (with Springer appearing just after Dr. Kessler).

"Dr. David Kessler is the commissioner of the FDA. He joins us this morning. Welcome. It's nice to see you again."

"Joining us to look at the rebound on Broadway is WCBS-TV entertainment editor Dennis Cunningham. Good morning, sir."

"Finding the right toy for your child can be a challenge. But you might find some help in the Oppenheim Portfolio, an independent guide that picks the best in toys, books and videos . . . And here with some examples is toy expert Joanne Oppenheim. Good morning. Welcome."

"Morgan Freeman is a two-time Oscar nominee for 'Street Smart' and 'Driving Miss Daisy' . . . And Morgan Freeman is with us. Good morning."

"Arlyne Brickman grew up on New York's lower east side in a world of loan sharks and hit men. It was a world she liked and became a part of before she turned and became a government informant. Author Teresa Carpenter takes a look at Brickman's life in 'Mob Girl: A Woman's Life in the Underworld.' And Arlyne Brickman joins us this morning. Good morning."

"Among the questions every reporter learns to ask are how and why and those are the questions we're about to ask Barry Holden, who joins us from the New York City borough of Queens this morning, with his floating house. Good morning, Barry."

Hosts' reactions: Microanalysis of this segment of the broadcast would be rewarding, although it goes beyond the scope of this study. Inter alia, it should be noted that praise of Springer began with the member of the show's team who enjoys least authority, and thus has greatest license to express unconventional opinions: the weatherman. Further, specific praises reflect a gendered division: the male host commented on Springer's principles and commitment, the female host on his courtesy, and the meteorologist on his courage and powers of articulation.

Wall Street Journal editorial: "The Hundredth Monkey Speaks," *Wall Street Journal,* 21 April 1992, p. A16.

Uncritical nature of deference: Relations of epistemic authority by their very nature involve suspension or, at least, some attenuation of critical judgment, since they are predicated on an asymmetry of expertise between audience and speaker that leaves the former incompetent to criticize the latter's pronouncements. The situation of executive authority differs somewhat, for as Michael Oakeshott and others have argued, taking their lead from Hobbes, those subject to such authority need not believe that those who hold it are particularly excellent, only that they have come to hold it in legitimate ways. Privates are thus free to think what they like of officers and the orders they give, provided they obey them. The argument is developed, inter alia, in Oakeshott, *Hobbes on Civil Association* (Berkeley and Los Angeles: University of California Press, 1975); R. E. Flathman, *The Practice of Political Authority* (Chicago: University of Chicago Press, 1980); R. B. Friedman, "On the Concept of Authority in Political Philosophy," in *Authority*, ed. Joseph Raz, pp. 56–91, and Joseph Raz, "Authority and Justification," in ibid., pp. 115–41. In essence, this analysis focuses on the person who speaks with authority rather than the speech or the speech situation, and further, dissolves that person into office and occupant, maximizing the import of the former and minimizing the latter. For my part, as I hope I have made clear, all of these aspects (speech, speaker, situation, office and occupant) have their importance, and none is analytically dispensable. Beyond this, with specific regard to the issue of how much space executive authority allows for criticism, I would pose three questions in any given instance: first, whether those "in authority" tolerate criticism precisely because (and only so long as) it remains private—i.e., invisible, inaudible, and inconsequential; second, whether such criticism, in which one finds the seeds of all the corrosive discourses we have considered, is really so impotent as this view would suggest; and third, in light of the potential such critiques have to undermine the authority of those against whom they are directed, whether such persons do not, in practice, attempt in one fashion or another to render their audiences incapable of advancing them, even within some restricted, private sphere.

INDEX

221